8 CORE PRACTICES
— of —
FACILITATIVE LEADERS

Michael Wilkinson

Published by Leadership Strategies Publishing
A division of Leadership Strategies – The Facilitation Company

800.824.2850 www.leadstrat.com

Publisher's Cataloging-In-Publication Data
(Prepared by The Donohue Group, Inc.)

Names: Wilkinson, Michael, 1957- author.

Title: 8 core practices of facilitative leaders / Michael Wilkinson.

Other Titles: Eight core practices of facilitative leaders

Description: First edition. | [Atlanta, Georgia] : Leadership Strategies Publishing, [2019] | Includes bibliographical references and index.

Identifiers: ISBN 9780972245883

Subjects: LCSH: Leadership. | Group facilitation. | Communication in management. | Business meetings.

Classification: LCC HD57.7 .W55 2019 | DDC 658.4092--dc23

Manufactured in the United States of America
Cover design by Talha Ahmad

FIRST EDITION

Dedicated to the fourteen people who, over my lifetime, have most influenced my development as a leader (in order of appearance in my life).

Mom　　　　　　　　　*Sherry Wilkinson*
Reverend Randy　　　*Mark O'Connell*
Dove　　　　　　　　　*Ken Blanchard*
Professor Galliard　　*Larry Hart*
Coach Piggy Clark　　*Patrick Lencioni*
James Ray　　　　　　*Jamie Drake*
Clive McAllister　　　*Ann Herrmann-Nehdi*

Table of Contents

Table of Contents

Table of Contents

Table of Contents

Acknowledgements

"How do you ever find the time to write a book?"

I suspect many authors are asked this question and the answer varies widely by author. For me, I am most productive when I can spend a year casually outlining chapters, blogging on content I will later use, and testing ideas and concepts in our classes and with our clients. But when it comes time to put pen to paper, I have to sequester myself for about a month to focus exclusively on writing without the distraction and the urgency of day-to-day concerns.

Yet to exit the command centers that surround my personal and professional life requires the support and love of a team of people. For when I exit, their individual plates become much fuller, their load becomes heavier, and their days can become longer. So, first and foremost I want to thank my leadership team for the tremendous job they do every day and especially during book writing to ensure we deliver the highest level of expertise and quality care to our many clients. To Sherry, our Chief Operating Officer, David, our VP of Sales, Dave, who heads our Facilitation Team, and Shellie, our head of Marketing, I simply say thank you for all you do.

To our Operations, Sales, and Marketing Teams, I want to thank each of you for the role you play in sustaining a fun, uplifting, and prosperous environment. We rock because you rock!

I say thank you to our highly skilled Core Team of facilitators who collectively are scored by our clients as 6.8 or higher on a 7-point scale, year after year. You have shown me, over and over again, that you are the most highly skilled group of professional facilitators I have ever had the pleasure of working with.

My editing team has been superb: John Rak, Kristin Summers, Jon Harrison, and Cher Paul. Thanks to each of you for your contribution to this work.

I want to thank the members of my content review team: Helene Lollis, Eileen Dowse, Dave Adelman, and Dorothea Brennan. Each of you offered unique insights and improvements that you will see reflected in the book. Thanks for taking the time to add great value.

Finally, Danielle and Gabrielle, my two twenty-somethings, I want to thank you for your emotional support, your laughter, our many talks, and your reminders to me to take the time to let people know how much I care. You are both precious.

8 Core Practices of Facilitative Leaders

Michael Wilkinson

Leadership
Strategies
Level up.

TAFA: Taking a Facilitative Approach

1

- What Is a Facilitative Leader?
- How Does a Leader take a Facilitative Approach?
- Benefits of TAFA
- How Your Role Changes with TAFA
- When Is TAFA Inappropriate?
- How This Book Can Help You
- Summary
- Spring Forward

Chapter 1.
TAFA: Taking a Facilitative Approach

It occurred to me the other day that I can divide my 40+ level-1 and level-2 managers into two categories: those who get it and those who don't. You can tell those that do because their people seem to be more engaged and proactive, taking more ownership over results. I don't know how these leaders do it, but the fact that they get it is unmistakable. Do you have any idea what I am talking about? Can you help me understand what 'it' is, and how more of my people can get 'it'?

Do *you* know what this leader is talking about? This book will make explicit both what the leader is describing and how to help others get "it."

A major shift is occurring in the workplace, and indeed, while some leaders get it and have adapted, unfortunately many have not. Many leaders and managers continue to view their role primarily as one of setting direction, allocating resources, and putting in place rewards, support, and development systems that ensure their people stay focused on achieving that direction.

In the changing workplace, this archaic view of leadership is completely inadequate. More and more, employees are seeking to participate in decision-making rather than merely being impacted by it. Employees are looking to understand where their organization is going and to influence the paths taken to get there.

> No longer willing to be just a pair of hands and feet waiting to be told what to do, employees want to be involved, engaged, and inspired to action.

This shift in the workplace requires a new set of leadership skills. The old days of "command and control" are long gone. Leaders must understand how to inspire people around a vision, foster trust, manage group interaction, build consensus, resolve conflict, and adapt their approach to the specific needs of each person they lead. They must be able to facilitate rather than dictate. This new direction calls for facilitative leaders.

What Is a Facilitative Leader?

A major difference between traditional leaders and facilitative leaders is that traditional leaders *tell*, while facilitative leaders nearly always *ask*. In my book, *The Secrets of Facilitation*, I describe how I learned what I call the fundamental secret of facilitation.

Learning the Fundamental Secret of Facilitation

I began understanding the secret during my career with the management consulting division of what was then one of the Big-8 accounting and consulting firms. In the eight years I spent in that practice, we had a standard way of addressing a client problem. We might be called in to review a particular department or activity. We would arrive with our army of bright people, interview those whom we believed were the key stakeholders, develop a set of recommendations based on our interviews and experience, and create what might be called the "100 percent solution." We would go away and come back a year later and perhaps, if we were lucky, 15 percent of the recommendations would be implemented.

In my final years with that organization, the practice in which I worked began taking a different approach. We would come in with a smaller group of consultants and work shoulder to shoulder with client personnel. Together we would convene group interviews (facilitated sessions) that typically included 8–20 people. In the facilitated sessions, the participants would create the recommendations, not the consultants. In most cases, they would only come up with what we might consider the 60 percent or 70 percent solution. So, we would float ideas based on our experience. Some they would accept, others they would reject as "not beneficial" or "not implementable" in their environment. When all was done, they might have created what we would consider the "85 percent solution." Yet, a year later, when we came back, amazingly 80–90 percent of the solution would be implemented!

Why wasn't more of the "100 percent solution" implemented? Why would the "85 percent solution," gained through facilitation, achieve far greater success? Therein lies the fundamental secret of facilitation and the power behind it.

The Fundamental Secret of Facilitation
If **they** create it, **they** understand it and accept it. You can achieve more effective results when solutions are created, understood, and accepted by the people affected.

As expert consultants, we were *telling* our clients what they needed to do. As a result, there was often very little buy-in by our sponsors or their people. As facilitative consultants, however, once we began *asking* the questions that resulted in the clients creating their own answers, the difference in implementation was staggering.

In *Transforming the Mature Information Technology Organization,*[1] Dr. Robert Zawacki from the University of Colorado put the secret this way:

$$ED = RD \times CD$$

Effective	**R**ight	**C**ommitment
Decision	**D**ecision	to **D**ecision

Dr. Zawacki's point is that even the best decision can be rendered completely ineffective if commitment to the decision is lacking. What does this mean to you as the leader in the organization? If you know the right strategy to implement, but your team has zero commitment to it, the effectiveness of your strategy will be zero because of the multiplication sign. Likewise, if you dictate the strategy and your team isn't committed to it, it will be as if you're pressing on the accelerator, while your team is stomping on the brake—a lot of energy expended and a lot of smoke in the air, but with little results to show for it.

To further illustrate this point, think about how, in a typical organization, decisions come down from headquarters that the people in the field know make absolutely no sense. The idea couldn't possibly work and many know it, but not the leaders. What happens? Time and energy are wasted implementing a "solution" that gets abandoned months later when the leaders figure out it was a bad idea. If they had only asked, the wasted time and resources could have been put to a much more productive use. If they had only asked….

Consider further how often a needed change is met with subtle subterfuge or blatant rejection simply because those expected to implement the change were not involved up front in its creation.

Facilitative leaders understand the issues that occur when there is a lack of buy-in. These leaders have redefined the meaning of leadership and the role of leaders.

What is a facilitative leader?
A facilitative leader is a person who takes a facilitative approach to making decisions, solving problems, managing people, and inspiring the performance of others.

Leaders who take a facilitative approach recognize that you can get better decisions and achieve higher levels of buy-in and commitment when those impacted by the decision are involved in creating it. Rather than setting direction and dictating action, they recognize the power of engaging their people in establishing direction and identifying priorities. Rather than identifying problems and determining solutions themselves, facilitative leaders provide the guidelines and empower their people to make things happen.

> Facilitative leaders create organizations where engagement
> is the norm, collaboration is the vehicle, and higher
> levels of achievement are the result.

How Does a Leader Take a Facilitative Approach?

This book describes eight specific practices common to facilitative leaders. You will find that a number of these practices borrow from some of the greatest leadership thinkers of our day, including Ken Blanchard, Jim Collins, Stephen Covey, Patrick Lencioni, Daniel Pink, Susan Scott, and Simon Sinek. These practices are not rocket science, but together form a framework of practices that guide new managers and veteran executives alike toward success in the new workplace.

In the past, when it came to managing and leading people, there have been three methods commonly delineated: directing, coaching and delegating. However, there is a fourth major method: the facilitative approach. This approach transforms the way leaders make decisions, solve problems, work with teams, coach individuals, develop strategy, et cetera.

What does it mean to TAFA, that is, what does it mean to "Take a Facilitative Approach" to solving a problem? The eight TAFA practices follow. For ease of memory, we start each TAFA practice with a verb to depict how a facilitative leader "SUCCEEDS."

1 Start with the Why, Engage with the How

A facilitative leader understands that inspiring people to higher levels of performance requires, among other things, a clear purpose. People are often inspired when they are connected and aligned with purpose. Unfortunately, most leaders communicate from the outside in: they start with what they want done and how to make it happen. In contrast, facilitative leaders understand the importance of communicating from the inside out. They start with the why and engage their team in determining how. This allows their team to buy in from the beginning and stay committed to the end.

> "People don't buy what you do. They buy why you do it."
> — *Simon Sinek*[2]

2 Understand and Empower, Don't Command and Control

Often leaders don't involve those impacted by decisions because they believe they need to control all aspects of what is done to achieve the desired result. However, facilitative leaders take the time to understand their people and individually empower them to perform at their best. Facilitative leaders know that they must give their people the authority, resources, support, and coaching that will enable them to develop and implement solutions that bring the "why" into reality.

3 Communicate in Their Language, not Yours

Facilitative leaders have highly tuned communication skills. They use questions and not statements to guide discussions and help people reach their own conclusions. They understand the basic communication styles and know how to recognize and adapt to each. Facilitative leaders know that whether talking to their superiors or their subordinates, they can communicate much more effectively by adapting to the communication language of the other person.

4 Connect First, Correct Second

Some leaders are expert at pointing out mistakes their people make. They seem to enjoy demonstrating their superiority by identifying errors and showing their people what they have done wrong. Leaders who take a facilitative approach understand the importance of connecting with people first and helping them discover their own errors. They recognize the power of being the "guide on the side" rather than the "sage on the stage." With every interaction, facilitative leaders strive to leave the person feeling elevated rather than beaten down.

5 Equip for Success, Monitor for Results

So many teams are essentially destined to fail from the start because they are not properly equipped for success. Facilitative leaders understand that teams require eight essentials, and they provide teams these key ingredients to accomplish their work. At the same time, many plans fall short of their desired ends due to lack of monitoring for results. (Case in point: how often do strategic plans get written and then put on a shelf?) Facilitative leaders understand the need to monitor for results every step of the way.

6 Engage Conflict, Encourage Disagreement

When faced with a challenging situation, leaders who lack the tools to effectively manage conflict tend to respond with either a "fight" or a "flight" strategy. Leaders who take the flight approach avoid addressing issues in hopes that the issues will go away on their own. Leaders employing the fight strategy tend to attempt to overpower the situation by enforcing their will without considering or inviting alternatives from others. Leaders skilled in TAFA, however, view conflict as a symptom indicating that perhaps something important is not being addressed. They understand the three reasons people disagree and have strategies for addressing each one. They believe that through disagreement even more effective solutions can emerge.

7 Drive Strategic Thinking throughout the Organization

One of the traditional leadership roles is to set a strategic vision for an organization and establish priorities for execution. Facilitative leaders aren't satisfied with reserving strategic thinking for the highest levels in an organization. They understand the benefit of having strategic thinking skills throughout the organizational hierarchy. They provide a strategic thinking process and promote a strategic thinking organization by modeling it in all that they do.

8 Start, Execute, and Close Every Meeting Masterfully

For leaders, meetings often serve as the primary vehicle for influencing action in their organizations. Whether these take the form of status meetings, working meetings, strategy retreats, 1-on-1 coaching sessions, or even "drive-by" updates when someone catches the leader in the hallway, meetings serve as the currency for leadership influence. Unfortunately, many meetings are a waste of time. Some are completely unnecessary; others are unfocused, unproductive, and ineffective. Bad meetings waste time, consume resources, and wear down people's energy and passion. Still worse, bad meetings often result in poor decisions: decisions which are inadequately thought through, void of innovation, and missing the necessary buy-in for success. Facilitative leaders understand the important role of meetings in sparking innovation and gaining buy-in. They use masterful meeting techniques to maximize interaction and results.

Benefits of TAFA

This book seeks to impart both an understanding of what it means to take a facilitative approach and a commitment to applying the practices in day-to-day leadership experiences.

This begs an obvious question. Why do this? Why TAFA? Why take a facilitative leadership approach?

Benefits to Your People

When, as a leader, you take a facilitative approach to making decisions and solving problems, you will likely see an almost immediate impact on your people:

- They will be more committed to the direction due to their greater involvement in creating it.

- They will be more engaged in their work because they were more involved in deciding what work will be done.

- They will feel more empowered to take action and better equipped for success because they understand your key principles of operation and the limits of their authority.

- They will feel more connected to the organization because they were given the opportunity to influence its direction.

- They will be more likely to believe that you care about them based on the involvement opportunities you have given them.

Benefits to Your Organization

While the benefits to your people will likely be felt almost immediately, the impact on the organization is longer-term as employee engagement increases. In his book, Employee Engagement 2.0,[3] Kevin Kruse defines employee engagement as "the emotional commitment an employee has to the organization and its goals, resulting in the use of discretionary effort." Higher employee engagement results in what Kruse calls the "Engagement-Profit Chain": employees who are engaged and care more are more productive, give better service, and stay in their jobs longer. This results in happier customers who buy more and refer more often, which drives higher sales and profits.

In this same way, when leaders take a facilitative approach, it is more likely that their organizations will achieve:

- Better decisions

- Higher levels of buy-in and commitment to action

- Lower turnover

- Higher productivity

- Stronger results

Benefits to You

The benefits to you as you implement the TAFA practices are significant as well.

- By starting with the why, and connecting first/correcting second, you will be able to inspire your people to higher performance levels.

- By equipping your team for success, driving strategic thinking throughout the organization, and monitoring for results, you will have greater trust in your people and feel greater comfort that the outcomes you want will be achieved.

- By encouraging disagreement, you will be able to get to better decisions through collaborative discussion and often faster decisions through the tools and techniques for effectively resolving conflict.

- Through the tools for creating masterful meetings, your group interactions will be move effective, more productive, and more engaging.

- Finally, by understanding and empowering your people to take higher levels of responsibility, you will reduce your stress, increase your own job satisfaction, be able to move from mundane management tasks to focus more of your time and energy on higher level, strategic leadership activities, and better prepare to grow your career and move on to other areas of the organization.

How Your Role Changes with TAFA

The TAFA practices require a fundamental shift in the way leaders see their role. As discussed, facilitative leaders recognize that they can achieve better results by involving the people impacted by a decision in the creation of that decision. To successfully do this, leaders must change what might be a more traditional perception of their role, as described in Figure 1.1.

Figure 1.1 How TAFA Changes the Leadership Role

From	To
• Sage on the stage	• Guide on the side
• Central hub of the wheel	• Outer rim setting the boundary
• Telling	• Asking
• Communicating what actions to take	• Communicating why action is important
• Autocratic decision-making	• Decision-making widely dispersed with defined authority

With this shift in their leadership role, many leaders find that they need additional strategies to ensure all voices are heard and to get their ideas on the table without overpowering the group, as described in the following.

Ensuring Voices are Heard

The fundamental secret of facilitation says that you can increase buy-in and commitment by inviting those affected by a decision to be involved in creating that decision. Does that mean that everyone affected by a decision should be at the table creating it? No, of course not. Nor is such an all-inclusive process necessary. Involvement doesn't necessarily mean being at the table. There are several ways to provide people with an opportunity for involvement.

- For some individuals, merely being given a chance to offer input through a survey or a suggestion box is adequate.

- For others, focus groups, one-on-one interviews, or other methods for gaining in-depth input may be more appropriate.

- And for other individuals, their responsibilities, influence, expertise, or perspectives are so important that it will make sense to have them seated around the table.

One of the most important leadership roles is determining who should be at the table and what avenues should be used to gain involvement from those who are not. Chapter 8 will dive deeper into the question of how to determine who should be in the room when decisions are made.

Getting Your Ideas on the Table without Overpowering the Group

Facilitative leaders understand that it is important that *all* voices be heard, including their own. Unfortunately, for most leaders, their voice can come with considerable baggage. When the boss speaks, people tend to listen, and they tend to listen differently than they do when other people speak.

There will certainly be some people in the room who treat your voice like every other voice. For them, whether an idea comes from you or a first-year manager is irrelevant; these people will state their agreement or disagreement in the exact same way. My experience, however, has been that in most organizations this typically is not the case. When the leader speaks, most may be quick to respond when they agree, and very, very slow to respond when they disagree—so slow, in fact, that sometimes they may never get around to it.

Lacking a challenge, the leader's views can easily overpower the group. Even when someone dares to challenge with a question, some leaders, often without knowing it, respond with statements that belittle the questioner or communicate that challenging the boss is unwelcome. Facilitative leaders use strategies similar to the following to ensure that their voice does not dominate the group.

Strategies to Avoid Dominating the Group

1. **Explain your role.** Let the team know how you see your role. Consider communicating the following.

- Your leadership title was left outside the door when you walked in.

- Inside the room, you are one member of the team and have one vote just like everyone else.

- The decisions being formulated inside the room are the *recommendations* of the team and will go to the leader for the final decision.

- Outside the room, you will put your leader title back on and will have the final say on the recommendations of the team. Should you, as the leader, decide to not accept a recommendation, you'll let them know why.

2. **Share your views appropriately.** If you have a recommendation that you know you want to have the team consider, be deliberate about getting it on the table.

- In some cases, it will be more helpful to state your view up front and gain feedback. (See "The Telemarketing Director" later in this chapter.)

- In other cases, it will be more helpful to give the team a chance to develop their ideas first and to suggest your idea only if the group didn't come up with it on its own.

How do you decide which approach is more appropriate?

- Generally, if your idea is focused on strategic direction or broad vision, consider stating it up front for reaction.

- If your idea is more narrowly focused or addresses how something will be implemented, it may be more appropriate to suggest your idea only if the group doesn't come up with it on its own.

3. **Don't be first.** Avoid being the first, second, or third person to respond.

- Many leaders find it difficult to sit back when a comment is made that is clearly off track or may take the discussion in what they believe is the wrong direction. As a result, they speak up and give their comments first, and, predictably, the rest of the group falls in line.

- When I facilitate executive sessions, I make it a point before the first session to ask leaders specifically to not be the first, second, or third person to respond to comments. I ask them to allow their people to speak up first and to comment only after at least three others have given their views. I ask leaders to adopt a personal ground rule: "Three before me."

4. **Use open rather than closed language.**

- When leaders say, "It won't work," they are responding with what I call closed language. Such words communicate that they have already made up their mind. And it follows that if people have a different opinion, they'll have to disagree with the boss, which many are reluctant to do.

- A more open language statement would be, "I don't see how that would work and still make us money." The simple phrase, "I don't see how..." implies that someone may be able to show you. This phrasing invites people to provide you additional information.

- As a leader, you will find that using open language gives people permission to make comments that they might otherwise keep to themselves.

Sharing Ideas in My Organization

As the leader of my organization, I've had to use these same strategies myself. For example, in one of our strategic planning sessions, I knew that I wanted us to seek to double our size in three to five years. I prepared a presentation to the team discussing why this expansion was important and providing general bullets of what it might require from each department. I then asked the team to respond first by saying what they liked about what they heard, and then what concerned them about it and ideas for how to make it better.

I was surprised by what came out. Several team members felt the target was too modest and that we should be looking to triple our size in three years, not double. Others felt that to achieve the growth rate that I was suggesting meant we had to focus on getting our processes more standardized and effective. Others felt that we needed to focus more on just a few products, while others felt we needed to add more products.

What followed was a rich discussion that resulted in essentially full buy-in to the target and excitement around developing the plan to make the target a reality.

Leaders Must Lead

While applying the TAFA practices, facilitative leaders never forget that leaders must lead. Facilitative leaders never lose sight of the fact that they are ultimately responsible for achieving results. While the engagement strategies inherent in the TAFA practices have time and time again helped leaders achieve sustainable results, facilitative leaders recognize that the goal is *not* engagement, the goal is results. Engagement is a valuable tool for maximizing your results.

Why is it so important that facilitative leaders remember that leaders must lead? Because there will be times when your team will be fully engaged and bought in to a solution that is simply unacceptable. For example, you may strongly believe that your team's proposed solution will take the team in the wrong direction or that the solution will waste considerable resources with little probability of success. *Leaders must lead.* You must step in to avoid what you believe is impending disaster. How you step in, however, is what makes facilitative leaders stand out.

Facilitative leaders know that if they veto a team's idea simply because they don't like it, or if they insist on a change because they believe that it will improve the solution, their people eventually conclude that putting in effort is a waste of time, as the leader is going make a unilateral decision without regard to the team's input.

While leaders must indeed lead, facilitative leaders understand the importance of going out of their way to lead without disempowering. How do they do it?

Strategies for Leading without Disempowering

1. **Explain the team's role.** When seeking input, be clear with your team what role you are asking them to play. What follows are a few examples.

   - "I would like for you to *brainstorm ideas* for how to address an issue. We will not be making a decision today. I just want to get your thoughts for me to reflect on."

   - "I need *your input* on something. I have a decision to make and I am leaning in a particular direction, but before I make the decision, I would like to hear your views. But I want to be clear, this is my decision, not the group's."

   - "We have a decision that is needed here. I am willing to go with whatever *the group decides*, and so I have just one vote like everyone else."

2. **Avoid vetoing unless necessary.** When individuals who have been empowered with decision-making authority make decisions with which you disagree, unless the decision is one which goes against a value of the organization or would do considerable harm, consider the following course of action.

   - Affirm that the decision is theirs to make.

   - Let them know you have concerns about the prospects for success and express those concerns.

   - Consider agreeing on an interim milestone and criteria that would confirm the validity of the direction, or that would indicate reasons to reconsider.

3. **If you veto, always explain why**. If you must veto a decision made, acknowledge to the group the downside of your vetoing a decision (i.e., it disempowers the decision owner), and explain why the decision was not appropriate. But, as discussed previously, it is highly important that leaders make every effort to minimize exercising their veto right.

Vetoing

In my own organization, we have a diverse leadership team with different levels of tolerance for risk and change, and multiple priorities. After discussion and debate, I frequently find myself on the short side of decision votes in our meetings. Yet in the 25+ years that I have led the firm, I have vetoed a leadership team decision less than a half-dozen times.

When Is TAFA Inappropriate?

Not every leadership situation requires taking a facilitative approach. There are indeed times when TAFA is inappropriate. Recall the fundamental principle of facilitation: *You can achieve more effective results when solutions are created, understood, and accepted by the people impacted.* Given this principle, there are several instances when a facilitative approach is not appropriate.[4]

- **When there is nothing to "create"**
  For example, if you have already made the decision to move in a specific direction, bringing people together to decide a direction to choose would be a waste of time. In fact, your people could perceive such a session as deceptive and misleading, as the decision has already been "created." However, bringing people together to discuss *how* to implement the decision would be appropriate.

- **When a situation or the related information is too complex or too sensitive for the group to "understand"**
  For example, in anticipation of a business downturn, you and your leadership team may meet to decide the order of department members who are candidates to be let go. Having those who would be directly impacted by the decision (i.e., the candidates for dismissal) involved in the decision-making is clearly not appropriate in most situations.

- **When time does not permit taking a facilitative approach**
  As an example, your facilitative hiring process provides the opportunity for all leadership team members to provide input on any high-profile hire. This increases buy-in and helps ensure that every leadership team member is invested in the new hire's success. However, after a first round of interviews that included just two of your six leadership team members, a highly desired candidate alerts you that she has another offer which she must accept or turn down in 24 hours. You recognize that you will not be able to involve all of your leadership team in the process and will have to make a decision with limited input.

When TAFA is not used appropriately, the result can be frustrating and quite ineffective. When used appropriately, however, taking a facilitative approach can yield better results with greater buy-in and stronger commitment to action. Figure 1.2 summarizes when TAFA is and is not appropriate.

Figure 1.2 When Taking a Facilitative Approach Is and Is Not Appropriate

	TAFA	Don't TAFA
Has the decision already been made?	No	**Yes**
Is the situation or the related information too complex or too confidential for a group to address?	No	**Yes**
Is adequate time available to take a facilitative approach?	**Yes**	No
Is the issue important enough to justify the time and expense of a facilitative approach?	**Yes**	No
Will the development of a solution require an understanding and analysis of the situation with input from a number of people?	**Yes**	No
Will the solution likely require buy-in or a change in behavior by a number of people?	**Yes**	No
Are the likely participants open to, or do they have a reason for, accepting a common solution?	**Yes**	No

The first two questions trump all others. If the decision has already been made or if the situation or the related information is too complex or too confidential for a group to address, then taking a facilitative approach to come up with a decision is not appropriate. If the answer to the first two questions is no, however, ideally you would use a facilitative approach in situations when the response to all of the other questions is yes.

If the response to one or two of the other questions is no, the conditions are not optimal for TAFA. You might choose not to take a facilitative approach, or you may be able to change the focus or the conditions so that TAFA is more appropriate.

How This Book Can Help You

This book is designed to be helpful to both senior leaders and relatively new, developing leaders. If you are already in an executive or senior leadership role, you will find that this book can help you in several ways.

- In some cases, you will find that this book reinforces strategies you already use. Some executives in our courses have commented that though they were already using some of the tools described, through the classroom experience they gained a better understanding of why the strategies worked and how to use them even more effectively.

- The book will also introduce you to new strategies that can be put into practice right away. Many executives, especially those who have never gone through a formal leadership development program, suffer from what can be described as "Swiss cheese" learning. That is, in some areas they have solid skills, but in other areas there are gaping holes in their knowledge. This book will help fill in the holes.

- You may also find, as other executives have, that the various models help you recognize mistakes you have made in the past—those wincing moments when you think, "I wish I had known that five years ago!" You will pick up strategies for addressing similar situations should they arise in the future.

- Finally, you will find tools and best practices that you can share with others in coaching the leaders that you lead.

If you are at an early stage in your leadership journey, you will find this book particularly insightful in several ways.

- It provides a roadmap detailing how you can develop over the three leadership levels. The book gives you tools for moving to higher levels of leadership.

- It lays out a comprehensive methodology for taking a facilitative approach in the way you make decisions, solve problems, work with teams, coach individuals, et cetera.

- Rather than just "telling" you what to do, the book includes examples and case studies that bring the facilitative leadership practices and strategies alive.

- Finally, at the end of each chapter the book includes the "Spring Forward" section which gives you specific actions to take to begin incorporating the strategies covered in the chapter.

How the Book is Organized

Following the next chapter, which describes the Level-3 Leadership Model, each subsequent chapter covers one of the eight core practices described earlier.

- Chapter 2: The three levels of leadership

- Chapter 3: Start with the why, not with the what

- Chapter 4: Understand and empower; don't command and control

- Chapter 5: Communicate in their language, not yours

- Chapter 6: Connect first, correct second

- Chapter 7: Equip for success, monitor for results

- Chapter 8: Engage conflict, encourage disagreement

- Chapter 9: Drive strategic thinking throughout the organization

- Chapter 10: Start, execute, and close every meeting masterfully

- Chapter 11: Pulling it all together

You will find that the chapters include a number of strategies for implementing each core practice. Furthermore, each chapter closes with a summary of the key concepts and includes one or more Spring Forward exercises that you can use to stimulate your implementation of the strategies found in the chapter.

The TAFA practices outline what it means to take a facilitative approach inside an organization. As more and more leaders adopt facilitation as a way of leadership, I expect to see greater business results driven by higher levels of buy-in and commitment throughout an organization. I believe facilitative leaders can make it happen.

Summary

1. The fundamental principle of facilitation: You can achieve more effective results when solutions are created, understood, and accepted by the people impacted.

2. A facilitative leader is a person in a leadership role who understands and applies the fundamental principle of facilitation. Facilitative leaders create organizations where engagement is the norm, collaboration is the vehicle, and higher levels of achievement are the result.

3. TAFA means "to take a facilitative approach" and applies to decision- making, problem solving, managing people, and a myriad of other leadership activities.

4. When a leader takes a facilitative approach, he/she **SUCCEEDS** by exercising the following practices:

   - Start with the why, not with the what

   - Understand and empower, don't command and control

   - Communicate in their language, not yours

   - Connect first, correct second

   - Equip for success, monitor for results

   - Engage conflict, encourage disagreement

   - Drive strategic thinking throughout the organization

   - Start, execute, and close every meeting masterfully

5. There are benefits to your people, to you, and to your organization for taking a facilitative approach:

   Benefits to your people

   - They will be more committed to the direction due to their greater involvement in creating it.

   - They will feel more empowered to take action because they understand key principles of operation and the limits of their authority.

Benefits to you

- You will have the time to focus on higher-level activities.

- You will feel greater comfort with and trust in your people.

- You will lower your stress level, increase your own job satisfaction, and be able to move from mundane management tasks to focus more of your time and energy on higher-level, strategic leadership activities. This will better prepare you to grow your career and move on to other areas of the organization.

Benefits to your organization

- Your organization will experience lower turnover rates.

- Your organization will achieve stronger results.

6. TAFA practices require a fundamental shift in the way leaders see their role, including moving from communicating what action to take and autocratic decision-making to communicating why it is important to take an action and widely dispersed decision-making authority.

7. With TAFA, leaders must exercise strategies to ensure that all voices are heard, including their own. And while facilitative leaders ensure their voice doesn't overpower the group, they also recognize that there are times when they must lead, and that may mean vetoing a group decision.

8. When is TAFA not appropriate?

- When there is nothing to "create."

- When a situation or the related information is too complex or too sensitive for the group to "understand."

- When time does not permit taking a facilitative approach.

Spring Forward

As you review the eight core practices of facilitative leaders, how would you rate them in terms of your knowledge, skill, and current application?

1. Improving—This is an area in which I look forward to improving and am seeking strategies that I can start using immediately.

2. Proficient—I have several solid competencies in this area but suspect there are strategies that can make me even better.

3. Masterful—I believe I understand this area well and actively apply strategies to exercise the practice on a regular basis.

	1 **Improving**	**2** **Proficient**	**3** **Masterful**
Start with the why, not with the what			
Understand and empower, don't command and control			
Communicate in their language, not yours			
Connect first, correct second			
Equip for success, monitor for results			
Engage conflict, encourage disagreement			
Drive strategic thinking throughout the organization			
Start, execute, and close every meeting masterfully			

The 3 Levels of Leadership | 2

- Manager versus Leader
- The 3 Levels of Leadership
- The Presentation to the CIO
- Questions about the Levels
- The Leadership Scorecard
- The Decision Matrix
- Holding the Decision Matrix Conversation
- Summary
- Spring Forward

Chapter 2.
The 3 Levels of Leadership

A surprisingly large number of people can't articulate the difference between a manager and a leader. Some people use the terms interchangeably, as if they essentially mean the same thing. Others have a sense that there is a difference, but have trouble articulating what the difference is. Before going into the practices of a facilitative leader, this chapter will provide clarity on what a leader is by defining the difference between a manager and a leader and by showing how leaders are developed.

Manager versus Leader

In our workshop, *The Facilitative Leader*, participants describe the difference between managers and leaders by choosing one-word verbs to describe what each one does across four dimensions: people, vision, problems, and client needs.

Figure 2.1 Manager versus Leader

	Manager	**Leader**
People	Supervises	Inspires
Vision	Implements	Creates
Problems	Solves	Eliminates
Client Needs	Satisfies	Anticipates

Figure 2.1 illustrates the types of responses given in workshops. While both managers and leaders play important organizational roles, there are several key distinctions based on the preceding table.

- While a manager supervises people, a leader *inspires* people.

- While a manager solves problems, a leader *eliminates* problems.

- While a manager responds to client needs, a leader *anticipates* client needs.

- While a manager implements the vision, a leader *creates* the vision.

To summarize, while a manager is reactive, a leader is proactive; while a manager tends to focus on today, a leader focuses on tomorrow; and while a manager ensures people are doing the job right, a leader ensures people are doing the right job.

The 3 Levels of Leadership

With this distinction between manager and leader as a starting point, we don't believe leaders are "born" as the saying goes, we believe instead that leaders are developed, and developed over three distinct levels as described in Figure 2.2.

Figure 2.2 The Level-3 Leadership Model

Level 3 – VISIONARY "Future Focus"	• Visioning the future • Linking to business objectives • Anticipating customer needs • Continuous improvement
Level 2 – COACH "People Focus"	• Communicating objectives • Delegating and grooming • Maximizing people's strengths
Level 1 – OVERSEER "Task Focus"	• Getting tasks done • Staying within budget • Meeting deadlines

Level-1 Leaders

When people are first appointed to a manager role, they tend to behave like overseers. They become very task-focused. This is "level-1" leadership. Level-1 leaders focus on figuring out what needs to get done, how to get it done, and how to get it done on time and on budget. For level-1 leaders, it is all about the work and getting the work done.

Level-2 Leaders

Once leaders understand what it takes to be successful in the work, they then begin to realize that they can be more effective if their people are more effective. When this realization occurs, leaders make the leap to level 2. They go from being an overseer to being a coach, and from being task-focused to people-focused.

Level-2 leaders direct their energies toward understanding their people's skills, maximizing their strengths, and minimizing their weaknesses. Level-2 leaders focus on communicating the overall picture of what they are trying to accomplish. They delegate, they groom, and they spend considerable time ensuring that everyone is clear on the goal. They understand that to be successful, their people must understand the leader's objectives and the key decision-making principles.

When you are in the presence of a level-2 leader, you know it because the difference from a level-1 leader is like night and day. Level-1 leaders talk about the tasks, the deliverables, and the factors related to accomplishing them. Level-2 leaders, however, tend to focus on people. They realize that their success depends on their people.

Level-3 Leaders

But while the difference between level-1 and level-2 leaders is significant, the difference between level-2 and level-3 leaders is even more so. While level-1 leaders focus on task, and level-2 leaders focus on people, level-3 leaders focus on the future. It is the visionary level.

Level-3 leaders want to know how decisions made today will impact the future. Regardless of the position in the organization, whether CEO, business unit director, department head, team leader, et cetera, level-3 leaders are consistently asking themselves questions such as:

- Where is the overall business going?
- How do we align our efforts with the overall business objectives?
- What will our customers want in the future?
- What do we need to be doing today to better prepare ourselves for the future?
- How do we continuously improve? How do we get faster, better, and cheaper?

Level-3 leaders create a vision of the future and strive to ensure that every decision they make is aligned to that vision.

The Presentation to the CIO

I started my career in information technology and at one point was an information systems consultant with what was then one of the Big Eight accounting and consulting firms. At the time, I was in charge of the account for a large metropolitan area. The city named a new chief information officer to head their systems area, and when she had been on board for about six months, I made an appointment to meet with her.

In the meeting, I explained that there were 23 major computer applications for the city and that of those 23 systems, eight of them had a resident database, each one acting like a silo system. Any time a resident moved it was a problem, because all eight of the databases had to be updated…separately…a very inefficient operation. But, frequently, not all eight databases were updated. And citizens would continue to get mail and other items at their old location. This was costly, inefficient, and poor customer service.

I presented to her the idea of creating an integrated systems architecture in which all eight systems would update a single resident database. Of course, the city could not spend the money all at once to move all these systems to this new architecture. But if they designed and created the architecture, as new systems were created, they would be designed around the integrated architecture—no more silos. And when an old system was updated, that system also could be moved to the integrated architecture. So, over three to five years, all systems would be on the new architecture.

Frankly, I thought it was a fantastic presentation. I gave her the reasons to change, a vision for change, and a way to change. I delivered the presentation with both passion and clarity. How could she possibly say no?

Her response: "You presented some interesting ideas for us to consider, but I just got a request in from the Police Bureau to implement a new system. Can you help us with this?"

I was devastated. I had presented to her a vision of integrated systems, and she was asking me to implement another silo database.

But here's the good news: that was not the end of the story. About two years later I got a call from the CIO. She indicated that she had just gotten a request in from the water department for a new system. She said that though they wanted a stand-alone system, her feeling was that it would be a better idea to figure out a roadmap for integrating their existing systems so that any new system like the one requested by the water department could be made a part of that integrated roadmap. She was wondering if we did that kind of work.

I practically fell out of my chair. She was asking me about developing an integrated architecture, the same thing I had proposed to her two years before. When I mentioned the presentation to her, she didn't even remember it!

Why didn't the CIO get the message the first time? Why did she have little interest in the idea when I presented it to her two years before? As might be surmised, I was presenting a level-3 concept to a leader who was operating at level-1. The presentation clearly didn't fit with the level at which she was operating. Remember, she had only been in her position six months. She was still operating in a "task focus" mode. My level-3 presentation had fallen on deaf ears. I had presented a solution to a problem that wasn't on her radar. I didn't know the Level-3 Leadership Model at the time. But had I known it, I would have recognized what it meant when, a year later, she began sending people to our classes. She had moved to level 2, and it was just going to be a matter of time before she would be ready to address level-3 issues.

Questions about the Levels

In our leadership workshops, we often get questions about the levels. Let's run through a few of them.

1. Are the levels the same as hierarchical positions in an organization?

   - No, the three leadership levels do not represent levels of organizational hierarchy. They are levels of development for a leader. Tragically, you can have the CEO of an organization operating at level 1. You can also have someone in an administrative position acting at level 3.

   - For example, examine the difference between a level-1 receptionist and a level-3 receptionist. A level-1 receptionist might be stressed daily by juggling the task of answering phone calls while greeting people who walk through the door. A level-3 receptionist, however, might be constantly looking for ways to improve how the phone and greeting processes could better support the business. A level-3 receptionist might arrange a meeting with the COO to suggest that, with the organization's emphasis on being customer-friendly, it might be more appropriate to replace the automated device that answers phone calls with a live person.

   - Organizations generally can gain significantly more value from people operating at higher levels because these people tend to be much more proactive in their thinking and in their actions.

   > Typically, the more people operating at level 3 in an organization, the better for the organization.

2. Don't leaders have to operate at all three levels? So how do I know at what level I am operating at?

   - Yes, to some extent all leaders have to operate at all three levels. But the key question is: Where is your focus? What is getting your mindshare? What are you spending your time thinking about and addressing? Is your principle focus on task, people, or the future? The answer will tell you at which level you are operating.

3. What must a leader have accomplished to move from level 1 to level 2?

   - To move from level 1 to level 2, you must understand what it takes to be successful in the job. You don't have to know how to do the job, just what it takes to be successful so you can recruit, coach, groom, and evaluate others. Until you are clear on what it takes to be successful, focus your energies on level-1 activities.

The Telemarketing Director

During the first five years in the business I run today, we decided that our growth was directly related to the number of people who knew about us. The Internet barely existed at the time, social media was not a "thing," and so we decided we needed a telemarketing department to increase awareness of our services. We knew we didn't know anything about telemarketing, so we hired a telemarketing director whose job it was to hire and oversee his team. However, while we didn't know anything about telemarketing, we did understand by then the Level-3 Leadership Model. So, before the telemarketing director hired anyone, we asked him to operate in the position for several weeks so that he would know the type of people he needed to hire and the challenges they would face.

As it turned out, that was a very smart move on our part! Though our newly hired director had been quite successful in telemarketing tangible products for other industries, he was quite ineffective with the conceptual services we provided. We let him go after 30 days. But imagine if he had gone ahead and hired a team before understanding himself what it would take to be successful. It would have literally been the blind leading the blind.

4. What must a leader have in place to move from level 2 to level 3?

   - Recall that level 2 is called, "Coach." Therefore, to have the luxury of focusing your energies on level 3 activities, you must have people in place who know what it takes to be successful and who can coach other people. If you do not have people who can coach others, this means *you* will be the one coaching, and you will be stuck at level 2. To move from level 2 to level 3, you must have people who know what they are doing, and those people must also know how to develop and coach other people.

5. What are the key reasons a manager might never advance beyond level 1?

   - There are many reasons a leader might get stuck at level 1. For example, some leaders enjoy focusing on tasks and aren't interested in moving to a higher level. Other leaders don't have competent people around them. In addition, they may lack the skills to develop such people, the authority to make personnel changes, or the budget to hire others. In other cases, leaders have the competent people, but don't trust them or empower them to make decisions.

   - But a surprisingly common and even more challenging reason that many managers never get beyond level 1 is because they don't know that there are other levels. Everyone who has ever managed them operated at level 1, so they believe that is what leadership is all about! They lack a vision of what higher-level leadership is.

6. What should leaders do when they take a new position?

   • When leaders change jobs, they must intentionally drop back to level 1 until they understand what it takes to be successful in that position. For people in new positions, I recommend them spending at least 30 days understanding how things work before making any changes.

From Level-3 Principal to Level-1 Entrepreneur

When I left the consulting firm, I had been a principal for three years. I had a good understanding of what it took to be successful as a principal and was operating pretty close to level 3. Then I left that consulting firm and became the first full-time employee of Leadership Strategies—The Facilitation Company. Our world headquarters was my second bedroom…but I had big plans!

What happened to the level-3 principal? I became a level-1 entrepreneur. I was struggling with just getting invoices out each month, not to mention paying bills, making sales calls, responding to inquiries, et cetera. But what would have happened if I hadn't dropped back to level 1? I more than likely would be working for someone else right now and not running one of the leading companies in the facilitation field.

---

7. Who is responsible for the development of an organization's leaders?

   • Some might say leadership development is the responsibility of the top executive. Others might say that all leaders are responsible for developing the leaders under them. And still others might say each individual is responsible for his or her own leadership development. So, which is it? Who is responsible for leadership development?

   • In our model, we believe *everyone* is responsible for leadership development. Yet consider the truism, "When everyone is responsible that means that no one is responsible for the result." However, when we indicate that everyone is responsible, we mean everyone is responsible for playing *his or her role* in leadership development. Figure 2.3 diagrams what this means.

   • Specifically, responsibility for leadership development starts at the top. Executive leadership team members have a responsibility to create an environment for leadership development (i.e., arrows "1" in Figure 2.3). Their role is to put in place the rewards systems for leadership development, to create the opportunities for people to learn how to develop others, and to instill in the culture that it is the responsibility of all leaders to develop the leaders under them.

- However, the story does not stop there. In addition, every leader is responsible for developing the people under him or her (the "2" arrows).

Figure 2.3 Responsibility for Leadership Development

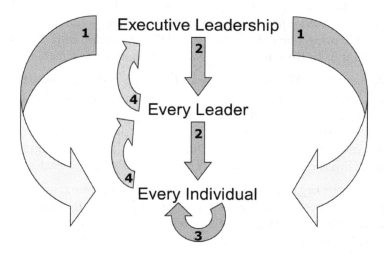

- The story goes on: every individual is responsible for grabbing these leadership opportunities (the "3" arrow). For if executive leadership is creating opportunities, but individuals aren't taking advantage of them, this is problematic.

- And, finally, every individual is responsible for developing the leaders above him/her (the "4" arrows). This is the feedback loop. Individuals are responsible for giving feedback to the leaders above them on how they are performing as leaders. (As the managing director of my own organization, I must confess I receive considerable feedback on my leadership skills—sometimes more feedback than I am seeking. This information is often humbling, but nearly always helpful.)

- Note that if any of the arrows are missing, that is, if any of the roles are not fulfilled, there is a breakdown of leadership development inside the organization. If the environment isn't created, or if leaders don't mentor others, or if individuals don't take advantage of the opportunities, or if individuals don't give feedback to their leaders, leadership development is hindered.

- Consider how strong the leadership development is in your organization. Where are the weakest links?

The Level-3 Leadership Model[5] is intended to encourage a culture where leaders strive for higher levels of leadership. For if the organization rewards only those people who get things done on time and under budget, your leaders will be encouraged to focus on level-1 activities.

Organizations must reward higher level activities including building leadership skills in others, anticipating customer needs, and inspiring vision.

The Leadership Scorecard

Okay, Michael, you give a pretty compelling case for the impact of effective leadership. But my leadership team is pretty stuck in the old paradigm. I can just hear one of them now saying, "I'm sorry, I don't have time for all this leadership stuff. I've got real work to do." Help me out here. How do I get my leadership team to focus on leadership?

That's a problem, isn't it? When the leaders of an organization see little value in "this leadership stuff," what do you do? First, to be very clear: a leader's number one priority must be the survival of the organization. And since getting the "real work" done is critical to organization survival, it is quite understandable that leaders would naturally focus first on level-1 activities such as getting the work done, on time, and within budget. Further, any leader struggling with these issues had better get back to the level-1 basics.

However, once past the organizational equivalent of food, clothing, and shelter, facilitative leaders recognize that these level-1 issues are not enough to ensure long-term success. They recognize the importance of such level-2 activities as coaching and developing people; therefore, they make investments in level-3 activities such as anticipating the changing needs of customers, shaping the organization's vision, and aligning resources to that vision.

How then do leaders inspire their leadership team to focus on leadership? One approach is to implement a leadership scorecard as a coaching tool for your leaders. While other scorecards are in place to get the organization to focus on the real work, the purpose of a leadership scorecard is to provide a vehicle to encourage leaders to focus on the work of leadership.

While the specific elements in a scorecard may differ by organization, you will find that the six elements shown in Figure 2.4 can provide a solid foundation. I recommend having every leader establish a quarterly goal for one or more of the six leadership elements. The goal and results are reviewed monthly and scored (1-10) at the end of the quarter.

A. Annual Outcomes Figure 2.4 The Leadership Scorecard

What are the 1–3 most important outcomes for your department <u>this year</u>?

Outcomes (Quantified results you will achieve)	Rating
1.	
2.	
3.	

B. Annual Initiatives

What are the 1–3 most important initiatives for your department <u>this year</u>?

Initiatives (Things you will do)	Rating
1.	
2.	
3.	

C. This Quarter

Category	Rating
Visioning What will you implement this quarter to help your team stay inspired and focused on achieving the outcomes and initiatives?	
Result	
Customers What will your department do this quarter to better understand or adapt to the needs of your entire customer base?	
Result	

Coaching
Whose performance are you most concerned about this quarter and what will you do to help ensure success?

Result

Resources
What is your most pressing resource constraint currently? What will you do to address the constraint?

Result

Continuous Improvement
What will you implement this quarter to improve the way your department operates?

Result

Execution
What is the priority initiative for your department this quarter that will drive the success of the organization and how will you ensure that it is successfully executed?

Result

The Decision Matrix

To achieve higher levels of leadership yourself, you must develop your people to accept higher levels of leadership responsibility. Figure 2.5a, The Decision Matrix, offers a vehicle for communicating the process.

Figure 2.5a The Decision Matrix

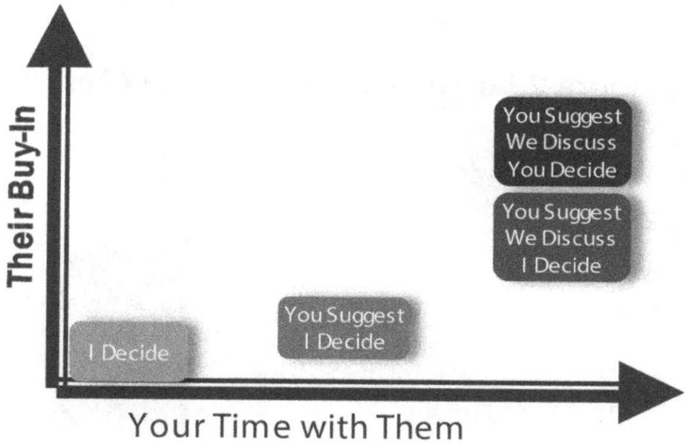

Consider the two axes. The X-axis is the amount of time you spend with your people in making a decision. The Y-axis is the level of their buy-in to the decision.

In Stage 1, I DECIDE, you are making all the decisions. You are neither seeking nor receiving input from your team. While it takes little time with them to make the decisions, the result is typically very low buy-in.

In Stage 2, YOU SUGGEST/I DECIDE, you are open to suggestions, but you still make all decisions. Taking suggestions tends to increase buy-in from your team, but it also requires more time with them.

Stage 3, YOU SUGGEST/WE DISCUSS/I DECIDE, requires even more time as you are discussing your team's suggestions. But as before, you are making the final decision. In this stage you have the opportunity to discuss your team's recommendations, hear their rationale, and help them understand why you might agree or disagree. In listening to their rationale and having them listen to yours, they learn how to anticipate your concerns and you're able to increase your level of comfort with their decision-making.

Stage 4, YOU SUGGEST/WE DISCUSS/YOU DECIDE, involves a significant shift in the decision-making. In Stage 4, you are open to the team's suggestions and you discuss them. However, the final decision is up to the team members. While this entails the same amount of time as Stage 3, notice that Stage 4 *significantly* increases buy-in. You can progress to Stage 4 only after increasing your level of trust in the team's decision-making ability.

Stage 5 is not shown in Figure 2.5a. With Stage 5, YOU SUGGEST/YOU DECIDE, all decisions are made by the other person without consulting with you at all. This begs the question, where does the box for this stage go in the Decision Matrix?

The Stage 5 box goes in the upper left as shown in Figure 2.5b. Stage 5 has an increase in buy-in, but a *significant* decrease in your time with the team. This final stage entails a major shift based on your trust in the others' decision-making ability. This shift allows you to be comfortable with completely delegating the decision-making authority and thereby reducing the time you have to spend with the team in decision-making.

Figure 2.5b The Decision Matrix (Part II)

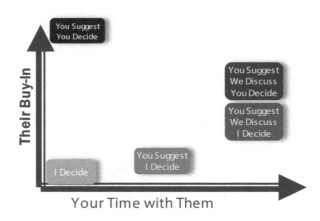

Of course, it is not advisable to hire people and automatically set them at stage 5. If you did that with every new hire it would not be long before complete anarchy would prevail, with little or no guidance, coordination, or integration. Instead, start people at the appropriate stage, based on the situation and the individual's skill and competence, and then move people through the decision matrix as they develop in the position and your trust in their decision-making increases.

The Decision Matrix and The Level-3 Leadership Model

It is important to note that the Decision Matrix correlates with the Level-3 Leadership Model.

In Figure 2.5c the first two stages represent a level-1 overseer. In these stages, you are making all the decisions. The third and fourth stages are level-2 coach, where you are helping the person understand factors to consider in decision-making. Over time, the final authority for making decisions shifts from you to the other person. The final stage is level-3 visionary, where the person makes all the decisions, freeing you to focus much more of your time on level-3 activities.

Figure 2.5c The Decision Matrix (Part III)

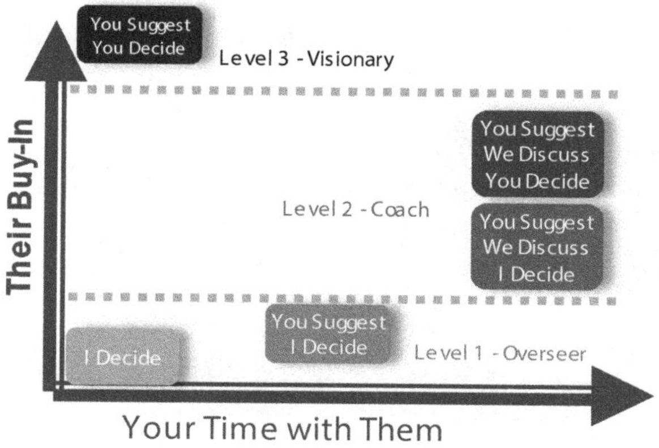

Notice in the diagram that as you progress a person from stage 1 through stage 5, both the level of empowerment and the level of buy-in increases. As you move through the middle stages (3 and 4), you invest more of your time, but it is temporary. The extra investment ends at stage 5. By moving more and more people to stage-5 decision-making, you become more productive and they are able to operate with much fuller autonomy.

Managing a New Marketing Director

If I only knew about the Decision Matrix before I hired my first marketing director. She was brilliant, coming to us with years of experience marketing consumer goods. She joined us in the days when direct mail through the postal service was a primary vehicle for making people aware of open enrollment training classes.

In those days, our standard mailing was a four-pager (11" x 17" folded in half). To save on mailing costs we used two-color rather than full-color brochures. Within a week of her arrival, the marketing director announced that she wanted to change our mail-outs from the four-pager to a postcard. (She didn't know when she changed jobs that it's helpful to drop to level 1 for at least 30 days!)

I was less than thrilled by her suggestion. I explained to our new hire that while postcards would certainly save us money in the short term and may have been quite successful for consumer goods, I was concerned that a postcard could not provide our potential buyers with enough information to build sufficient interest for them to pick up the phone and call us. Keep in mind that in those days there was no website to refer people to, as most people didn't have Internet access.

She believed that when we overwhelm people with too much information like the four-page brochure, they don't bother to read any of it and we lose the potential sale anyway.

I then showed her the brochures of three of our competitors. Two of the brochures were eight pages (compared to our four) and the third was twelve pages. She was still adamant that her approach would work. I wasn't open to it.

This was how the relationship started, and within a year, the marketing director left for another position because she felt I wasn't allowing her to do her job. She was right.

If I had only known about the Decision Matrix back then, I would have been able to hold the Decision Matrix conversation with her.

Holding the Decision Matrix Conversation

We've discussed the decision matrix, and it is now valuable to discuss how to have a conversation about it, so you can maximize the value from it. Consider these steps in the conversation.

1. Meet with the team member individually and introduce the Decision Matrix.

2. Gain agreement on the current decision box by asking her to indicate the stage at which most decisions involving her area are being made currently. Discuss further if your view is different from hers.

3. Gain agreement on the desired decision box by asking her to identify the stage at which she desires decisions to be made. Discuss further if your view is different.

4. Identify why the desired decision box isn't the current decision level.

5. Identify what needs to happen to achieve the desired level.

6. Outline a possible plan of action.

7. Confirm agreement.

8. Ensure monitoring.

The Decision Matrix can help those who feel they're being micromanaged to see the possibility for change. My first marketing director believed that I would be micromanaging her for the rest of her time with the company. If I had known this model two decades ago and held the Decision Matrix conversation, we would have both agreed that we were at stage 3, and that we both wanted marketing decision-making to be at stage 5. We would then have been able to discuss a plan for trying some of her ideas in a limited form with specific, pre-defined results required to continue the investment. Over time, we would both have learned what works and what doesn't, with the potential for new ideas to prove their worth. At the same time, the model would have provided the time needed for the marketing director to learn our industry. If only I had known the model!

Summary

1. There are significant differences between managers and leaders.

    • While a manager supervises people, a leader *inspires* people.

    • While a manager solves problems, a leader *eliminates* problems.

    • While a manager responds to client needs, a leader *anticipates* client needs.

    • While a manager implements vision, a leader *creates* vision.

    • While a manager is reactive, a leader is *proactive*.

    • While a manager tends to focus on today, a leader focuses on *tomorrow*.

    • While a manager ensures people are doing the job right, a leader ensures people are *doing the right job*.

2. Leaders are developed over three distinct levels.

    • Level-1 leaders are overseers and tend to focus on completing tasks on-time and on-budget.

    • Level-2 leaders are coaches and tend to focus on developing people.

    • Level-3 leaders are visionaries and tend to focus on the future, including anticipating client needs and linking to business objectives.

3. To move from level 1 to level 2, a leader must understand what it takes to be successful in the job.

4. To move from level 2 to level 3, a leader must have people who can coach other people.

5. Many leaders don't progress beyond level 1 because they don't know that there are other levels. Everyone who has ever managed them has operated at level 1, so they believe that is what leadership is all about!

6. To some extent all leaders have to operate at all three levels. But the key question is: Where is your focus? What is getting your mindshare? What are you spending your time thinking about and addressing?

7. To achieve higher levels of leadership, leaders must progress their people to higher levels of leadership. The Decision Matrix offers a vehicle for communicating and executing the process.

Spring Forward

Your Leadership Level

At which leadership level are you operating today?
What can you do to begin moving to the next level?

Your People

For your direct reports, list their leadership level, where your interaction is with them in the decision matrix (e.g., you suggest/I decide), and how you can help them move to a higher level.

Person	Leadership Level	Decision Matrix	Action to a Higher Level

Start with the Why, Engage with the How **3**

- The Two Stone Masons
- Mission Statement: State the Why
- Meetings: Start with Why
- The Benefits to Them
- Summary
- Spring Forward

Chapter 3.
Start with the Why, Engage with the How

All too frequently leaders start with *what* they want people to do rather than focusing on the *why*. It's easy to understand why this happens. Leaders tend to focus on the outcome and the work needed to get there. They have already visualized the end point and need their people to begin doing the things required to reach that end point. So, what words do leaders tend to use? The words that describe what needs to get done. They start with the *what*. Unfortunately, when leaders start with the *what* they are back to treating their people like hands and feet that need to be directed.

Facilitative leaders, however, understand the impact of starting with the *why*.

The Two Stone Masons

In his groundbreaking book, *Start with Why*,[6] Simon Sinek tells the story of two stone masons approached by a traveler who asks them both whether or not they like their jobs. The first explains that the work of laying one brick upon another is terribly monotonous, and the stones are heavy, the sun is hot, but the job pays the bills. The second explains that he loves his job, and though the work is monotonous and the stones are heavy and the sun is hot, he is a part of a team that is building a great cathedral.

Though they are doing the exact same job and experiencing the exact same conditions, there is a fundamental difference in attitude, motivation, and engagement. However, by all appearances, the difference seems to be due to the second stone mason's understanding of, and buy-in to, the why.

Facilitative leaders understand that there are many moments in the typical workweek when bringing forth the why is beneficial and, in some cases, essential. Here are just a few examples.

- Presentations
- Project kick-offs
- Meetings
- Coaching sessions
- Delivering praise
- Delivering constructive feedback

Whether you are leading an enterprise, a division, a department, a team, or just a small group, more times than not, the why can be defined as purpose.

- You are thinking about starting up a new division…why? What's the purpose?
- You are considering increasing investments in a product line…what's the purpose?

- You want to bring a task force together to address customer satisfaction issues... what's the purpose?

- You are thinking about holding a meeting...what's the purpose?

Once you identify your purpose, it is important to communicate that purpose right from the beginning. Consider the following two vastly different examples: mission statements and meetings.

Mission Statement: State the Why

As you will see in Chapter 9, a mission statement should answer three important questions:

1. What do we do?

2. For whom do we do it?

3. What is the benefit?

The third question answers the why. A mission statement should clearly state the why. Here are three examples:[7]

- *To organize the world's information and make it universally accessible and useful* (Google).

- *To discover, develop, and deliver innovative medicines that help patients prevail over serious diseases.* (Bristol-Myers Squibb Company)

- *To help our clients achieve their financial objectives by serving as their tax and financial partner* (H&R Block).

While all three mission statements state the benefit, notice how the first two start by answering, "What do we do?" The third one, however, starts by answering, "What is the benefit?" Mission statements often have greater impact when starting with the benefit.

Unfortunately, some mission statements miss the point entirely. They leave out the why, at least from their target customer's perspective. Consider the example that follows.

- *The Company's primary objective is to maximize long-term stockholder value, while adhering to the laws of the jurisdictions in which it operates and at all times observing the highest ethical standards.*

While the case could be made that the benefit is to stockholders, the end customer is lost in this mission statement. As well, it would be difficult to guess in what industry this organization competes.

Meetings: Start with Why

Consider the simple example of starting a meeting. I believe meetings should generally start with the leader sharing the meeting's purpose and the products that will be created as a result. A meeting leader might state something similar to the following.

"The purpose of this meeting is…. When we are done, we are going to walk away with…."

By starting this way, right from the very beginning everyone at the meeting understands why they are there (the purpose) and when they can leave (when the products are created). Note, however, that it is not enough just to state the purpose; it is important to elaborate on it. Consider two examples[8] of how to start a meeting, with an eye toward which is the better choice.

Meeting Opening #1

- Good morning. The purpose of this meeting is to find ways to improve our performance review process. When we are done, we will have a list of recommendations that we will submit to the senior management team.

- Let's start by reviewing our agenda for today.

Meeting Opening #2

- Good morning. The purpose of this meeting is to find ways to improve our performance review process. When we are done, we will have a list of recommendations that we will submit to the senior management team.

- Why is this important? As you all know, we've been having significant difficulty with our performance review process.

- Your people have likely complained about wide differences among our departments on what is considered "meets" versus "exceeds" versus "far exceeds" expectations. Your employees may have also commented that the review process is all about how well people are liked and not how well they perform. Additionally, we have had cases of people receiving high ratings just a few months before being terminated for poor performance. You may have seen the impact on your team's motivation and your team's morale. In summary, it doesn't appear that our performance review process is very effective.

- This is your opportunity to make sure we have a performance review process that you feel good about, one that will allow you to ensure your top performers are fairly evaluated and rewarded compared to others in other departments. You will be creating a process that can make your job easier: fewer problems, fewer complaints, better morale, which should translate into better performance for your people, for your department and for our company.

- Let's start by…

Which meeting would you rather attend? When you focus on the why, people are more likely to feel engaged and a part of something that is important.

The Benefits to Them

There is an additional point here related to starting with the why. The full start of a meeting covers four key concepts in particular.

Inform   Provide the purpose and product, that is, explain why the meeting is being held and what products will be produced as a result of the meeting.

Excite   Describe the benefits to the participants for achieving the purpose and the products.

Empower   Let them know what they are being asked to do. Are they making a decision, making a recommendation, just brainstorming ideas, or some other activity?

Involve   Get them involved and interacting by posing a question to them that will further the work of the meeting.

As described above, after you explain the purpose and product (*inform*), you then *excite* by describing the benefits of achieving the purpose and product. The key, however, is to describe the benefits *to the participants*, not the benefits to the department or organization.

The excite component plays an integral part in helping people understand the why. In the training world, I describe the excite this way:

> Everyone in the world is tuned in to the same radio station, WII-FM: "What's in it for me?" If you broadcast at that frequency, people will hear you.

With your excite statement, it is important to describe the WII-FM. This makes *the why* personal to the participants. It's now time to take a second look at the last portion of Meeting Opening #2. Did you notice the number of times "you" and "your" appear?

- This is **your** opportunity to make sure we have a performance review process that **you** feel good about, one that will allow **you** to ensure **your** top performers are fairly evaluated and rewarded compared to others in other departments. **You** will be creating a process that can make **your** job easier: fewer problems, fewer complaints, better morale, which should translate into better performance for **your** people, for **your** department and for our company.

That is the key to making an excite statement personal. Include "you" or "your" at least four times. This will help ensure that when you state the why you are broadcasting on the WII-FM frequency.

Summary

1. All too frequently, leaders start with *what* they want people to do. Facilitative leaders understand the impact born of starting with *the why*.

2. There are many moments in the typical work week when bringing forth the why is beneficial, such as the following:

   - Presentations
   - Project kickoffs
   - Meetings
   - Coaching sessions
   - Delivering praise
   - Delivering constructive feedback

3. Mission statements should include the why by answering three questions: What do we do? For whom do we do it? What's the benefit?

4. Meetings should generally start with the meeting leader stating the purpose of the meeting and the products that will be created as a result. Note, however, that it is not enough just to state the purpose; it is important to elaborate on it in order to describe the why. When you focus on the why, people are more likely to feel engaged and a part of something that is important.

5. Since most people are tuned in to the same radio station, WII-FM (What's In It For Me?), if you broadcast at that frequency, people will hear you.

6. Therefore, after you explain the purpose and product, you then describe the benefits of achieving the purpose and product. The key, however, is to describe the benefits *for the participants*.

7. You can be sure to do this by using the words "you" or "your" at least four times. This will help ensure that when you state the why you are broadcasting on the WII-FM frequency.

Spring Forward

For many, starting with the why is not a natural activity and requires practice for it to become rote. You can practice with activities in the present, past, or future. Accordingly, take the time to list below three important activities, initiatives, or meetings that you will lead, are leading, or have led in the past. Write out the why and the WII-FM for the participants.

Activity	The Why: "The reason we are doing this is…" The WII-FM: "This is exciting/matters because…" (you/your)

- Leadership Styles
- Applying the Appropriate Style
- When Leaders Use an Inappropriate Style
- The Promotion
- The 5 Cs of Trust
- The Trust Conversation
- Delegation Dysfunction
- Steps for Effective Directing
- Steps for Effective Delegation
- Steps for Effective Coaching
- Principles of Operation
- Decision Trees
- The "Managing Your Boss" Memo
- Summary
- Spring Forward

Chapter 4.
Understand and Empower, Don't Command and Control

Facilitative leaders recognize the importance of understanding their people and empowering them appropriately to achieve higher performance levels. This chapter starts with a focus on two key concepts when it comes to understanding your people: leadership styles and trust. The chapter closes with several tools based on those concepts used to empower people to achieve stronger results.

Leadership Styles

How and when you empower a person depends in large part on the individual and the situation. Paul Hersey and Ken Blanchard in their landmark work, *Management of Organizational Behavior*,[9] defined a situational leadership model that includes four leadership styles: directing, coaching, supporting, and delegating. A fundamental principle of situational leadership is that there is no "best" style, but that a leader adjusts the style used based on the needs of each situation. Situational leadership, therefore, can be defined as the process of adjusting the way one engages subordinates based on the specific circumstances and on their skills, experience, and attitude.

Leaders have a natural leadership style, a style that they will use by default. It is the style that they find most natural, and the style with which they are most comfortable. Facilitative leaders recognize that they must understand their people and the needs of the situation to maximize the outcomes and their people's success.

This discussion incorporates the supporting style into the coaching style for clarity's sake, and delineates the three remaining styles as follows. As you review them, consider which might be your natural leadership style.

Directing

Some leaders naturally direct others. Their highest aspiration is for their team members to be clear about what is expected of them. They want team members to understand the outcome they desire and how to go about achieving it. They tend to detail their expectations and to closely monitor the execution to avoid a less than preferred result.

As an example, assume that a leader was meeting with a direct report in a conference room, and there were people holding a loud conversation outside the closed door. A leader using a directing style might say, "That noise is disturbing our meeting. Please go and let them know that they are disturbing us and that if they could be quieter or move to a different location that would be great."

Coaching

While some naturally direct, other leaders naturally use a coaching style. Their highest desire is to help people realize their potential. Such leaders enjoy engaging their direct reports in conversations that help their people learn what to do and how to do it. They derive satisfaction from developing others and watching them mature in their decision-making and take on higher levels of responsibility.

Going back to the example, a leader using a coaching style might say, "The noise is disturbing our meeting. What do you think we should do about it?"

The subordinate might respond, "I think I should go out there and tell them to show some respect and shut up."

The leader might then ask questions, "How do you think that would make them feel about engaging with you in the future? Might there be a way to approach them so that you get the behavior you want without the negativity? People often like being empowered with a choice; is there a way to give them a choice here so that it doesn't feel like you are insisting on a solution?"

Delegating

Finally, some naturally delegate to others. Their highest desire is to let people use their expertise to achieve the desired result. Delegators generally do not require a specific outcome or a specific way of securing an optimal result. Instead, they tend to express what the need is in general terms and then trust that their team members will get the job done in a suitable way with a suitable outcome.

Going back to the example, a leader using a delegating style might say, "That noise is disturbing our meeting."

The other person might respond, "I'll take care of it." That would be the end of the conversation.

Applying the Appropriate Style

Though each of us has a natural leadership style, facilitative leaders recognize their own leadership bias while developing the ability to use all three. They will then apply one of the three leadership style based on what is most appropriate for the team member and the situation. So, when should a leader use a directing, coaching, or delegating style?

When to Direct

- Lack of experience—The person lacks sufficient experience or expertise.
- Lack of time—There is not sufficient time to coach.
- Lack of trust—While the person has sufficient experience and expertise, you have little trust that the subordinate will accomplish the task successfully.

When to Coach

- Plenty of time—There is adequate time to coach the person.

- Preparing for greater responsibility—You are preparing the person to take on higher levels of responsibility.

When to Delegate

- Plenty of experience—The person has sufficient experience or expertise.

- Plenty of trust—You believe that the subordinate will accomplish the task successfully.

It is important to note that the appropriate leadership style is not only impacted by the other person, it is also impacted by the circumstances and the task. As an example, you might delegate to a budget analyst when it comes to developing a financial report. However, when this same budget analyst is charged with leading a cross-functional team focused on improving expense reporting, you may have to do significant coaching.

When Leaders Use an Inappropriate Style

Consider the following two examples of what happens when leaders apply an inappropriate leadership style.

Directing instead of Delegating

What happens when leaders direct someone for whom delegating is more appropriate? As you can probably imagine, such subordinates can become quite frustrated with not being allowed to exercise their expertise and creativity. For them, it can be de-motivating. They might label their leaders, "micromanagers." (This might sound awkwardly familiar to those who are natural directors!)

Delegating instead of Directing

What happens when leaders delegate to someone for whom directing is more appropriate? In the prior case, the subordinates become frustrated; in this case the leaders become frustrated because the results are not what were expected, or the methods used produce undesired consequences. In some cases, the leaders find themselves having to accept something they didn't like or having to redo a task themselves or assign it to someone else to redo. (This might sound awkwardly familiar to those who are natural delegators!)

Both these examples share a common title: mismanagement. The leaders are mismanaging their resources by applying an inappropriate leadership style. What follows is an example of what can happen when leaders mismanage.

The Promotion

In my prior career as a management consultant, Jim Jacobs[10] served as my senior consultant on most of the projects I led. I grew to rely on him as a highly effective consultant who could deliver in just about any situation. After working alongside me for several years, he received a promotion to another department. I was very happy for him, for the promotion was richly deserved, but I was losing my "right-arm man," and must confess to having had some ambivalent feelings about it.

About three months later I received a call from his new manager, who explained that he was calling me out of courtesy to let me know he was going to have to let Jim Jacobs go. I was shocked. I remember responding, "Jim Jacobs? Are you kidding? Jim was my best consultant. Why are you letting him go?" The new manager explained that every time he gave Jim an assignment, what Jim came back with was nothing like what he expected, and the manager had to redo the work himself. I explained to the new manager that I had never had that problem with Jim. He and I would sit down and we would discuss how to go about doing each assignment; he would share his ideas, I would provide him feedback, and off he would go. He delivered on my requests, every time.

While I am sure there were many factors involved, one of the major issues in the above scenario appears to be based on leadership style. While the senior consultant was quite effective when a coaching approach was used, he was quite ineffective in a new role with the delegating approach.

Unfortunately, when leaders mismanage people by applying the wrong leadership style, it's not the leader who looks bad, but the person being led! Imagine people who are very creative but underperform and are disgruntled because they are de-motivated by the directing style of their leader. Or people, as in the case of Jim Jacobs, who need direction and coaching but work for a delegator and perform badly because of lack of guidance. In both cases, because of mismanagement, the person being managed looks bad, not the manager. For Jim Jacobs, he perceived the end was near and found a position in another company. Through mismanagement, the organization lost a talented contributor.

The 5 Cs of Trust

Before describing tools that facilitative leaders use to successfully direct, coach, and delegate, this chapter will focus on one more topic related to understanding your people: trust.

Trust is one of those topics that most people know is important, yet many find difficult to talk about because they see it as a soft, mushy, and intangible "thing." They know when it is present, they know when it is not, but they can't distinctly describe it.

One of the most exciting aspects of what we do in my company is the work we do to take soft concepts and break them down as best as we can into tangible ideas with practical strategies that people can grasp and execute.

Figure 4.1 The 5 Cs Trust Model

In this same way, in our work with literally thousands of people around the globe, we have broken down trust into five critical aspects which we call, "The 5 Cs of Trust" as shown in Figure 4.1.

To validate the model in our workshops, we ask participants to think about someone they trust. We tell them that it may be someone in their personal or professional lives. We ask them to think about that person and what he/she does that lets them know they can trust the person. We have them write down specifically what it is about that person that tells them that they can trust him/her.

We then walk through the 5 Cs of Trust and have each person read what they wrote and answer the question, "Which C is it?" We haven't found a sixth "C" yet. Inevitably, each person describes trust in one or more of these five ways.

When I say I trust you, it means I believe:

- You have the necessary skills and expertise to get the job done (Competence).
- We truly hear and understand each other when we communicate (Communication).
- You are committed to the success of the endeavor (Commitment).
- You care about me and take my interests into consideration (Caring).
- You are honest and ethical (Character).

Likewise, when you do not trust one of the people that you lead, it is likely because of one of these 5 Cs. Your lack of trust in that person is typically due to their competence, communication, level of commitment, lack of caring about you and your concerns, or character issues that you perceive.

Trust Symptoms and Actions

I want to make one additional point about the 5 Cs Trust Model. Our experience is that the lower the C is in the Trust Triangle, the more difficult the C is to overcome. Figure 4.2 walks through each of the Cs and gives a sample description of a symptom of that C (i.e., how you would know that the C is the cause of mistrust) and the process for addressing it.

So, while you can address competence issues through skill-building activities, addressing communication issues involves verbal habits—often a little more difficult than skills. Commitment issues require changing how one behaves, which can be even more difficult than changing verbal habits. Addressing caring issues requires, to some extent, addressing how you "feel" about the other person and the behaviors that demonstrate a level of caring. Changing feelings and the way you express them is typically more difficult than changing behaviors. Finally, character issues are the most difficult to address. It can be extremely difficult to change behaviors that are based on character or change the mind of a boss who feels an employee is dishonest or unethical. Once more, "freeing up the future" of an employee with character issues might be the only alternative.

Figure 4.2 Trust Symptoms and Actions

The C	Typical Symptom	Typical Actions
Competence	Mistakes, insufficient deliverables	Hold training, coaching sessions
Communication	Misunderstandings, disagreements about what was said or what was intended	Verbally play back agreements, document in writing
Commitment	Missed meetings, late deliverables, last-minute changes	Gain agreement on behaviors to be done differently and consequences
Caring	Actions that don't address your concerns, lack of questions about your needs or desires	Gain agreement that, prior to any key action, the person will come to you with a list of concerns he/she believes you might have
Character	Dishonesty, deception, subterfuge	Consider involuntary transition if confession, remorse, and regret are not present or are not believed.

I have talked about leadership styles and trust as key concepts in understanding your people. What follows are a series of strategies and tools that can help you apply these concepts to a number of different situations.

The Trust Conversation

If you find yourself faced with a subordinate or a superior with whom trust appears to be an issue, I recommend that you hold the trust conversation as follows as a structured approach to introducing and engaging the other person.

1. Introduce the 5 Cs.

    • "One of the things that I have learned is that there are five Cs to trust. The first C stands for…"

2. Express your desire for trust.

    • "I think the organization would benefit, and you and I would as well, if we had a more trusting relationship. Do you agree?"

3. Acknowledge the current situation.

- "I am not sure that we have that relationship completely today. Do you agree? Which C or Cs do you think we need to improve on?"

4. Suggest an approach to build trust.

- "In order to increase our level of trust, here is an idea I would suggest..."

5. Ask for feedback and other suggestions.

- "What do you like about this suggestion? What concerns do you have about it working for us? How might we improve it? What other suggestions come to your mind?"

6. Decide and confirm agreement.

- "So, let's agree on an approach we can use.... We are agreed then that we will..."

7. Ensure monitoring.

- "I would like to make sure we have a way of monitoring how we are doing.... Might we...?"

Delegation Dysfunction

Early in my career as a management consultant, a partner in the firm asked me to go off and do a study of handheld inventory devices. There was no Internet at the time, so I went to the library and spent two days identifying, researching, and documenting the various alternatives for handheld inventory devices. When I came back to the office, I had a 12-page report which I proudly handed to the partner. As the partner slowly looked through the pages he said, "Wow, you put a lot of time into this." Again, proudly, I said, "Yes, I did." I had no idea that the partner was NOT complimenting me. When the partner finally got to the last page, he asked, "Where's your recommendation?" "My what?" I asked. "Well, which of these devices should we use with our client?" he asked. "Client? What client?" I asked. The partner just shook his head and walked off. It was at that moment that I realized that the partner was a poor delegator, and I was a very poor "delegatee."

What was the problem here? Sure, the partner could have done a much better job of delegating. But I should never have accepted the assignment without asking some very important questions. So, don't let this happen to you, and don't do this to the people who report to you! With that said, the following section outlines effective directing, delegating, and coaching strategies.

Steps for Effective Directing

If you have a subordinate that you choose to direct, prior to meeting with the subordinate you should:

- Identify the work to be done and why it is important.
- Develop a clear picture of the specific deliverable to be achieved.
- Select a person who has the time, expertise, and disposition to accomplish the task.

Once you have done your preparation work, meet with the person and consider the following steps

1. Start with the why by explaining why the activity is needed.
2. Describe at a high level what needs to be done.
3. Explain why the person was selected and the benefits to him/her.
4. Begin with the end in mind[11] by describing the specific deliverable to be produced; ensure understanding.
5. Describe the steps that should be taken; ensure understanding.
6. Gain agreement on the time frame for completion.
7. Ask the person what additional support he/she needs to be successful.
8. Set interim review times.
9. Upon completion, provide praise and feedback.

Steps for Effective Delegation

Clearly, the steps for directing are specific. At this point it is prudent to turn to delegation. Which of the directing steps would you keep and which would you eliminate for effective delegation?

In our facilitative leadership workshop, we have had wide differences in the responses to what effective delegation looks like based on which of the directing steps to keep. What follows are the three most frequent responses.

- **2-3 Steps**: Some have felt steps 1 and 6 are enough when delegating and maybe step 9. But they have been quick to add, "If you have to include 9, go light on the praise. We don't need it."

  1-Start with the why by explaining why the activity is needed.

  6-Gain agreement on the time frame for completion.

  9-Upon completion provide praise and feedback.

- **6 Steps**: Others have felt steps 1-4 should be done whether you are directing or delegating and also steps 6 and 9.

    1-Start with the why by explaining why the activity is needed.

    2-Describe at a high-level what is needed to be done.

    3-Explain why the person was selected and the benefits to him/her.

    4-Begin with the end in mind by describing the specific deliverable to be produced; ensure understanding.

    6-Gain agreement on the time frame for completion.

    9-Upon completion provide praise and feedback.

- **8 Steps**: And still others have said ALL the steps are needed for delegation except step 5 (Describe the steps to be taken).

    1-Start with the why by explaining why the activity is needed.

    2-Describe at a high-level what is needed to be done.

    3-Explain why the person was selected and the benefits to him/her.

    4-Begin with the end in mind by describing the specific deliverable to be produced; ensure understanding.

    6-Gain agreement on the time frame for completion.

    7-Ask the person what additional support he/she needs to be successful.

    8-Set interim review times.

    9-Upon completion provide praise and feedback.

Consider what works for you based on experience. Leaders whose natural style is directing may find themselves using more directing steps than necessary when delegating. Likewise, leaders whose natural style is delegating may find that they use fewer of the directive steps when delegating than might be necessary. However, the feedback you receive from delegatees may provide insights as to whether you are under-guiding or over-guiding when you delegate.

A final note on delegation. For those who naturally direct, and to some extent for those who naturally coach, there are two significant obstacles to delegation: time and trust.

- Time because delegation typically does take significantly more time than just doing it yourself. Therefore, many people do exactly that the first time, the second time, the third time, ad nauseam. However, successful delegators recognize that it does take more time the first time. The second time usually requires less of their time, and the third time even less until, once the activity is completely delegated, it takes very little if any of their time.

- Trust because the leader has trouble trusting that direct reports will do it as well as he or she would do it. Once more, they may not do it as well the first time, or even the second or third time. But over time, with proper directing and coaching, a delegatee who has the time, expertise, and disposition will likely achieve the level of mastery needed.

Steps for Effective Coaching

A facilitative leader views the coaching process through two lenses: long-term career growth and short-term learning moments. In both situations, the facilitative leader predominately uses questions to help the subordinate discover his/her own answers so as to build understanding and commitment to action.

Coaching for Long-Term Career Growth

Assume you are meeting with a direct report at the beginning of the year to help develop goals. Chapter 9 covers in detail the Drivers Model, a structured process for taking a team through strategic thinking around goals, objectives, critical success factors, barriers, and strategies. The Drivers Model is also very effective in the coaching context for career growth as shown in Figure 4.3. Accordingly, the Drivers Model concept is introduced here.

Figure 4.3 Coaching with the Drivers Model

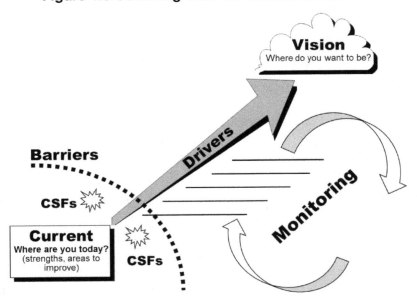

1. The Drivers Model starts with answering the question, "Where are we today?" In the coaching context this means the facilitative leader might ask questions such as:

   • What are you doing well? What are your strengths?

   • What is not going so well? What do you see as your areas for improvement?

2. The second Drivers Model question is, "Where do you want to be?" In the coaching context the questions are:

   • Where do you want to be in your career three years from now? Five years from now? Ten years from now?

   • What are one-year outcomes or measurable objectives that might indicate you are moving in the direction you desire?

   • What other one-year outcomes might the company need you to achieve?

3. Next, the facilitative leader asks about barriers.

   • Why aren't you there already?

   • What barriers are standing in the way?

   • What are the things preventing you from getting there?

4. Following the barriers discussion, the facilitative leader asks about critical success factors, a term covered in greater detail in Chapter 10.

   • What are the critical success factors for your vision? That is, what are the key conditions that, if you create them, will accelerate you to your vision?

5. Once barriers and critical success factors are known, the next concept to cover is drivers.

   • What are the things that you can begin doing to overcome the barriers, create the critical conditions for success, and drive you to your vision?

   • Which of these should you start on first?

6. The final step is monitoring.

   • How shall we monitor your progress toward accomplishing your drivers and moving toward your vision?

   • How often should we meet to discuss this?

Coaching for Short-Term Learning Moments

Consider short-term learning moments to be those opportunities during the workday in which you are interacting with a subordinate and you recognize a teachable moment. This might be when making a decision, assigning a task, reviewing a deliverable, et cetera.

Take the example of assigning a task. Using the same flow of conversation for directing and delegating, the conversation might proceed as follows. (The emphasized items and bullets indicate differences from the directing approach).

1. Start with the why by explaining why the activity is needed.

2. Describe at a high level what is needed to be done.

3. Explain why the person was selected and the benefits to him/her.

4. Begin with the end in mind by *discussing* the specific deliverable to be produced; ensure understanding.
    - Ask, "What are your thoughts about what the deliverable might look like?"
    - Ask follow-up questions and, only if needed, add your thoughts to ensure a suitable deliverable.

5. *Discuss* the steps that should be taken; ensure understanding.
    - Ask, "What are your thoughts about the steps that should be taken?"
    - Ask follow-up questions and, only if needed, add your thoughts to ensure a reasonable approach.

6. Gain agreement on the time frame for completion.
    - Ask, "What are your thoughts about the time needed to get this done?"
    - Ask follow-up questions and, only if needed, add your thoughts to ensure a reasonable timeframe.

7. Ask the person what additional support he/she needs to be successful.
    - Ask follow-up questions and, only if needed, add your thoughts to ensure the person has the support needed.

8. *Discuss* interim review times.
    - Ask, "What are your thoughts about how frequently you and I should meet to review your progress?"
    - Ask follow-up questions and, only if needed, add your thoughts to ensure reasonable review times.

9. Upon completion, praise and *discuss* feedback.
    - Ask, "How do you think it went? What do you feel good about? What didn't go as well as you would have liked? What learnings did you gain here?"
    - Provide your words of praise and encouragement.
    - Ask follow-up questions and, only if needed, add your thoughts to ensure a comprehensive review.

Principles of Operation

The discussion of the Level-3 Leadership Model in chapter 2 explains the importance of level-2 leaders communicating objectives so that people can operate independently. As the case that follows demonstrates, it is also important to communicate principles of operation.

The Unhappy Customer

At Leadership Strategies we offer public, open enrollment classes in a number of cities across the U.S. Imagine that a call comes into our office from a person complaining about a class he took. The person might say, "I took that facilitation skills course last month and I hated it, and I want my money back." Now, I would want the person from my organization who answers that call to answer it the same way I would. And that person will do this if he/she understands our three basic principles of operations.

1. *We are in business to make money. If we are not making money, we will not be in business long.*

2. *We only deserve to make money when we have satisfied a client need. If we haven't satisfied a client need, we do not deserve to make money.*

3. *We do not fix problems; we eliminate them. We do not want that problem coming back again.*

Now, suppose the person from my organization who answers the call understands our first principle of operation only: We are in business to make money. How will the person answer the call? I suspect the response would be something like, "Sorry we don't give refunds. Have a nice day." Well, let's just say that's not the way I would want that call handled!

Suppose the person who answers the call understands our first two principles of operation only: We are in business to make money, and we only deserve to make money when we have satisfied a client need. How will the person answer the call now? Perhaps something like, "We are so sorry that we didn't satisfy your need, we will gladly refund your money." Of course, that is a better way to handle the call, but still not quite the way I would want it done.

But suppose the person understands all three principles of operation: We are in business to make money, we only deserve to make money when we have satisfied a client need, and we don't fix problems, we eliminate them. How would the person answer the call in this case? Perhaps something closer to the following: "We are sorry our class wasn't helpful to you. We will gladly refund your money. But would you mind helping us? We don't want another client to have the experience that you had. So, help me understand what were you looking to gain from the class?"

In this case the person might say, "I was looking to understand how to work better with my clients, how to build stronger relationships, how to do a better job of defining their needs." And the person from my organization will readily recognize that the person took the wrong class because those are skills and techniques we address in our consulting skills class, not our facilitation skills class.

Our person might ask, "Who talked with you from our organization when you signed up for the class?" The person might answer, "I didn't speak with anyone. I signed up online on my own." "Did someone contact you after you signed up?" The person might say, "Oh, is that what that call was for?" Now we've learned that we need to make sure that we contact everyone who signs up on the Web for a class, to help avoid this mistake from happening again.

Our person would then add, "It sounds like we had you in the wrong class. It sounds like you wanted to learn how to diagnose your clients' needs, build stronger relationships with them, get to consensus, and communicate in their style. These are the exact skills that we teach in our consulting skills class, not in our facilitation skills class. If you're okay with it, instead of refunding your money I would love to transfer your registration to the consulting class at no additional cost to you, so that you get exactly what you need. Would that be okay?" As you can see, we really are in business to make money!

Principles of operation provide a simple vehicle for you to define how you want people to operate in your organization. For if you have not defined and communicated YOUR basic principles of operation, people will operate based on THEIR principles of operation, which might not match yours! Principles of operation can be for a team, a department, a business unit, or for an entire company. When done for a company, these often are called values or guiding principles, as outlined in Chapter 10.

Decision Trees

While principles of operation help your people understand how you want them to engage in the workplace, facilitative leaders also provide clarity on what the people who work for them are empowered to do. This empowerment includes delineating actions their people can take on their own, those actions which need the input of others, and those that require approval. In her book, *Fierce Conversations*,[12] Susan Scott uses the analogy of a tree as a way of delineating the level of decision-making authority a person has over an area. I have adapted the descriptions in Figure 4.4 that follows to incorporate the principles of involvement and buy-in essential to facilitative leadership.

Figure 4.4 Decision Tree Decision Types

Decision Type	Description
Leaf	The decision only impacts you or your area; make the decision.
Branch	The decision is one that others need to know about; make the decision and notify others.
Trunk	The decision is yours to make but impacts others or needs their buy-in for success; involve others in developing the decision and gain leadership approval before action.
Root	The decision is not yours to make, as it significantly impacts other areas that also have a significant stake in the outcome.

For each of your subordinates, consider developing with them a decision tree which communicates their authority. Figure 4.4 provides a sample decision tree for a marketing organization.

Figure 4.5 Sample Marketing Decision Tree

Area	Decision	Leaf	Branch	Trunk	Root
Brand	Re-establish brand and logo.				X
Campaigns	Execute marketing campaigns.		X		
Collateral	Design look-and-feel for company collateral.		X		
Finance	Make monthly marketing expenditures under $10,000 or expenditures with existing vendors under $25,000.	X			
Finance	Make non-routine monthly marketing expenditures over $10,000 or with existing vendors in excess of $25,000.			X	
Outgoing	Manage social media, involving/ notifying others as appropriate.		X		
Plan	Establish marketing plan.			X	
Plan	Make minor adjustments to marketing plan based on results.	X			
Plan	Make significant changes to marketing plan based on results.			X	
Reporting	Report marketing results.		X		

Area	Decision	Leaf	Branch	Trunk	Root
Survey	Implement customer surveys.		X		
Team	Coach team members.	X			
Team	Establish individual targets.		X		
Team	Establish rewards for team members.			X	
Team	Recruit/terminate team members.			X	
Trade show	Select trade shows/events.			X	
Webinars	Execute monthly marketing webinars.	X			
Websites	Redesign websites.			X	
Websites	Provide search engine optimization.	X			

Note that not only does a decision tree provide clarity related to levels of responsibility, it can also be a development tool to track progress as a leader moves up the decision matrix. As an example, the decision tree can be updated with more and more items initially designated as trunk or root being downgraded to leaf or branch as people mature in their decision-making and the level of trust you have in them grows. As your people take on more decision-making responsibility, you are able to move to higher levels in the Level-3 Leadership Model.

The "Managing Your Boss" Memo

A final strategy that many facilitative leaders have found helpful in empowering their people is what I call the "Managing Your Boss Memo." Recall instances when you took a job where you were reporting to someone new. You likely remember the lengthy time it took for you to learn how to work with your new boss. It may have taken awhile for you to understand what your boss valued, how to best communicate, what to do to gain approval, and what to avoid doing so as to stay in your boss' good graces. Wouldn't it have been helpful to have had a cheat sheet that explained these things clearly and concisely?

The "Managing Your Boss" memo, drafted by the manager and disseminated to his/her reports, is intended to do this and more. The memo is a gift that you can give to empower the people who work for you. The memo contains the following sections.

- Overview of my objectives
- What I expect from you
- How to communicate with me
- Principles to guide your actions

- Your decision authority
- When you make a recommendation to me
- If you want more responsibility

Figure 4.6 provides a sample of a Managing Your Boss Memo.

Figure 4.6 Sample Managing Your Boss Memo

The Secrets to Managing Your Boss

Things to consider if you work for James

I. Overview of My Objectives

If you work for me, it is very important that you understand my key objectives, the barriers I am facing, and what I believe my critical success factors are.

Area	Comments
My Objectives	• Ensure first the stability and then the growth of the company in revenues and profits. • Maintain a positive, uplifting working environment—a place where people want to come to work. • Ensure a strong leadership team with aligned values and goals.
The Barriers I Face	• A developing leadership team • Weaknesses in several key markets
My Critical Success Factors	• A high-performing sales team • A superior marketing engine for branding and market awareness • A continuous stream of customer-centric products that meet performance expectations

II. What I Expect from You

At a minimum, I expect you to do the following.

- Be clear in your thinking by providing support for your ideas, or by indicating that you aren't sure why you feel a certain way.
- Speak up when you don't agree; avoid passive aggressive behaviors.
- Contribute actively to a warm, positive team environment.
- Live up to your commitments. Let me know in advance if you will miss a deadline.

III. How to Communicate with Me

When you speak with me, it would be very helpful if you understand that I typically communicate in a Hi-D/Hi-S/Hi-C style. I greatly appreciate those who can get to the point, communicate with warmth, and back up their positions with facts when needed. Therefore, here are the things you should consider doing and not doing when communicating with me.

Communication Dos

- Let me know how much time you need; don't assume that I have the time. It makes me feel bad to have to cut you off.
- Start with your end point—what do you need from me? Once I understand this, I know what to listen for. If you start talking without me knowing where you are going, I don't know what information to hold on to, and will likely have to ask you to back up and reiterate what you told me.
- Communicate, communicate, communicate. Keep me updated on important issues that you are facing or that are facing the company. If I am out of the office, an FYI email works best for me rather than a phone call or text.
- If you need me to take an action, add to the end of the subject line in caps, "(subject) – ACTION NEEDED" and in the body, include a deadline. If immediate action is needed, say that in the subject line. It is okay to indicate something like, "If I haven't heard from you in 24 hours, I will..."

Communication Don'ts

- Avoid "hit-and-runs"—catching me walking down the hall and starting immediately in on an important conversation. Instead give me a warning such as, "Can I get 10 minutes to talk with you about..."
- Avoid coming to me with a problem without having spent some time thinking about solutions. I like talking about solutions. Talking about problems is not nearly as enjoyable. If you come to me with a challenge, try to have at least one possible solution. It shows me that you are not just complaining; but instead, you have thought it through and are taking initiative.

IV. Principles to Guide Your Actions

These are the things I would like you to keep in mind on a day-to-day basis as you do your duties.

- Take initiative (e.g., be willing to offer help where help is needed).

- If you make a mistake, tell me, own it, and correct it. Be sure to take the time to understand why the mistake occurred and what you can do to help ensure that the mistake doesn't happen again.

- Maintain good relationships with everyone inside and outside the organization.

- I am open to new ideas, so feel free to challenge me (e.g., "Why are we doing it that way? Have you considered..."). Challenging gives opportunity for improvement. But don't be confrontational (e.g., "That's stupid. That won't work.") Confrontation makes people defensive.

- Communicate, communicate, communicate. Listen to your colleagues to understand their points of view, not just to get yours across. Look for solutions that can address all needs.

IV. Decision-Making

I would like to give you as much authority as possible to make decisions for our organization. Accordingly, there are three types of decisions. I welcome your coming to me with a recommendation of the types of decisions that you believe should be leaf versus branch versus trunk.

Leaf Decisions	• Leaf decisions affect only you and your area. These are decisions that you should make on your own. You do not need my input. Just notify me after the fact.
Branch Decisions	• Branch decisions can have an impact on other departments or other people and you should come to me with a recommendation that we should discuss prior to implementation.
Trunk Decisions	• Trunk decisions can impact the entire organization. These decisions will likely require the involvement of the entire leadership team.

Adapted from Fierce Conversations, Susan Scott.

V. When You Make a Recommendation to Me

When you have a recommendation for me, it would be most helpful if you use the following format. This will help make sure you have fully thought through your recommendation and you give me the ammunition to take it to the next level. Here is a sample.

Finding (Facts)	**Conclusion** (What the facts mean)
Recommended Action	
Benefit	
Risks	

When you want us to make a significant investment that is outside your spending authority, usually you should identify a minimum of three alternatives. Show the pricing for each, the strengths and weaknesses of each, and the reasons why you are recommending a specific alternative.

VI. If You Want More Responsibility

If you feel you are ready to take on more responsibility, recognize I need to be able to trust you first. It is helpful to view trust as having five components.

Competence

...You have the necessary skills and expertise.

Communication

... When we speak, we truly hear and understand each other.

Commitment

...You are committed to our success.

Caring

...I know you have my interest at heart.

Character

...You are ethical and honest.

I will most likely use the following decision graph to give you more and more responsibility. As we work together through the stages, you will gain greater responsibility as I gain greater trust in your ability to make decisions that take into account the things I believe are important.

Summary

1. How and when you empower a person depends in a large part on the individual and the situation. This book delineates three leadership styles.

   - Directing

   - Coaching

   - Delegating

2. All leaders have a natural leadership style, a style that they will use by default. Facilitative leaders recognize that they must understand their people and the needs of the situation and adapt their leadership style to maximize outcomes and their people's success.

   - Direct when the person has a lack of experience, when you have a lack of trust, or there is a lack of time to coach.

   - Coach when there is ample time to coach and you are preparing a person for greater responsibility.

   - Delegate when the person has extensive experience and you have significant trust in his/her ability to be successful in the task.

3. When you direct instead of delegate it can frustrate the person you are trying to lead. When you delegate instead of direct, it can frustrate you! Both are forms of mismanagement.

4. When you trust or distrust someone it is likely due to the presence or lack of one or more of the 5 Cs of the Trust Triangle.

   - Competence

   - Communication

   - Commitment

   - Caring

   - Character

5. As you go deeper in the Trust Triangle, the more difficult it is to address the issue.

6. This chapter includes several other tools for empowering:

   - The Trust Conversation

   - Steps for Effective Directing

   - Steps for Effective Delegation

   - Steps for Effective Coaching: Long-term Career Growth

   - Steps for Effective Coaching: Short-term Learning Moments

7. Principles of Operation
8. Decision Trees
9. Managing Your Boss Memo

Spring Forward

Consider the individuals reporting directly to you. Record the appropriate leadership style for each individual and any specific actions you might consider taking.

Name	Direct	Coach	Delegate	Comment

Consider which, if any, of the other tools you might begin implementing right away.

- The Trust Conversation
- Steps for Effective Directing
- Steps for Effective Delegation
- Principles of Operation
- Decision Trees
- Steps for Effective Coaching: Long-term Career Growth
- Steps for Effective Coaching: Short-term Learning Moments
- Managing Your Boss Memo

Communicate in Their Language, Not Yours

5

- Communications Bigotry
- High-Ds: Break through the Wall
- High-Is: Motivate People to Take on the Wall
- High-Ss: Help Others over the Wall
- High-Cs: Develop Detailed Plans
- Adapting to the Style of Others
- Identifying the Style of Others
- Natural Style Clashes
- Recovering When You Miscommunicate
- Tailoring Your Communication
- Pigeonholing? Manipulation?
- Detect, Adapt, Beware, Refresh, Expand
- Summary
- Spring Forward

Chapter 5.
Communicate in Their Language, Not Yours

To be able to engage and inspire people successfully, facilitative leaders must have a firm grasp of different communication styles and understand how to adapt as needed to the styles of others.

Communications Bigotry

I have a confession to make, and I don't think I am alone in this. For a significant portion of my life I found myself quite frustrated with the way many people communicated. I felt strongly, and I hate to admit it but I did, that if the rest of the world communicated the way I did, the world would be a much better place! I was essentially a communications bigot. If you didn't communicate the way I did, you were wrong and a poor communicator.

When I was exposed to the material covered in this chapter, I had an awakening experience. I realized that the way other people communicated wasn't wrong, it was just different. This alone was enough to move me from being nearly dismissive of other styles to at least being tolerant of them. As I used this material more and more, my attitude moved from tolerance to actual appreciation of the differences. For I could see how, in many situations, the communication style of others was actually more beneficial and more effective than my own.

This change in my view of communications transformed relationships in both my personal and professional life. I moved from judging people to trying to understand how to improve my ability to communicate with them. I moved from "looking out the window" and blaming others to "looking in the mirror" and adapting what I was doing. For me, this information about communication styles has truly been transformative.

There are a number of models for understanding behavioral and communication styles, including Meyers-Briggs Type Indicators, Hermann Brain Dominance Indicators, and DISC Communication Styles. In our organization, we use the DISC Communication Styles from TTI Performance Systems to focus on communication styles. I find that it is an insightful yet simple model that is easily understood, retained, and applied by casual users of the information.

In this model, there are four basic communication styles, referred to as drive (or dominance), influence, steadiness, and compliance (DISC).[13] Although all of us have the capacity to communicate using each of the four styles, for most of us one of the styles tends to dominate the way we communicate. It is illuminating to begin with a summary of the four basic styles, using the analogy of standing in front of a brick wall and having the task of getting to the other side of the wall.

High-Ds: Break through the Wall

In the DISC model, D stands for drive or dominance. High-Ds get things done. They take a direct, assertive approach to solving problems. What do high-Ds do at the wall? They lower their shoulders, get a running start, and break through the wall. They enjoy challenges and get satisfaction from overcoming them. While the rest of us wake up and wonder what day it is, high-Ds wake up and immediately begin thinking about what they are going to get done that day.

When you think of a high-D, think of entrepreneurs, team leaders, and directors. High-Ds bring value to organizations by focusing efforts on getting the job done. They address problems directly, and they make tough decisions quickly.

Figure 5.1 High-D Communication Dos and Don'ts

HIGH-D	Key Factor: Getting Things Done
Communication Dos	**Communication Don'ts**
• Be prepared – tell them what you are going to tell them. • State your points clearly, briefly, specifically. • Give only as much detail as necessary.	• Don't waste their time with idle chatter. • Don't ramble or tell long stories. • Don't be too detailed unless they ask for it.
Shorthand: Be prepared, be brief, be gone.	

Unfortunately, this communication style also has a down side. You know when you are in the presence of a high-D. They tend to be always pushing. They want to win—no matter the cost. They also tend to be so concerned about the goal that they often don't consider the impact on people. And they tend to make decisions very quickly before having all the facts. Why do they do this? Because of their driving factor: getting things done. When you think of high-Ds, think 'time'—don't waste their time because they have too much to do.

Whether communicating with a boss or a subordinate who is a high-D, consider the dos and don'ts shown in Figure 5.1, which can be summarized with the shorthand: be prepared, be brief, and be gone!

High-Is: Motivate People to Take on the Wall

The second major style in the DISC model is "I" and stands for influence. High-Is enjoy influencing others and helping people see the big picture. They motivate and inspire others to succeed. While high-Ds break through the wall, high-Is motivate people to take on the challenge. They are the ones with the megaphone yelling, "Hey everyone. We have a wall to get over. Come on. It will be great on the other side. We can do it. Go Team! Go Team!"

When you think of high-Is think of sales people, teachers, and facilitators. High-Is bring value to organizations by helping people see the big picture. They are great at motivating and selling others. They create a dynamic environment that is almost always fun. They like relationships and working with people. They are also highly creative and the ones who naturally come up with innovative solutions.

But, as with high-Ds, this communication style also has a down side. First, high-Is can be so talkative that they don't listen. They can spend so much time on the vision that they never execute. And, because they focus on ideas, they tend to overlook details.

Figure 5.2 High-I Communication Dos and Don'ts

HIGH-I	Key Factor: Being Heard
Communication Dos	**Communication Don'ts**
• Give them the big picture before going into details. • Give them a chance to share their ideas. • Keep the conversation friendly and warm.	• Don't dwell on details and facts, provide these in writing instead. • Don't tell them what to do without giving them an opportunity to respond. • Don't allow them to ramble too long.
Shorthand: Let them sell themselves.	

Why do high-Is do this? Because of their driving factor: being heard. High-Is like the stage. They enjoy having an audience with whom to interact. When communicating with high-Is, keep in mind the shorthand: let them sell themselves. If you are trying to sell a high-I on something, the wrong person is speaking! Give high-Is the stage. You have to get them talking about your solution. Ask them what they need in a solution. Ask them to describe how it would work. Then after outlining your solution, ask them to talk about the benefits. Remember, you have to let them sell themselves, as shown in the Figure 5.2 summary.

High-Ss: Help Others Over the Wall

The third major style in the DISC model, the high-S stands for steadiness. High-Ss tend to be the stabilizing force within an organization. They tend to be dependable, loyal workers who prefer a stable and secure environment. They love to help.

What are they doing at the wall? While the high-Ds are busting through the wall and the high-Is are cheering people on, the high-Ss are quietly at the wall lending people a hand, helping people over it. For the person needing a boost, the high-Ss will supply it. For those needing a lift, the high-S will crouch down, link hands and provide the lift. And for those who need a step, some high-Ss will even get down in the mud on their hands and knees and allow you to step on their backs to help you over the wall.

Classic occupations for high-S individuals include social service workers, civil servants, and retail clerks. They bring value to organizations by being supportive and dependable workers. They are people-oriented and good listeners. They are accommodating and tolerant of others. As an example, when high-Ds are being pushy and abrasive, people with the high-S communication style understand that this is just the way high-Ds are. When high-Is are blabbing away, high-Ss are there, listening. They understand that high-Is can ramble sometimes.

Unfortunately, the high-S communication style also has a down side. First, they can avoid dealing with issues until they become big problems. This happens because they dislike confrontation. So, if you do something that upsets a high-S, he will likely take it and not say anything or do anything. If you do something else that upsets a high-S, once more, he will take it as well. Do something else, and he will take it. Do something else, and he will explode. And when a high-S explodes, you really want to be somewhere else, because when the frustration gets so high that they express it, high-S individuals tend to explode in a big way. Many of us might think, "I don't understand, all I did was…" because we don't see all the things that have been building up to the explosion.

Another high-S downside is that they can seem to lack vision and creativity. That's because they are trying to make things work and ensure that everyone is comfortable. They tend not to be the ones thinking outside the box. And finally, they can be slow to accept change, and they hold grudges. They want stability, not change. For the typical high-S, change is a four-letter word because for them change is chaotic, causes instability, and disrupts relationships.

One of the reasons high-S individuals dislike confrontation is because of their key factor: being liked. High-Ss want to be liked. They want harmony. They want everyone to get along. Therefore, it is important when communicating with a high-S not to be demanding or abrasive. Let me explain why by way of a comparison. If a high-D is demanding and abrasive to another high-D, the other high-D will be demanding and abrasive back. If a high-D is demanding and abrasive to a high-I, the high-I will tell everyone how demanding and abrasive the high-D has been. The high-I will tell peers, co-workers, the spouse, the dog—anyone who will listen. But, if a high-D is demanding and abrasive to a high-S, the high-S will shut down. The high-S will not say anything. And this gets us to the final point about high-S individuals: don't assume silence means consent. When high-Ss agree with you, they nod their heads. When they disagree, they do nothing. Be careful, you may miss it. You may believe, because they don't say anything, that they are in agreement. It may be just the opposite. It may be that they are simply avoiding conflict.

Figure 5.3 summarizes the dos and don'ts of communicating with a high-S, including the short hand recommendation: Start personal; don't assume.

Figure 5.3 High-S Communication Dos and Don'ts

HIGH-S	Key Factor: Being Liked
Communication Dos	**Communication Don'ts**
• Start with a personal comment. • Present ideas deliberately and clearly; provide assurances. • Make sure they are in agreement before moving on.	• Don't dive straight into business. • Don't be demanding or abrasive. • Don't assume silence means consent.
Shorthand: Start personal; don't assume.	

High-Cs: Develop Detailed Plans

Moving on to the last style in the DISC model, the high-C. "C" stands for compliance. High-Cs tend to comply with rules. They rely on logic and evidence to reach conclusions. They make sure that things are done by the book.

While the high-Ds are busting through the wall, the high-Is are cheerleading, and the high-Ss are helping people over the wall, the high-Cs are doing their homework. First, they measure the height of the wall and enter the information into their computer. Then, they use the scaling equipment to determine that the wall is at an 84.5 degree angle. They then check the wind speed and their own weight. After entering all the data into the spreadsheet, they produce a four-page report that details how, if they stand exactly twenty feet five inches from the wall, take 7 strides averaging 2.7 feet each, leap with a force equivalent to the correct proportion of their body mass, they will clear the wall by 2 inches and land 2.1 feet beyond the wall on the other side. And if you have a few minutes, they would like to walk you through each detailed calculation!

When you think of typical occupations for high-Cs, think of researchers, accountants, engineers, analysts, and other detailed or quantitative professions. High Cs bring value to organizations because they tend to be organized and detail-oriented. They make sure decisions are well supported. They ensure that procedures are properly followed. It's the high-C individuals who are looking for why things won't work. It's the high-Cs who are helping to ensure that the organization maintains high quality. It's the high-Cs who help keep processes efficient.

Unfortunately, like all the other communication styles, high-Cs also have a down side. First, high-Cs can be perfectionists and very hard to please. Not only do they have high expectations for themselves, they also can have high expectations for those around them. And people generally don't enjoy having to live up to someone else's high expectations. High-Cs can also be so focused on facts and figures that they ignore the people side, resulting in them sometimes being considered cold and calculating by others. Finally, high-Cs can be overly cautious and suffer from analysis paralysis: taking far too long to make even the smallest of decisions.

Why do they do this? Because of their key factor: getting it right. High-Cs want to get it right. They would rather make no decision then make the wrong decision.

Therefore, in communicating with high-Cs, it can be helpful to keep in mind the shorthand indicated in Figure 5.4: Give them time for the details.

Figure 5.4 High-C Communication Dos and Don'ts

High-C	Key Factor: Getting it Right
Communication Dos	**Communication Don'ts**
• Present ideas in a logical fashion. • Stay on topic. • Provide facts and figures that back up claims.	• Don't be disorganized or make random comments. • Don't rely on emotional appeal to gain agreement. • Don't force a rapid decision.
Shorthand: Give them time for the details.	

Adapting to the Style of Others

We've taken a look at the four communication styles as a basis for creating better communications. Now, I want to continue laying the foundation by looking at how one can adapt to the style of the person with whom you are communicating.

First Words

I want to start this discussion by taking a simple example of communicating with your boss about a problem that has arisen in your area. You have fully researched the problem and have created an eight-page document which delineates the problem, specifies four possible alternatives, and gives the strengths and weaknesses for each. You favor alternative four. (Note that you have done the "high-C thing" well!)

You are about to meet with your boss to talk about the problem and your proposed solution. Your boss knows nothing about the problem and is not anticipating your visit. You knock on the door. You hear, "Come in."

Depending on your boss' communication style, what would be the first words out of your mouth? For example, if your boss is a high-D, what would be the first words you would say? What if your boss is a high-I, or a high-S, or a high-C? Based on the key factors and shorthand communications described in the prior section, think about what each style would want from you when you walk through the door and what, accordingly, might be the first words out of your mouth. Figure 5.5 provides sample responses.

Figure 5.5 First Words for Each DISC Style

Style	Key Factor	What They Want from You	First Words
D	Getting it done	A concise explanation of what you want and how much time it will take	"Can I get eight minutes to get your decision on...?"
I	Being heard	To be given the stage	"How was your weekend?"
S	Being liked	A friendly interaction and affirmation of a positive relationship	"How are you? How's the family?"
C	Getting it right	Detailed information and the time to make a quality decision	*(Email report in advance)* "If now is okay, I would like to take as much time as you need to step through the information I sent you last week..."

We've looked at the first words out of your mouth. Now, focus on the rest of the conversation with your boss. Figure 5.6 shows nine potential topics to be covered in the conversation. Think about each style and the activities you would and would not do, as well as the order in which you would do them. What follows is a detailed walk through for each of the styles. If you want to peek ahead, the fully completed chart, Figure 5.7, appears at the end of this section.

Figure 5.6 Holding the Conversation with Each DISC Style

	D	I	S	C
Pleasantries				
Explanation of the problem - High-level problem explanation				
- Detailed problem explanation				
Asking how to solve the problem				
Offering solution(s) - High-level solution explanation				
- Detailed explanation, each solution				
Benefits of solution(s) - Asking for the benefits				
- Explaining the benefits				
Reaching agreement on next step				

The High-D Conversation

If your boss is a high-D and you are having the conversation we just talked about, where would you start first? Pleasantries? No, absolutely not with a high-D. High-level explanation of the problem? No, not there either. With high-Ds, you start with the solution. High-Ds are the type of people who read the end of a book first and then decide whether they want to read the rest. So, give them the solution you want first.

After starting with the solution, give a high-D a high-level explanation of the problem, then describe the benefits of the solution, and then reach agreement on the next steps. In essence the conversation is, "I would like to do this…because it solves this problem…. As a result, we get these benefits…. Can I get your approval to act?"

With high-Ds do you describe all four solutions? No, just the one you think is the best. But be prepared with the others, in case the high-D doesn't like your first solution.

The High-I Conversation

Where do you start? With pleasantries? Of course. "How was your weekend?" This gives them the stage right from the beginning. Be prepared, however, for they may want to spend quite some time on this topic. After pleasantries, you can transition to the second step, a high-level explanation of the problem.

But it is the third step that is the critical one: You ask the high-Is for their ideas regarding how to solve the problem. Now, if you are a high-C, you might be wondering, "Let me get this straight. I just spent days researching a problem, identifying four solutions, analyzing the strengths and weaknesses of each, and preparing an eight-page report. Now you are telling me that I am supposed to ask my boss, who has spent all of two minutes hearing me describe the problem, how to solve the problem? How much sense does that make?"

To someone who may be a high-C, asking high-Is to give their ideas of how to solve a problem they just heard about makes no sense at all. But to high-Is it makes perfect sense. For many high-Is the fun part of discussions is in brainstorming ideas. They enjoy the creativity of coming up with potential solutions. They don't want to hear your solution yet. They wouldn't want your thoughts to hamper their creativity.

But consider high-Ds for a brief moment. Think about what would happen if you took this same step with a high-D. What would happen if you asked a high-D how to solve the problem? You can imagine that a high-D might say, "Excuse me. Are you asking me how to solve *your* problem? Are you saying I have to do my job and *your* job too? If that's what you are saying, then we probably don't need both of us, do we?"

To recap, with high-Is, step one is pleasantries, step two is a high-level explanation of the problem, and step three is asking them how to solve the problem. With step four, you describe the solution you want. Once more, describe only the solution you want, not the others. Step five is also an interesting step. Remember the shorthand for dealing with high-Is: *let them sell themselves.* This is exactly what happens in step five: You ask the high-I to describe the benefits of your solution. They are now describing what they like about what you are suggesting. Then, finally in step six, you get agreement to move forward.

The High-S Conversation

The high-S conversation is perhaps the simplest. You start with pleasantries of course. Then the flow is very much like telling a story: high-level explanation of the problem, high-level explanation of the solution you prefer, explain the benefits, and get agreement to move forward. High-S individuals will be able to follow your flow, and if the solution makes sense to them and takes into account concerns about people, high-Ss will tend to go along with you.

A key point: don't put high-Ss on the spot. Don't ask them to come up with solutions or to come up with the benefits. Don't treat them like high-Is. Instead, provide assurances that the solutions will solve the problem and yield the benefits you have documented in your report.

Likewise, since high-S individuals don't like confrontation, it is better that you don't ask," What don't you like about my suggestion?" or "What are the weaknesses you see?" A different way to get this same information that can be much more productive with high-S people is to ask, "What do you like about this? What are things we might do to make it even better?" The positive wording of a potentially negative idea often yields greater response from a high-S.

The High-C Conversation

Recall that high-Cs prefer that you email them the document in advance to allow them to review the information at their own pace. So where do you start once you are in front of a high-C? Do not open with pleasantries. High-Cs have little interest in the so-called touchy-feely. Start first with a high-level explanation of the problem. You will then need to go into a detailed explanation of the problem because, with high-Cs, you have to convince them that there really is a problem that needs solving. You must explain to them what the problem is, how big the problem is, how long the problem has been occurring, the root cause of the problem, the cost to the organization of the problem, et cetera.

Once you have convinced them that there is a problem and the problem is worth solving, you then give high-Cs a high-level explanation of the solutions, followed by a detailed review of the solutions you analyzed, including the strengths and weaknesses of each. Why do you have to review every one of the potential solutions instead of just the one you favor? High-Cs want to know that you have done a comprehensive analysis. They will want to understand why you concluded that alternative four is the best. The high-Cs will want to hear your rationale to ensure you have made a quality recommendation and that they would reach the same conclusion.

Once they are comfortable with your recommendation, explain the benefits and ask if they are ready to make a decision, or if additional information is needed.

While Figure 5.7 details the flow of each conversation, it is also important to focus on time. Which of these conversations would likely take the longest? Which would be the shortest?

- The high-C conversation might well be the longest. Why? Because *you* will be doing a lot of the talking as you go through all the details.

- The second longest? Probably with the high-Is. Why? Because *they* will be doing a lot of the talking as they share their thoughts in each of the steps.

- The shortest? Without question, the high-D. Why? Remember their short-hand: be prepared, be brief, and be gone!

- The time required for the high-S conversation would likely fall between the time of the high-D and the high-I. There will not be a lot of details covered, and high-Ss generally don't do a lot of the talking, but you will be spending some time on pleasantries.

Figure 5.7 Holding the Conversation with Each DISC Style (completed)

	D	I	S	C
Pleasantries		1	1	
Explanation of the problem - High-level problem explanation	2	2	2	1
- Detailed problem explanation				2
Asking how to solve the problem		3		
Offering solution(s) - High-level solution explanation	1	4	3	3
- Detailed explanation, each solution				4
Benefits of solution(s) - Asking for the benefits		5		
- Explaining the benefits	3		4	5
Reaching agreement on next step	4	6	5	6

Which Conversation with Your Boss?

In our leadership classes, once we have covered the information about the DISC styles, we put this challenge to the class:

> *I would bet that at least 75 percent of the people in this room have the exact same conversation with their boss. Which conversation is it? Is it the high-D, the high-I, the high-S, or the high-C conversation?*

I then ask people to raise their hand if they think it is the high-D conversation. Many hands typically go up. Our response: "No, it is not." I then go through each of the other styles, high-I, high-S, high-C, and ask people to raise their hands. I give the same answer, "No, it is not." I then ask, "If it is not the high-D, high-I, high-S, or high-C, then which conversation is it?"

Inevitably someone gets it, "It's OUR conversation. If we are a high-D we have the high-D conversation, if we are a high-I, we have the high-I conversation and so on."

And we ask, "If that's the conversation we ARE having, which conversation SHOULD we have?" And of course, by this time everyone catches on that we should be having the other person's conversation.

Facilitative leaders understand that they can be more effective if they communicate in the other person's style. Unfortunately, in most interactions, there is a conversation battle going on in which each person is insisting that the other person communicate in his or her style. I say, "Stop the battle; you can be more effective by adapting to the style of the person with whom you are communicating."

A Typical Communications Battle

Consider an example of a communications battle. Consider the example above of a person having a conversation with his/her boss about a problem. In this case, assume that the employee is a high-C and the boss is a high-D.[14]

High-C	I sent you an eight-page document describing a problem we are having and four potential alternatives for addressing it. Did you have a chance to…?

(The high-D interrupts the high-C in mid-sentence.)

High-D	Right, I remember that long e-mail. I haven't had a chance to look at it. Why don't you net it out for me? What is it that you think we should do and why?'
High-C	Let me start with the problem. I was doing some research last week and while reviewing customer complaint data, I noticed a significant increase in the percentage of complaints related to a specific part. See, over the past two years, less than 1 percent of our complaints were about this same part. Last month, however, this part made up 15 percent of the complaints. And when I looked back at the prior month, it was 11 percent, and the month before was 7 percent and the—

(Again, the high-D interrupts the high-C in mid-sentence.)

High-D	Okay I get it. There's been an increase in the problem. What's the problem and what do you want to do about it?
High-C	I just want to make sure that you understood that this has been an increasing issue, so it is important that we solve it because it could continue to get worse. The problem is that we are getting failures with part number K75226, which as you know we import from a Korean manufacturer. When we were seeking a manufacturer for this part several years ago it had come down to this vendor and one other. We chose this vendor because of their track record of higher quality. When I talked with the Korean manufacturer, they told me…

(By this time the high-D has determined that he is not going to get the information he wants from the high-C quickly. Therefore, while the high-C continued to go into detail, the high-D found and opened the e-mail and scanned the document. The high-D interrupts again.)

High D	I see your analysis of the problem here. It looks like you isolated the problem to be a manufacturing issue and you have identified four recommendations. Your primary one is to have the manufacturer recall all parts manufactured

over the past six months and for the manufacturer to pay for the recall. I'm fine with that as long as we make the recall voluntary to our customers.

High C   Yes, after careful consideration I do believe that this is our best alternative. But I think it would be prudent for us to take adequate time to examine the other three alternatives because they have strengths as well.

High-D   I see your strengths and weaknesses here. I can't think of anything you may have missed. I am fine with what we've just discussed. You should bring me in again only if the manufacturer balks at the recall. Anything else? Otherwise I need to get back to work.

Could you see the conversation battle? This happens every day in workplace conversations around the world. Once more, the key is to stop the battle by communicating in the other person's style.

Yet you may be wondering, "If each person understood communication styles, and the high-C was adapting to communicate like the high-D and the high-D was adapting to communicate like the high-C wouldn't it still be a dysfunctional conversation?" Review the following conversation with both people adapting to the style of the other.[15]

An Adaptive Conversation

High-C   Do you have ten minutes? I need to get your approval to take action to solve the problem we're having with part K75226. (*The high-C started in the high-D style by stating why he was there and how much time he needed.*)

High-D   Actually, I am a little pressed now. But if you can take eight minutes to introduce the problem, then if we need more time we can decide on the back end of this conversation when to have a follow-up discussion. Tell me what's going on. (*The high-D offered the high-C more time later if needed.*)

High-C   Let me start with my end point first. I believe we should ask for the Korean manufacturer of the part to recall all parts manufactured over the last six months. The reason for the recall is this part has gone from being less than 1 percent of our complaints two years ago to 7 percent, 11 percent and now 15 percent for the last three months. The manufacturer has isolated the problem and by doing the recall, we let our clients know that we are being proactive in solving a problem that they may not even be aware of. This will help us to continue to build trusting relationships with our client base. Assuming we can get the manufacturer to go along, does this meet with your approval? (*The high-C went straight to solution, briefly described the problem it solves, gave the benefit, asked for approval.*)

High-D	It sounds like you've done a great job of researching this. I like it. We should, however, make the recall voluntary for our customers. But let me ask you: Are there other alternatives we should be considering? *(The high-D was sensitive to the High-C's need for quality and thoroughness.)*
High-C	I did analyze three other alternatives and identified the strengths and weaknesses of each. I do believe the one we have discussed is the best of the group. However, if you would like I can go over the others and discuss the strengths and weaknesses of each. *(The high-C put the high-D in control of how much detail to go into.)*
High-D	No, that won't be necessary. But why don't you put that analysis and recommendation into an e-mail for me in case we need to come back to this. Assuming the Korean manufacturer doesn't balk at the recall, do we need to meet again on this, or are you comfortable we have given it the time needed to come to a reasonable solution?*(The high-D confirmed that the high-C was comfortable with the time put in.)*
High-C	No, I think we are fine. Thanks, and I'll let you get back to work. *(The high-C acknowledged the high-Ds need to get things done.)*

In adapting to the style of others, you may find it helpful to keep in mind the key factor and shorthand in communicating with the other style. In the preceding example, it may have been helpful for the high-D to be thinking, "Am I giving enough time to ensure that this is the right decision?" For the high-C, it may have been helpful to be thinking, "Am I covering what the high-D wants covered and am I covering it quickly?"

Identifying the Style of Others

We've looked at the four styles and how to adapt to them. But how do you go about determining another person's style? The good news is people "leak" their communication style; that is, they reveal their style through their words, non-verbal cues, actions, and more. What follows is an examination of how to identify the styles of others so that you can adapt to any particular style and improve the communication.

The Dimensions

To identify the styles of people we look across two dimensions: direct versus indirect and task-oriented versus people-oriented, as shown in Figure 5.8

Figure 5.8 DISC Dimensions

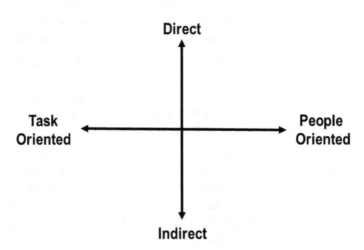

The direct-indirect dimension is the first axis we will consider. Imagine a situation where you are giving a presentation and someone has a question. People who are more direct in their orientation will ask the question as soon as it occurs to them. People who are more indirect in their orientation will likely wait until you finish, perhaps being more courteous to you or perhaps expecting that you will cover their question as you go along.

Similarly, if a direct communicator came into a room and the temperature was about 60 degrees, the direct communicator might say, "It's cold in here." The temperature needs to be higher." A direct communicator might even add, "I am going to get someone to turn up the heat." On the other hand, if an indirect communicator came into the same room, he/she might ask, "Is anybody uncomfortable?" or "Does it feel cold to anyone?"

Consider how direct-oriented people walk. They tend to walk with purpose. They have somewhere they're going. They look straight ahead and march to that place. On the other hand, people who are indirect will likely take their time, enjoy the journey, and perhaps pause to take in the scenery. It is a different orientation.

The other dimension is task-oriented versus people-oriented. Those who are task-oriented concentrate on getting tasks done. Their focus is on activities and accomplishments. People-oriented individuals are more interested in relationships. They focus on people and the impact of activities on people. Again, it is a different orientation.

As an example of the task-orientation versus people-orientation, assume your boss has been on vacation for two weeks. On her first day back at the office, she sees you walking down the hall. If she is people-oriented, the first words out of her mouth might be: "How are you doing? How's your family?" However, if she is task-focused the first words out of her mouth might be: "How is the project going? What's the status? Anything I need to be aware of?" Once more, it is a different orientation.

Figure 5.9 DISC Dimensions and DISC Styles

Direct

D
DRIVE
Getting it Done

I
INFLUENCE
Being Heard

Task Oriented

People Oriented

C
COMPLIANCE
Getting it Right

S
STEADINESS
Being Liked

Indirect

Figure 5.9 illustrates how these dimensions delineate the DISC styles. People who are direct and task-oriented tend to communicate like high-Ds. People who are direct and people-oriented tend to communicate like high-Is. High-S individuals tend to be people-oriented and indirect, and high-Cs tend to be indirect and task-oriented.

Notice that the styles on the left tend to be about achieving: "getting it done" and "getting it right." The styles on the right tend to be about being: "being heard" and "being liked." Once more, a different focus.

To take an example of applying the dimensions, Table 5.10 depicts the dimensions and the likely communication style of six U.S. presidents. It is clear that the quadrants can be very helpful in identifying someone's communication style.

Figure 5.10 Likely Communication Style for U.S. Presidents

U.S. President	Dimension 1	Dimension 2	Style
George H. W. Bush	Indirect	Task-focused	High-C
Bill Clinton	Direct	People-focused	High-I
Jimmy Carter	Indirect	People-focused	High-S
George W. Bush	Direct	Task-focused	High-D
Barak Obama	Direct	People-focused	High-I
Donald Trump	Direct	Task-focused	High-D

The Voicemail Message

While the dimensions can work with people you know, what about people you don't know? The good news when it comes to identifying the style of others is that people are leaking hints to you all the time as to how they want you to communicate with them. All you have to do is pay attention and look for the signs. Take an example of a voicemail message.

You call someone on the phone and you get his voicemail message and you hear:

> *You know what to do. <Beep>*

Which style is this? This person is clearly saying, "I'm a high-D. Communicate with me like a high-D: be prepared, be brief, and be gone!" You didn't even get the person on the phone. You got the voicemail message. In fact, the person just said five words. But in those five words are hints that tell you to communicate with this person like a high-D.

Consider a second example. You get the voicemail message and you hear:

> *I'm sorry we're not here to take your call right now. But your call is very important to us. Please leave your message, and we will get back with you as soon as possible. Have a nice day. <Beep>*

The cue phrases such as "I'm sorry" and "very important to us" shout out a high-S mantra: Relate to me! I'm a person. You're a person. Let's treat each other kindly.

How about this message:

> *No one is available to take your call at the moment. At the sound of the tone, please leave your name, telephone number, the date and time of your call, and a brief message explaining why you are calling and I will get back to you at the earliest possible time. <Beep>*

The very detailed instructions let you know, if you are paying attention, that this person is most likely a high-C.

A final example: the telephone rings and when the voicemail message starts, you hear eight seconds of music followed by a bright and energetic message:

> *No one's here right now. Leave a message! <Beep>*

Once more, the message shouts out, "I'm a high-I! Communicate with me in a high-I style."

The Office

Always be aware that, because people leak their communication style, you can gain insights into someone's possible communication style if you know what to look for.

If you walk into someone's workspace and you see a wall full of awards, plaques, certificates, and other items indicating his or her accomplishments, which style would you think that person is, most likely? Most likely a high-D, as the awards seem to be communicating, "See what I've accomplished; I get things done." Keep in mind, however, that for some professions, such as doctors and lawyers, it is customary for plaques and certificates to be displayed, and there are plenty of high-Is, high-Cs, and high-Ss in those professions. So, plaques don't necessarily mean high-D. They are just a sign to be aware of and another piece of input, just like the voicemail message and other information. But it is important to recognize the likely signs, adapt based on the conclusions you reach, and readjust if the person's behavior tells you that you are communicating in the wrong style.

What about the high-I's workspace? What would you expect to see? Perhaps pictures with inspirational messages like "Teamwork" and "Success." You might also find a lot of "distractibles" such as koosh balls for squeezing, a basketball hoop over the trash can, or a Newton's cradle (the balls on the string that clang against each other)–fun things that help spark their creativity, relieve stress, or reduce their boredom with a detailed task.

For the workspace of a high-S, you might see pictures of family and friends, or treasured personal items. It might be like walking into someone's living room.

The typical high-C's workspace comes in two forms. One form is immaculate organization: the desk is clear, books are lined up evenly on the shelves, and the file folder labels are typed. The other is organized chaos: stacks and stacks of paper everywhere, but every stack has a purpose and specific information. If you ask the high-C for something, the high-C will turn to a stack, go two-thirds down in the pile and pull out exactly what you were seeking.

Natural Style Clashes

Certain communication styles tend to clash, and it is important to recognize what they are, why the clashes occur, how to recognize them, and what to do about them. Looking back at Figure 5.9, DISC Dimensions and DISC Styles, high-Is tend to be direct and people-oriented. Which of the other styles would likely have the greatest problem with high-Is? Most likely the high-Cs because they are indirect and task-oriented. However, it is important to dig deeper. Think about what the high-Cs would say about the high-Is, What would be their biggest complaint? They might say something such as, "They talk, talk, talk. They are dreamers with big ideas, but seldom if ever follow through. They don't get anything done on time and are always shoddy about the details."

Now to reverse the question. What would the high-Is say about the high-Cs? What would be their biggest complaint? They might say, "High-Cs are detailed to a fault. They are real killjoys when it comes to discussing ideas. They always focus on why something can't happen. And when they do decide to do something, they won't start until they have detailed it to death instead of just trying it and seeing what happens."

But consider this: What do high-Is need? They need someone to rein them in and give their ideas substance; something high-Cs happen to be very good at. And what do high-Cs need? Someone with ideas, creativity, and a sense of fun. Again, this is a great job description for a high-I. In essence, the high-I/high-C partnership is a match made in heaven, or a match made in the other place, depending upon whether each person learns how to value and work with the other's communication style.

The same occurs on the other diagonal. A high-S is indirect and people-oriented. So, of course the style which is least like the high-S is the high-D, which is direct and task-oriented. High-Ss would likely complain that high-Ds are aggressive to the point of being pushy and demanding, and too focused on task and not people. The high-Ds would consider the high-Ss too soft on people. They probably would complain that the high-Ss don't speak up often enough and don't seem willing to step up and address the tough issues.

Just like the high-I/high-C combination, the high-D/high-S can be a partnership made in heaven, if each learns to value the other's style. What do high-Ds need? People to follow them. What do high-Ss desire? A great leader or a cause that they can believe in and support.

Yes, the styles are different. But by valuing the strengths of the other styles and by communicating with each of them in their style, we can increase the strength of the relationship and can greatly enhance the effectiveness of the organizations we lead. Our people are more likely to be engaged and inspired because we understand them, speak their language, and work with them in a way that maximizes their effectiveness and feeling of worth.

Recovering When You Miscommunicate

What happens when you guess wrong? What if, with all that you now know about recognizing communication styles, you still get it wrong and you miscommunicate by using the wrong style with someone? How will you know and what do you do about it?

Figure 5.11 summarizes a recommended approach for recovering from miscommunicating with each of the styles. A detailed walk-through of the high-D information in detail will demonstrate how to use this information.

- The key factor for high-Ds is getting things done.
- So, if you are abusing their key factor, it means that they feel they are not getting things done with the time they are spending with you; that is, they feel you are wasting their time.
- What are their typical behaviors when they feel you are wasting their time? They get impatient. They look at their watch. They multi-task.
- What should you do when you see these behaviors? You might say, "Let me cut to the chase here and give you the bottom line." This will likely get their attention because you would have shifted to their communication style.

Watch carefully for people exhibiting behaviors in the third column. You should consider these signs that you are miscommunicating. The point of the recovery behaviors is to provide you with a tool to quickly bounce back from a miscommunication.

Figure 5.11 Recovering from Miscommunications

	Their Key Factor	Your Miscue	Their Behavior in Response	Your Recovery Approach
D	Getting it done	Wasting their time	Impatience, looking at watch, multi-tasking	*Let me cut to the chase here and give you the bottom line.*
I	Being heard	Not giving them a chance to speak; being too detailed	Interrupting, checks out mentally	*I would like to get your thoughts on... Brainstorm with me how to...Let's save the details for later...*
S	Being liked	Being pushy or abrasive	Shutting down, becoming passive-aggressive	*There may be good reasons for not doing this; let's identify potential strengths and weaknesses*
C	Getting it right	Forcing a rapid decision	Objecting, arguing, finding fault	*Let's not rush into something unnecessarily... Let's identify what we know and where we need more information*

Tailoring Your Communication

The four figures that follow summarize the information from this chapter and provide additional guidance to help you adapt to the styles of others, so that you can be more effective as a leader by tailoring your communication.

Figure 5.12 High-D Tailoring Tips

High-D Tailoring Tips	
In general...	• Let them control the conversation. • State your points directly and concisely. • Focus on the benefit to be achieved.
Avoid...	• Wasting their time with information, details or activities that they may consider unnecessary.
To start...	• Be direct; put the high-D in control. (*What can I do for you?*)
When conversing...	• Let the high-D control the flow of the conversation. • Be clear and concise with your questions and direct with your responses.
When presenting...	• Give the recommendation first followed by the problem it solves, and the benefits to be achieved. • Use visual displays and graphs to clarify points.
When writing...	• Be as brief as possible. • Use bullet-points. • Provide one-page summaries.
When asking for a decision...	• Don't offer many alternatives; high-Ds want your best recommendation and only need to know you have considered other options. • Stress the impact of your proposal and how it will bring tangible results.
They will tune out if...	• You take too long to get to the point.
To regain their attention...	• Let me get straight to the point. • Suppose I skip the details and just hit the highlights?
In summary...	• Be prepared, be brief, and be gone.

Figure 5.13 High-I Tailoring Tips

High-I Tailoring Tips	
In general...	• Be warm, friendly, and upbeat. • Start with the big picture ideas first. • Give them plenty of time to talk.
Avoid...	• Diving straight into business. • Focusing on details. • Telling versus asking.
To start...	• Be warm, friendly, and upbeat.
When conversing...	• Let them take their time getting to the point. • When making a point, ask for their feedback; give them a chance to share their ideas. • Stress uniqueness; they respond to new or out-of-the-ordinary.
When presenting...	• Allow time for people to network by planning a gathering time in the agenda. • Give them the big picture before going into details. • Provide them an opportunity to share their ideas before presenting your own. • When sharing your ideas, provide them a picture of the future. • Focus them on your ideas by asking them to give the benefit.
When writing...	• Start friendly and warm. (*I hope your weekend was great.*) • Describe the overall purpose. • Invite their input. • Suggest a meeting. • Avoid writing if you can; high-Is prefer to interact face-to-face.
When asking for a decision...	• Dream with them by describing the vision and result their decision will create. • Be conceptual; relate to a broader concept or idea. • Give high-level information, not the specific detail.
They will tune out if...	• You focus on facts and figures or don't make it interactive.
To regain their attention...	• I would like to get your thoughts on... • Brainstorm with me how to... • Let's save the details for later.
In summary...	• Let them sell themselves.

Figure 5.14 High-S Tailoring Tips

High-S Tailoring Tips	
In general…	• Keep the atmosphere friendly and warm. • Provide assurances that your solution will work. • Stress the positive impact on people.
Avoid…	• Starting with business. • Being pushy or discourteous. • Asking questions that put them on the spot. • Assuming that they agree with you.
To start…	• Be personable; let them know you are wanting to help. (*Hi! I'm…How can I help you today?*)
When conversing…	• Show an interest in them and their needs. (*What are the most important things to you in making this decision? Will that help you by…?*) • Make it easy for them to say yes or no. (*I'd love to hear what you like about this as well as any concerns you have about this working.*)
When presenting…	• Allow time for people to connect with one another. • Present ideas deliberately and clearly. • Stress the positive impact on people. • Show how the idea has worked well in the past.
When writing…	• Start with a personal connection. (*I hope your family is doing well.*) • State your ideas as suggestions that have benefited others. (*We may find it helpful to do something like what organization XYZ did. They…*) • Suggest meeting or holding a telephone conversation. • Avoid writing if you can; high-Ss prefer to interact face-to-face or holding a telephone conversation.
When asking for a decision…	• Focus on how their decision will positively impact others. (*By doing this, our team will like that they will be able to…*)
They will tune out if…	• You become pushy, demanding, or forceful.
To regain their attention…	• What's really important here is to make sure you are completely comfortable and you make the decision that you deem best for our people. • Is this a good time to recap what you are comfortable with and what is not quite comfortable yet?
In summary…	• Start personal; don't assume.

Figure 5.15 High-C Tailoring Tips

High-C Tailoring Tips	
In general...	• Present ideas in a logical, linear, step-by-step manner. • Provide the details needed and give time to get comfortable with them. • Include alternatives, outline pros and cons of each. • Provide supporting evidence to back up claims. • Do what you say you are going to do.
Avoid...	• Being disorganized or making random comments. • Making statements that you can't prove. • Trying to use emotion to convince. • Forcing a rapid decision.
To start...	• Send information ahead of time if possible. • *I have several approaches for you to look at.... Let's walk through this step-by-step.*
When conversing...	• Stay on topic. • Take your time; provide a sense of unhurriedness. • Offer to walk through supporting data.
When presenting...	• Present in chronological order or use a structured flow such as finding, conclusion, recommendation, benefit. • Be precise; use ranges and probabilities when precise facts aren't available.
When writing...	• Get straight to the point. • Have a clear, logical flow. • Provide options. • End by suggesting a deadline for a decision.
When asking for a decision...	• Provide options with strengths and weaknesses for each.
They will tune out if...	• You make claims without providing evidence or try to force a rapid decision.
To regain their attention...	• Let's not rush into something unnecessarily. • Let's identify what we know and where we need more information.
In summary...	• Give them time for the details.

Pigeonholing? Manipulation?

When we cover communications in our leadership workshops, we often get a comment similar to the following, "This feels a lot like we are pigeonholing people. You said up front that each one of us has some level of all four styles in us. We are all very complex. How could it possibly make sense to try to fit each person in the world in one of these four buckets?"

Indeed, we are all individuals and very complex. The goal here isn't to pigeonhole people. The only goal is to figure out how to communicate with people in a way that works better for them. I use communication styles to help lead people better by having an idea of how to better communicate with them. If more leaders just knew what to look for, it could make a significant difference in their leadership.

Another comment we frequently hear in our workshops is about manipulation. For example, someone might ask, "Isn't this manipulation? We adjust our style just to get people to do what we want. It doesn't seem right that we would be using these clever communication techniques to get our way. Isn't that manipulation?"

For this communication styles information to be useful to leaders, they have to be comfortable using it. And for some, if they feel they are manipulating people, they may not feel good about using the tools. So, consider a different perspective. Imagine an elderly relative who is a little hard of hearing. If you want him to hear you, you have to speak louder. Do you speak louder to manipulate him? No, you speak louder so he can hear you. Speaking louder is the *vehicle* you use to help him hear you. Now, if your *intention* is to manipulate him, you can use speaking louder as a *vehicle* for manipulation.

In the same way, if you want to propose something to a high-D, you need her to hear you. So you will adjust your communication style so that you are prepared, brief, and then gone. This is the *vehicle* you are using so she can hear you. Now, if what you are proposing is not in her best interest, and your *intention* is to have her do it anyway, then you might be using the *vehicle* for manipulation. My point is that communication styles—like speaking louder—is a vehicle to help people hear you. Manipulation is determined by your intent and how you use the vehicle. Whether you use the vehicle in a manipulative way is based on your intention.

Detect, Adapt, Beware, Refresh, Expand

To implement the information from this chapter, consider focusing on five key words: detect, adapt, beware, refresh, and expand.

- Be a detective. Actively look for the clues your people give that tell you how they want you to communicate with them. Your people have been giving out these clues for years. Now you know how to read the clues to detect their communication styles.

- Once you understand their communication style, adapt your style to match that of the people with whom you communicate. To quote Ann Herrmann-Nehdi, the Chair of the Board of Herrmann International and one of my mentors, "Don't become a prisoner of your own preference!"

- Beware of the signs that you are communicating in the wrong style. If the person with whom you are communicating becomes impatient, if they are interrupting, if they are actively objecting, if they shut down—these are all signs that you may be communicating in the wrong style.

- Keep the information fresh. Communication styles strategies can be quickly forgotten if you don't intentionally begin using the information on a regular basis. Consciously apply the information with your boss, with your subordinates, with peers, et cetera. Review the information daily or weekly to keep it fresh.

- Expand the use of communication styles. As more and more people in your organization understand and apply DISC, the greater the impact can be on promoting more effective and harmonious communication. Consider workshops and other vehicles for raising awareness and expanding use.

Detect, adapt, beware, refresh, and expand; these are the keys for long-term success with communication styles.

Summary

1. To be able to engage and inspire people successfully, facilitative leaders must have a solid appreciation of different communication styles and understand how to adapt as needed to the styles of others.

2. In the DISC model, there are four basic communication styles, referred to as drive (or dominance), influence, steadiness, and compliance. Although all of us have the capacity to communicate using each of the four styles, for most of us one of the styles tends to dominate the way we communicate.

3. There are specific communication dos and don'ts for each of the styles which can be summarized with the following:

   - High-D: Be prepared, be brief, and be gone.

   - High-I: Let them sell themselves.

   - High-S: Start personal; don't assume.

   - High-C: Give them time for the details.

4. In most interactions, there is a conversation battle going on in which each person is insisting that the other person communicate in his or her style. Facilitative leaders understand that they can be more effective if they communicate in the other person's style.

5. People often "leak" their preferred communication style through their words and actions. You can identify people's preferred style if you know what to look for.

6. The four styles can be delineated through two dimensions: direct/indirect and task-focused/people-focused

    - High-D: Direct and task-focused

    - High-I: Direct and people-focused

    - High-S: Indirect and people-focused

    - High-C: Indirect and task-focused

7. Given that they are complete opposites in their dimensions, high-Ds and high-Ss form a natural style clash, as do high-Is and high-Cs. However, because the style pairings are so opposite, they can be very complementary if each learns to appreciate the strengths of the other style.

8. When you are miscommunicating with a style, the person begins exhibiting specific behaviors. Should you observe these behaviors, you can recover by taking specific actions.

9. Adapting to communication styles is not intended to be either pigeonholing or manipulative. The intention is to use the tools to improve leadership through better and more effective communications.

10. To implement the information from this chapter, consider focusing on five key words: detect, adapt, beware, refresh, and expand.

    - Be a detective. Actively look for the clues your people give that tell you how they want you to communicate with them.

    - Once you understand their communication style, adapt your style to match.

    - Beware of the signs that you are communicating in the wrong style.

    - Keep the information fresh. Consciously apply and review the information daily or weekly.

    - Finally, expand the use of communication styles through workshops and other vehicles for raising awareness and expanding their use within your organization.

Spring Forward

List below the people you interact with on a regular basis. Make an educated guess concerning the person's communication style. Indicate the behaviors or other signs that lead to your conclusion. Specify the approach you will take to better communicate with each person.

Person	Style	The Signs	Approach
Your Boss			

Connect First, Correct Second

- Seagull Management
- Separating the Facts from Our Story
- Praise by Giving a GIFT
- Constructive Feedback through PERCS
- Using PAC to Connect then Challenge
- Behavioral Issue Types
- Reasons People Change
- Summary
- Spring Forward

Chapter 6.
Connect First, Correct Second

When people aren't doing what we believe they should be doing or aren't performing at the level we believe they should, the natural response for most leaders is to take corrective action.

Seagull Management

I was the project manager on a six-month project to implement a payroll system for a retail chain of 500 stores. It was the first time I was managing a project and I was working until 8:00 or 9:00 p.m. most evenings. I wanted it to be the best payroll implementation in the history of humanity!

We were nearing the end of the first month when the CFO, the project sponsor, came into my office and declared, "You are doing a terrible job. I was just talking with the controller and he is upset because he doesn't understand how this new payroll system is going to update the balance sheet accounts. You need to do your job." He stormed out.

We often refer to this type of leadership style as "seagull management:" the leader flies in, makes a lot of noise, dumps on everybody and flies out. For a payroll system, the update to the balance sheet accounts is called "an interface." For a six-month project, you generally design the interfaces in month two and implement them in month five. We were nearing the end of month one and he was blasting me for something we weren't even scheduled to get to yet. I was livid: "This ungrateful jerk. Here I am working extra hours to get this system done for him and he comes in here and criticizes me for not doing something that's not scheduled to be done yet!"

But, suppose he had come into my office and said, "I know you have been putting a lot of hours in and I really appreciate it. And there is something else I need you to do. I was speaking with the controller earlier today and he is upset because he doesn't understand how this new payroll system is going to update the balance sheet accounts. Would you sit down with him and get him comfortable with how all this is going to work? Can you do this for me in the next day or two?"

If he had approached me in that way, my response likely would have been, "Of course, I'll be glad to do that for you." Note that he is delivering the same message: You aren't doing something that I need you to do. But because of his approach, my response would have been, "Of course." Compare that to my actual response and to the fact that I still get a little upset when I think about the situation over 30 years later!

The difference in the CFO's second way of approaching the project manager represents a core practice of facilitative leaders: Connect first, correct second. Facilitative leaders understand that correction is essential for improvement. But they also understand that if you try to pour water into a jar that has a cap on it, all you are going to make is a mess! To help uncap the jar so that their people are open to receive the input, facilitative leaders connect first. This chapter covers the following concepts and strategies facilitative leaders use for engaging, connecting, and correcting:

- Separating the facts from our story

- Praise by giving a GIFT

- Constructive feedback through PERCS

- Using PAC to connect then challenge

- Behavioral issue types

- Reasons people change

Separating the Facts from Our Story

In *Crucial Conversations*,[16] the authors introduce the importance in our communications of separating the facts from "the story" we make up about the facts. I use the diagram depicted in Figure 6.1 to describe this to people desiring to become more facilitative in their leadership style.

- Something happens in the workplace: an event, a behavior, a conversation. The behavior is a fact. In the seagull management case that started this chapter, the fact was that I had not spoken to the controller about the new payroll system.

- This fact then passes through the CFO's filter. Assume that the CFO has previous experiences with consultants, or may have had a past experience with me, that leads him to believe that consultants just focus on getting the job done and don't focus on the people impacted by the change.

- As a result of his filter, he has formed a story that says I don't care about his people and I am not doing my job.

- That story causes him to have a feeling of irritation and anger.

- As a result of his feeling, he takes action: seagull management!

Figure 6.1 Separating the Facts from Our Story

The diagram makes it clear: we don't react to facts; we react to the story that we make up about the facts. The CFO's strong reaction was not because I had not spoken to the controller. His reaction was based on the story he had made up about it: the consultant doesn't care about my people. But while the facts are true by definition, the story we make up may not be. Unfortunately, many leaders don't recognize the difference between the facts and the story, and react based on the belief that their story is true.

Facilitative leaders intentionally attempt to separate the facts from their story. You will hear from them such phrases as, "When you did this, it led me to believe that…" or "When I saw this happen, the story I made up was…" Comments such as these deliberately communicate that the leader recognizes that the story may or may not be true. Whether praising superior performance or correcting underperformance, be sure to recognize the difference between the facts and your story.

Praise by Giving a GIFT

Questionable Praise

Over a decade ago, one of our facilitators received an email of praise from a client. Let's say the name of the client was Q-Health Systems. The next time I ran into the facilitator, I said, "I saw the Q-Health email. Great job."

In a different conversation with the same person a few weeks later, the facilitator mentioned to me, "You really should praise people more." I was surprised at the comment, and, just by way of an example, I reminded the person of the praise that I had given regarding the Q-Health letter. The facilitator said, "That was praise?"

> *I was shocked at the question. But the facilitator was right. It didn't feel like praise, at least not to that facilitator. The message I was trying to send was clearly not received.*

In *Whale Done!,*[17] Ken Blanchard describes the power of praise to encourage the behaviors leaders want. However, facilitative leaders understand the distinction between typical praise and giving a GIFT. Typical praise might sound like the following:

"You did a superb job with the presentation!"

However, I recommend that facilitative leaders give a GIFT when they praise, as follows:

The GIFT Praise Process

- **General to specific.** Start with a general comment and then identify one or two specific behaviors to praise.

- **Impact.** Indicate the impact or benefit of the behavior.

- **Feeling.** Let the person know how the behavior made you feel.

- **Thank you.** Thank the person.

Using the GIFT method, the leader might instead comment this way.

Jane, you did a superb job with the presentation! Right from the beginning you gave them your recommendation, explained the problem that it solved, enumerated the benefits, and went straight to the close. They were so impressed, how could they not say yes and give our department the budget? I have to say, it made me feel so proud to see a member of my team give such a stellar presentation to the management team. I know it was a lot of work, but your preparation really showed. Please keep it up, it was magnificent. Thanks so much.

How is the GIFT form of praise different from how praise is typically given? People have commented that receiving a GIFT feels more personal and feels like the person giving the praise really means it. Others have mentioned that with typical praise, they are waiting for the person to counter the praise with the dreaded, "But..." followed by an admonishment about what they did wrong. But not so when they receive praise in the GIFT format.

Another reason giving a GIFT may be more effective: it appeals to each of the four DISC styles, as shown in Figure 6.2.

Figure 6.2 How GIFT appeals to the DISC Styles

	D	I	S	C
General to specific				X
Impact	X			
Feeling		X	X	
Thank you		X	X	

Constructive Feedback through PERCS

Along with delivering effective praise, facilitative leaders also need to provide constructive feedback to help their people develop. I recommend using the PERCS process to give constructive feedback.

The PERCS Approach for Constructive Feedback

Approach Privately.	Meet with the person one-on-one or with perhaps one additional person.
Empathize with the Symptom.	Connect first with the person by praising the effort put forth, the level of participation, the quality of input, or anything else that is both sincere and worthwhile.
Address the Root Cause.	Identify the critical issue and causes for it. Avoid saying, "But..." Instead, consider using "And, one area that I want to address..." Provide your thoughts and check in with the other person to gain the person's understanding of the issue.
Get Agreement on a Solution.	Seek a mutually agreeable approach to addressing the symptom and root cause.

In using the PERCS model, it is especially important to separate the facts from your story. When you describe the facts and then the story you have made up, it allows the other person to better understand why you are reaching the conclusion that you reach.

Using PAC to Connect Then Challenge

There are times when a team member may make a recommendation that you, as the leader, disagree with. The typical approach is "listen-respond" which, as might be surmised, involves listening to what the person says and then responding directly with our objection.

Review how the leader in the scenarios below responds in the brief dialogue that follows—classic "listen-respond."

Joe: I've been thinking about this for some time. I think we should close down the home office and just operate the business out of our three satellite locations.

Leader: Are you out of your mind? That's a bad idea and couldn't possibly work.

A different approach is to build a PAC with the other person by taking the following steps between listen and respond.

Figure 6.3 PAC Steps

```
        ┌──────────────────┐
        │     LISTEN       │──┐
        └──────────────────┘  │
                    ┌──────────▼──────┐
                    │    Playback     │
                    └─────────────────┘
                              │
                    ┌─────────▼───────┐
                    │     Agree       │
                    └─────────────────┘
                              │
                    ┌─────────▼───────┐
                    │   Challenge     │──┐
                    └─────────────────┘  │
    ┌──────────────────────┐             │
    │      RESPOND         │◄────────────┘
    └──────────────────────┘
```

- **Playback**: *It sounds like what you are saying is…is that right?* First, playback what the person said to ensure you heard correctly.

- **Agree**: *I certainly agree that…*
  Next, connect with the person by agreeing with what you can agree with. For example, if part of the suggestion makes sense to you, say so. Or if there is an obvious benefit of doing the suggestion, share the benefit.

- **Challenge**: *If we do that, how…*
  Then, ask the challenge question. The challenge question embodies the reason you

disagree with the suggestion. Through the challenge question, if the person can answer it, you might be more open to the suggestion.

Now to redo this last conversation using the PAC.

Joe:	I've been thinking about this for some time. I think we should close down the home office and just operate the business out of our three satellite locations.
Leader:	It sounds like you are suggesting we eliminate our headquarters altogether. Is that right? (*playback*)
Joe:	That's right.
Leader:	I certainly agree that if we eliminate our home office it could significantly reduce the overhead of an additional office (*agree*). But let me ask you, if we eliminate the home office, how would you address the increased costs resulting from each office having to hire staff to do billing, collections, IT, legal, and all the other things our home office does today (*challenge*)?

The person at this point might say, "Oh, I get it. I hadn't thought about that." Alternatively, the person might say, "My thought is that we still keep those functions centralized, but in a field office. For example, one office could handle billing and contracts, another could handle IT and purchasing, and so on. This would eliminate the overhead of the home office, but still allow us to get the work done by distributing people in the field."

Based on the person's response, you would then give your response or, if necessary, build another PAC to confirm that you are hearing how the person would address the challenges you see. The playback-agree-challenge process is designed to have you and the other person connect and work together to address issues with the suggestion.

Types of Behavioral Issues

Facilitative leaders understand that there are essentially only three types of behavioral issues: awareness, skill, and will, as Figure 6.4 delineates.

Figure 6.4 Types of Behavioral Issues

- **Awareness:** Awareness issues are the simplest by far to address. The real issue is that the person isn't aware that there *is* an issue.

- *Solution*
  Bring the issue to the person's awareness. If it is simply an awareness issue, the person will likely address it because the person has the skill and the will to do so.

- **Skills:** However, in some cases, awareness isn't enough. After bringing the issue to the person's attention, he/she may accept that there is an issue and have the will to make a change, but lack the skills to make it happen.

- *Solution*
  In this case, additional support, coaching, development and/or training might be needed.

- **Will:** In other cases, there might be a will issue. That is, the person is aware of the issue and has the capability to change, but doesn't want to or is not willing to put forth the effort to bring about the change.
  Solution
  For many, will issues are the most difficult to address. Will issues often require a change in perspective and attitude to overcome.

How do will issues show up? What does the behavior look like? Will issues often show up as change resistance, often due to disagreement or lack of alignment. Not surprisingly perhaps, change resistance appears differently by communication style type, as shown in Figure 6.5.

Figure 6.5 Change Resistance Behaviors

DISC Style	When There is a Will Issue, This Style Will Likely...
D	Argue with you; attack your position; attempt to go above you or around you
I	Spread their dissatisfaction by telling everyone around them about their concerns
S	Shut down; become passive-aggressive
C	Object by providing facts and figures to justify their position; attempt to slow down the process

In the next section, I describe strategies for addressing these will issues based on appealing to the person's reason for change.

Reasons People Change

As leaders take their journey through the three levels of leadership, they inevitably find that they have to implement programs of change. Whether it is a new strategy, a new process, a new computer system, a redesign of the organization, or what have you, change happens.

Some people get excited about change while others take a more "wait and see" attitude; and still others actively, or passive-aggressively, resist. Facilitative leaders understand that there are essentially four reasons why people change, and try to connect with their people accordingly. Once more, the reasons people change correspond more or less to the DISC types as shown in Figure 6.6.

Figure 6.6 Reasons People Change

Reason	Associated Style	Explanation
Higher Vision	I	Some people are willing to change when you provide a vision of the possibilities of what can be. High-Is tend to fall into this category.
Desired Outcomes	D	Others, especially high-Ds, are motivated by the specific outcomes and benefits to be gained by the change.
Fear of Consequences	C	High-Cs frequently are motivated to take action to reduce risk or avoid a potentially negative outcome.
Pain	S	Finally, some people don't respond to a higher vision, desired outcomes, or fear of consequences. They are more likely to endure the hardships of the current reality rather than face the instability, uncertainty, and insecurity that they believe comes with change. This group, often dominated by the high-S communication style, often has to be in considerable pain to be willing to change.

Grades and the Teenager

Shortly after I started the company I run now, I had my 14-year old nephew come to live with me and my family for several years. After he had spent several weeks with us and before he went off for his first day of school, I explained to him that I had gone to public school and knew that in many classes, if you just show up and pay attention, you will get a C. If you do all your homework and do a little studying for the tests, you will get a B; and on top of that, if you apply yourself and have above average intelligence you will easily get a B+, A- or an A. And I pointed out to him the several occasions where he had already demonstrated that he was above average in intelligence. This got a smile out of him.

But that was about all it got out of him. His first quarter grades: one B and five Cs. Clearly higher vision didn't work! I took a different approach: desired outcomes. I told him that for any A he brought home, whether a test or homework, I would give him $5. Any B would receive $1. Unfortunately, this was not adequate motivation. Next quarter grades: one B, four Cs, and one D. This was not going in the right direction.

I talked with his teachers and learned that the major problem was that he wasn't submitting all of his homework. Talking with him about it, I learned that frequently he didn't know there was an assignment, because he didn't write it down. The next approach: I worked with him to create a one-page daily form where he would write in his assignment and have each teacher sign the form. Any day he came home without it signed by all teachers, he would be grounded and lose all electronic privileges (i.e., phone, video games, TV, et cetera) for the night. Impact on grades? The decline continued: four Cs, two Ds.

So I tried higher vision, I tried desired outcomes, I tried fear of consequences. All that was left was pain. How do you put a teenager in pain? I removed his door. No privacy for the entire quarter. Amazingly, grades dramatically improved: four Bs, two Cs. By the way, my nephew is a high-S!

The Surround Strategy

In our workshops, when discussing the four reasons people change, we often are asked a question like the following:

> *I have a boss who is a high-S. He is so change-averse, I can't get him to take action on anything that looks like change, even though I provide clear benefits to our department. What do I do? How do I legally put my boss in pain?*

As you can probably detect from the comment, the person who is asking the question is a high-D who is frustrated because the high-S is not responding to the potential benefits that the high-D would respond to. Once more, there is a tendency for listeners to expect people to respond as they would, given their own communication style.

In the case of a high-S reluctant to implement change, the "surround strategy" can be quite effective. As you recall, the key factor for a high-S is being liked. If multiple people surrounding the high-S let the high-S know how not making the change hurts them, it increases the likelihood that the high-S will relent and make the change.

Summary

1. When people aren't doing what we believe they should be doing or aren't performing at the level we believe they should, the natural response for most leaders is to take corrective action.

2. Facilitative leaders understand that correction is essential for improvement. Yet they also understand that if you try to pour water into a jar that has a cap on it, all you are going to make is a mess! To help uncap the jar so that their people are open to receive the input, facilitative leaders connect first.

3. Facilitative leaders know that we don't react to facts, we react to the story that we make up about the facts. Therefore, facilitative leaders intentionally attempt to separate the facts from their story. You will hear from them such phrases as, "When you did this, it led me to believe that…"

4. When facilitative leaders praise, they give a GIFT:
   - Start with a **General** comment and then identify one or two specific behaviors to praise.
   - Indicate the **Impact** of the behavior or the benefit.
   - Let the person know how the behavior made the leader **Feel**.
   - **Thank** the person.

5. Along with delivering effective praise, facilitative leaders use the PERCS process to give constructive feedback.
   - Approach **Privately**.
   - **Empathize** with the Symptom.
   - Address the **Root Cause**.
   - Get agreement on a **Solution**.

6. When a team member makes a recommendation that you, as the leader, disagree with, build a PAC to connect first then challenge.
   - **Playback**: "It sounds like what you are saying is…. Is that right?"
   - **Agree**: "I certainly agree that…"
   - **Challenge**: "If we do that, how…"

7. Facilitative leaders understand that there are three types of behavioral issues: awareness, skill, and will, and apply appropriate strategies for addressing each.

8. There are essentially four reasons people change: higher vision, desired outcomes, fear of consequences, and pain. Facilitative leaders apply the appropriate strategy to help influence people into changing.

9. The communication style that is frequently most resistant to change is the high-S. The surround strategy is an approach that can be effective in helping high-Ss be willing to change to meet the needs of their people.

Spring Forward

This chapter including several concepts and strategies for connecting and correcting:

1. Facts versus stories

2. GIFT

3. PERCS

4. PAC

5. Awareness, skill, will

6. Change resistance behaviors

7. Reasons people change

8. The surround strategy

Using the same list from the prior chapter of the people you interact with on a regular basis, indicate one or more of the strategies that you might implement to be more effective in connecting and correcting, and indicate the goal you hope to achieve by using the strategies.

Person	Style	Strategies to Use	To Achieve What Goal?
Your Boss			

- Teams versus Groups
- 8 Team Essentials
- Anticipating Team Issues: Based on the Leader
- Purpose and Deliverable
- Composing the Team
- Anticipating Team Issues: Based on the Team
- Selecting Project Team Members
- Team Norms
- When Do We Have a Decision?
- Happy Talk
- Work Processes
- Developing and Delivering Recommendations
- Accountability and Monitoring
- Summary
- Spring Forward

Chapter 7.
Equip for Success, Monitor for Results

Facilitative leaders understand that their role is to equip their teams for success and then monitor their efforts as the team produces results. Facilitative leaders understand that when they don't adequately equip a team or when monitoring is haphazard, the risk of team failure increases significantly. This chapter describes the 8 Team Essentials—the eight key elements every team needs—and the role of the facilitative leader in helping to bring them about. However, it is best to start with the basics, or an understanding of the critical differences between teams and groups. This will help define the key essentials for every team.

Teams versus Groups

Any project team, even the strongest ones, can fall into dysfunctional patterns. As facilitators, my organization is called in from time to time to help project teams and intact teams (i.e., people who work together on an ongoing basis) get back on track. As one of the critical activities in our team-building workshops, we ask participants to define the difference between a team and a group in a polarity form (i.e., "While a team is this, a group is that"). Figure 7.1 gives a list of typical responses from participants.

We then split the participants into sub-teams and ask them to classify a list of items as a team or group. The list includes relatively easy items like a "symphony orchestra" which sub-teams quickly classify as a team. There are also more difficult ones such as the U.S. Congress, volunteers rescuing a child out of a well, and a major league sports team that finished in last place. For each item, the sub-team participants have to come to consensus on whether the item is a team or a group, *and* they have to justify their decision by indicating one or more of the reasons (A-G) from the list they created for the difference between a team and a group.

Figure 7.1 Difference between a Team and a Group

		Team Members	Group Members
A.		Common goal or purpose	Self-interests, individual goals
B.		Defined responsibilities	No role definitions
C.		Work together	Act independently
D.		Have a leader	Don't have a leader
E.		Communicate continuously	Communicate if necessary
F.		Take responsibility	Blame others
G.		Rely on one another	Rely on self

The discussion fosters a deeper understanding of the differences between how teams are organized and how teams operate. For example, Figure 7.2 indicates an organization that is organized as a team but operates as a group.

Figure 7.2 Organized as a Team / Operates as a Group

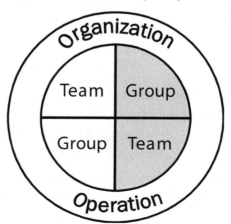

In our workshops, participants often place the U.S. Congress in this category. While our forefathers organized Congress to have a common purpose to work together on behalf of the nation, unfortunately Congress all too often operates based on self-interests, with members acting independently and blaming one another (Item A in our list).

Contrast this with Figure 7.3, which portrays a team that is organized as a group but operates as a team.

Figure 7.3 Organized as a Group / Operates as a Team

The neighborhood volunteers might fall into this category. Prior to coming together, they had no common goal and no defined responsibilities. However, to save a child stuck in a well, they operated collectively to achieve the goal.

However, the most effective teams are those that are organized as a team and operate as a team, as shown in Figure 7.4.

Figure 7.4 Organized as a Team / Operates as a Team

The symphony orchestra would fall into this category. They have a common purpose. They have a leader and defined responsibilities. Though the leader is the only one perceived to be communicating continuously during performances, the orchestra works together to create an amazing blend of sounds that results in beautiful music.

Note, however, that being organized as a team and operating as a team do not guarantee success. You can still miss achieving your ultimate goals. As an example, consider a sports team that is organized and operates as a team, but still does not win the league championship. Two other components have to be in place: a strong strategy and the focused execution of that strategy. I will cover these elements in Chapter 9.

By the way, the last entry in the list of team-versus-group items is always "your organization." The sub-teams have to indicate whether they believe their organization is a team or a group. This exercise can be quite effective, regardless of whether they choose "team" or "group." The real learning is in discussing the reasons for the choice. What inevitably results is a discussion around their team's strengths and areas for improvement.

Before leaving this topic, it is important to underscore two additional, clarifying points.

- It is not unusual for an organization to be composed of a "group of teams" with each team working independently from the other teams, with no common purpose or vision. This is a common pitfall for government agencies and large businesses where individual departments can have their own agendas without working for the good of the whole.

- I have also seen a "team of groups." The leadership team is strong, but each of the individual operating units is plagued with self-interest and conflict.

Consider *your own* organization. Is it organized as a team? Does it operate as a team? Is it a group of teams? Is it a team of groups?

8 Team Essentials

With the foundation of the difference between a team and a group in place, I want to focus on what is needed for a team to be successful. Through experiences with a variety of teams, my organization has identified what we believe are the "eight essentials"—that is, the eight things every team needs to be successful. I have found that a team missing one of the essentials can still be successful through the persistence and skills of the individual team members, but it is just more difficult. A team missing two essentials is severely handicapped and our experience has been that the chances of success are very low.

> But for a team missing three or more of the team essentials, the likelihood of success is so low, one can predict with high probability that failure will be the result!

Figure 7.5 provides a summary of the 8 Team Essentials.

Figure 7.5 The 8 Team Essentials

Purpose	The mission or reason for being
Deliverable	The product or results expected, how success is defined
Constraints	The time by when the deliverable is to be completed, additional limitations/conditions
Sponsorship	The person or authority from whom the team receives its charge, by whom the charge is changed, or to whom the team reports
Resources	The people who participate on the team, as well as funding, etc.
Leadership	The method used to make decisions, assign tasks, establish policies, address issues, etc.
Work Process	The method used to produce the deliverables
Teamwork	The level of team trust, communication, and accountability

Note the bold line separating the first five essentials from the last three. The line is significant in that the top five are different from the bottom three in a number of ways, as shown in Figure 7.6.

Figure 7.6 Focus of the Top 5 Essentials versus Bottom 3

Top Five Essentials	Bottom Three Essentials
• How the team is organized	• How the team operates
• What the team is tasked to do	• How the team will get it done
• Essentials that should be given to the team	• Essentials that should be created by the team

The last bullet in each list is critical. In most cases, the top five should be given to the team. Your job as a facilitative leader is to ensure that you equip the team adequately with the top five items. A team that is not given the top five essentials may be poorly chartered. But once a team is chartered, the team members need to focus on ensuring they develop the bottom three.

In our work with teams, we have found teams that failed because they were poorly chartered (missing one or more of the top five) as well as teams that failed because they executed poorly (the bottom three). Consider the teams that report to you, as well as the teams of which you are a member. Do they have each of the eight essentials?

Anticipating Team Issues: Based on the Leader

Imagine you have chartered a team and assigned a high-D to be the leader of the team. Consider the 8 Team Essentials and the ones the high-D team leader might be most concerned about, and those essentials that a high-D team leader is more likely to ignore or overlook. How does that change if your team leader is a high-I, high-S, or high-C? Based on our work with teams, Figure 7.7 answers these questions by identifying what each style leader likely would be most (M) and least (L) concerned about.

Figure 7.7 Most and Least Concerns by DISC Style

	D	I	S	C	Explanation
Purpose		M		L	The mission or reason for being
Deliverable	M		L		The product or results expected, how success is defined
Constraints		L		M	The time by when the deliverable is to be completed, additional limitations/ conditions
Sponsorship					The person or authority from whom the team receives its charge, by whom the charge is changed, or to whom the team reports
Resources	L	M	M	L	The people who participate on the team, as well as funding, etc.
Leadership	M		L		The method used to make decisions, assign tasks, establish policies, address issues, etc.
Work Process		L		M	The method used to produce the deliverables
Teamwork	L		M		The level of team trust, communication, and accountability

Given the essentials that likely would be of least concern to a project leader with a particular DISC style, consider the issues that you might anticipate the team to have, and the actions you might take in response. Figure 7.8 provides potential issues and possible preventive measures you might take. In each case, one strategy is to assign a team member with a balancing DISC style to focus on preventing the issue.

Figure 7.8 Potential Team Issues Based on the Team Leader

	Potential Issue	Suggested Prevention Strategies
D	Low team morale	• Include a high-I/high-S to focus on morale. • With team check-ins, ask the team to rate morale and suggest strategies to improve.
I	Lacking details or consistent process	• Include a high-C to focus on details. • Provide a sample deliverable to demonstrate the level of detail needed. • Ensure the team adopts and steps through a solution process (*see later in this chapter*).
S	Over focus on people versus results	• Include a high-D to focus on results. • Have team create a timeline of activity with deliverables due.
C	Lack of creativity and innovation	• Include a high-I to provide creativity. • Ensure plan includes steps to collect creative input from others outside the team.

The remainder of this chapter will focus on several elements of the eight essentials:

- Purpose and deliverable
- Composing the team
- Making decisions
- Work processes and recommendations
- Accountability and monitoring

Purpose and Deliverable

Facilitative leaders understand that when they charter a team it is essential to provide a clear purpose and deliverable that together define team success. When clarity is lacking, teams may create their own definition of success which might not match yours. Perhaps even worse, a lack of clarity can cause internal team turmoil. Team members themselves can differ on what is expected and push and pull the project in different directions due to the lack of alignment caused by insufficient clarity from the leader.

Facilitative leaders understand the role clarity plays in empowering people. Having a clear purpose statement and specific defined outcomes allows team members to align their actions around a common focus.

How do you ensure the purpose and deliverable provide clarity? Purpose must answer, "Why are we doing this?" The deliverable must answer, "What must we have when we are done?" What follows is an example to be refined to provide clarity.

You have assigned a team to exhibit at a trade show. What's wrong with this purpose and deliverable?

Version #1

The purpose of this project is to exhibit at the upcoming XYZ tradeshow. When we are done, we will pass cold leads to the marketing team to do nurturing and distribute the warm and hot leads to the sales team for immediate follow-up.

You may be surprised by the number of purpose and deliverable statements that get written this way. The purpose is a "what" statement, explaining only *what* the project is. The statement doesn't speak to *why* we are undertaking the project. The second sentence explains *how* results will be processed; it does not define the *expected outcome* in terms of success. Because the term "leads" (plural) is used, the implication is that if the exhibit produces just two cold leads and two warm and hot ones, the project is a success.

Version #2

The purpose of this project is to raise awareness of our services by exhibiting at the upcoming XYZ tradeshow. We define success as collecting a minimum of 85 leads from the effort.

This purpose statement is certainly better than the previous version. It does answer the why. And the deliverable (the definition of success) is also improved. However, is the purpose solely to raise awareness? Isn't the purpose also to gain revenue from leads? In addition, as a way of clarifying success, we recommend setting targets at three levels: minimum acceptable, expected result, and stretch target, as shown in Version #3.

Version #3

The purpose of this project is to raise awareness of our services and create revenue-generating leads by exhibiting at the upcoming XYZ tradeshow. We define success as follows:

	Minimum	Expected	Stretch
Number of cold leads to marketing for nurturing	75	150	250
Number of warm and hot leads to sales for immediate follow-up	10	20	30
Number of closes from leads within 9 months (to determine if we exhibit again next year)	2	5	8
Sales generated from leads within 9 months	$25K	$100K	$250K

Clarity of purpose allows you to increase specificity in the definition of success. Having a specific definition of success allows the entire team to align their activities around achieving a handful of well-selected outcomes. Using the minimum-expected-stretch format gives the team a clear target (expected), but also communicates what would be considered minimally acceptable. So, for example, if the trade show does not achieve all, or at least most, of the target minimums, the team would likely question the benefit of attending the tradeshow the following year.

Composing the Team

Missing a High-C

When we were a start-up with just six employees, we had one high-D, three high-Is and two high-Ss. There was not a single high-C in our group. If you were DISC knowledgeable and had visited our offices during that time, you would have looked around and noted exactly that. We were unorganized, we were chaotic, we were just having a great time working with clients and getting things done.

We decided to take "affirmative action." Our goal was to increase DISC diversity on our team by ensuring that one of the next people we hired was a high-C. We did just that. She lasted two weeks. At the end of that time she was ready to resign—the environment was way too disjointed for her. I begged her to stay, explaining, "We need you! We hired you purposely to help change the way we do things." She has been with us ever since, keeping the high-Ds, high-Is, and high-Ss in line!

As the preceding case implies, having all DISC styles on a team can improve performance. But examine what would happen if there were a team of people all with the same communication style. In other words, assume a team in which all of the team members were just one style, either all high-Ds, high-Is, high-Ss, or high-Cs.

Figure 7.9 delineates what I believe would likely occur related to four questions.

- What would be the key dysfunction in the room?

- Would they finish the task?

- What would be the quality of what they did finish?

- How would they feel about each other when the assignment was completed?

Figure 7.9 All Team Members with Same DISC Style

	Key Dysfunction?	Would they Finish?	Quality of What They Finished? Why?	Feel?
D	Who leads	Yes	Low Fast, low cooperation	Dislike
I	Who speaks	Maybe	Low High-level, unfocused	Like
S	Who challenges	Yes	Low Low creativity & challenge	Love
C	Who stops the analysis	No	High	Neutral

To better understand the results for each style, imagine that a team has been given two days to identify key problems and develop potential solutions and a detailed implementation plan to improve the organization's hiring process. What would be the result at the end of the two days if everyone on the team had the same style?

High-D

- **Dysfunction**: The key factor for a high-D is "getting it done." So, if everyone in the room was a high-D and trying to get it done, the key dysfunction would likely center around who will lead the team. Each high-D would be trying to take over and lead. You would have all generals, no soldiers. You probably can imagine the constant clashing of egos as each tried to get his/her way. Here is an example of what a conversation might look like.

  1st High-D: So, the assignment is for us to identify problems and develop recommendations with the hiring process. Here's how we will go about it—

2nd High-D:	*(interrupting)* Excuse me. Who died and appointed you king of this group?
3rd High-D:	We had this same problem at our old company and I was on the team that solved it. So, here's what we should do—
4th High-D:	*(interrupting)* In case you haven't figured it out, you're not at your old company. You're at a new company, so let me tell you what we're going to do.

And the fight for control continues. Tough crowd!

- **Finish**: Would a high-D group finish? Of course. They get things done. However, if there are ten high-Ds in the room, you might end up with ten different solutions because they couldn't agree on who would lead!

- **Quality**: The quality would likely be low for two reasons in particular. First, there would be little teamwork as described earlier. Second, high-Ds act very quickly and tend to be satisfied with the first answers received rather than analyzing deeper for better solutions.

- **Feel**: Due to ego contests in the room, the high-Ds would likely walk away not liking each other. I can imagine each one leaving the room saying exactly the same thing: "We could have gotten a lot more done if they would have just listened to me."

High-I

- **Dysfunction**: The key-factor for a high-I is "being heard." Imagine the competition for air time in that room and the effort needed to keep the discussion on topic. I can visualize the conversation.

1st High-I:	Hey, it's been great catching up with everyone and I've loved the discussion, but we probably should start in on what we are here to do. We are supposed to be giving our ideas for improving the hiring process. Maybe we can—
2nd High-I:	*(interrupting)* That's a good idea because last week I hired a guy from Iowa who—
3rd High-I:	*(interrupting)* Iowa? I was born in Iowa. Do you know which city he's from?
4th High-I:	I think some of my best people are from the Midwest. Do you think it is because of their diets?

From the hiring process, to Iowa, to diets all in less than two minutes!

- **Finish**: A group of high-Is may or may not finish the task. It could depend upon whether there is at least one high-I in the room who also has a moderate-to-high dose of high-D and therefore feels motivated to corral the conversation.

- **Quality**: Like the group of high-Ds, the high-Is would have difficulty with quality. First, the amount of time spent on the task would be limited by all the other topics that came up. In addition, high-Is would spend little time on the details.

- **Feel**: The high-Is would likely walk out of the room liking one another. I can imagine each saying the same thing, "That was fun. I had trouble getting a word in, but really great people."

High-S

- **Dysfunction**: The key-factor for a high-S is "being liked." This would be a highly supportive group. When one of the members came up with a good idea, you would likely hear, "Great idea!" When someone came up with a mediocre idea, you would likely hear, "Great idea!" The room would be very warm and supportive and every idea, no matter how good or how bad, would make the list. Why? Because of their dysfunction: no one would be willing to challenge what was said.

- **Finish**: High-Ss would certainly finish since they don't want to let down the person who assigned them the task.

- **Quality**: The reluctance to challenge ideas has two impacts that together would likely yield a low-quality result. First, as described before, without any challenge mediocre ideas would appear on the list. Second, low creativity. Creative abrasion[18] is a term used to describe what happens when conflicting ideas push against each other to create even better ideas. An environment that avoids the challenge of ideas decreases the possibility for more creative and innovative solutions emerging.

- **Feel**: With such a supportive environment, high-Ss would likely experience the discussion as a love fest, with each one walking away making similar comments, "Wow, what a wonderful experience. The world would be such a nicer place if every experience was like this one."

High-C

- **Dysfunction**: The key-factor for a high-C is "getting it right." A team of all high-Cs will take whatever time was necessary to ensure that they did a high quality and comprehensive job. They would analyze, analyze, and analyze some more. And, if they weren't satisfied that they had looked at all angles, they would go back and analyze some more. Why? Because there was no one in the room who would stop it; no one who would say, "That's enough. We have to finish this."

- **Finish**: Would they finish? No way. As you recall, the first task was to create a list of problems with the hiring process. While the high-D list would be fairly short, and the high-I list of problems would list all kinds of items including problems, solutions, and ideas about unrelated issues, the high-C list would be a substantive product. It would likely include every problem in the history of the company that had ever occurred related to the hiring process. The problems would be cross-referenced by root cause and the root causes would be pair-ranked to ensure that the most significant ones appeared first. But then the two days would be over. You might ask the team, "Where are the recommended solutions and the implementation plan?" And they might respond, "Surely you knew this would take more time. You can't expect a quality job to be done in just two days."

- **Quality**: While they wouldn't finish the job, the quality of what they were able to deliver would be extremely high.

- **Feel**: How would they feel about each other when it was over? Neutral is the safe answer. Recognize, however, that they might not even understand the question. "Feelings? What do feelings have to do with this?"

As you can tell from Figure 7.9 and the explanation, no style got the complete job done well. So, which style would be best at which task? Figure 7.10 answers this question.

Figure 7.10 The Style Best at Each Project Task

	D	I	S	C
1. Identifying problems				X
2. Brainstorming solutions		X		
3. Developing the detailed plan				X
4. Documenting the plan			X	
5. Selling the plan		X		
6. Overseeing plan execution	X			
7. Executing the work plan			X	

Figure 7.10 underscores the point that it takes all styles to be completely successful. Keep in mind that a single person might cover two or three styles. For example, it is not unusual for someone to be both a high-I and a high-S, or a high-D/high-C, or a high-D/high-I.

Anticipating Team Issues: Based on the Team

The Marketing Team

At one point in our organization's history, we had a three-member marketing team. The marketing leader's style was high-C/high-S, the content marketing specialist was a high-C/high-I, and the digital marketing specialist was a high-S/high-C. Can you guess what one of the biggest issues for the team was? Getting things done! There was not anyone in the group with a high-D.

The team worked hard and started a number of initiatives, but many things just never got completed. The managing director began requiring detailed action plans for each of the major projects just to ensure projects were finishing. When the completion of projects began to stall, he put a moratorium on starting anything new until several projects came to completion. Sometimes, when your team is missing a style-type, it might mean that you have to adopt that style!

In an earlier section of this chapter, I talked about anticipating team issues based on the leader. Now we will anticipate issues based on your team missing a DISC style. Figure 7.11 makes recommendations for each style. As we will see, the recommendations are just the opposite of the recommendations when your leader had a particular style (Figure 7.8).

Figure 7.11 Potential Team Issues Based on Team Missing a Style

	Potential Issue	Suggested Prevention Strategies
D	Bringing projects to completion	• Have the team create a timeline of activity with deliverable due dates.
I	Lack of creativity and innovation	• Ensure the plan includes steps focused on creativity, including steps to collect creative input from outside the team.
S	Lack of focus on people and morale	• With team check-ins, ask the team to rate morale and to suggest strategies to improve.
C	Lack of details or a consistent process	• Provide a sample deliverable to demonstrate the level of detail needed. • Ensure the team adopts and steps through a solution process (*see later in this chapter*).

Selecting Project Team Members

There is a common saying in the facilitator world, "If you are not *at* the table, you could be *on* the menu!" The implication, of course, is that if you are not participating in the decision-making, it is possible that decisions will be made that negatively impact you. Facilitative leaders are conscious to select team members who have the knowledge, skills, focus, and insight needed, while being representative of the diversity of views of those who will be impacted by the decision.

In our work, we recommend that leaders consider three key questions when addressing those impacted by the issue.

- Who are the people who will be impacted by the decision?

- What level of involvement should they have in the process?

- Whose perspectives, involvement, and buy-in are so critical that they should be at the table or represented by someone who is?

The first question allows you to consider all those impacted by the decision. The second question helps you differentiate levels of involvement. For example, some people may only need to be informed of decisions after the fact. Others might provide input prior to the decision. And still others might participate in the decision-making. The final question helps you consider preliminary criteria for selecting those to have at the table.

Desired Characteristics

To have a fully functioning team, I recommend seeking team members with the characteristics shown in Figure 7.12.

Figure 7.12 Desired Characteristics of Team Members

All team members should...	As a group, and as much as practical, the team members should...
• Understand the issue under study • Have a stake in the outcome • Be empowered to make decisions or recommendations • Be perceived as leaders by peers • Be open to solutions other than their own	• Represent diverse communication styles • Be knowledgeable of all the major activities included in the team's focus • Be cross-functional and representative of all groups with a major stake in the outcome • Be drawn from various levels within the organization structure (e.g., managers, supervisors, and workers)

Why are these criteria important? What follows examines these criteria a little more closely, starting with each individual criterion.

- **Understand the subject under study**. Participants who don't understand the topic will likely take one of two positions. Either they slow down the rest of the group by requesting explanations of unfamiliar topics, or they decide to reduce their level of participation because they don't feel they understand enough to make a valuable contribution.

- **Have a stake in the outcome.** There are times when it is helpful to have people on a team who are not impacted in any significant way by the outcome of the project. For example, you might include outside industry experts on a team attempting to address a company problem. However, in many cases people who do not have a stake in the outcome may become non-participants in the discussion, or can detour the group to topics of greater personal interest for them.

- **Be empowered to make decisions or recommendations**. It is not unusual for people to be assigned to a team as a representative from another group, with specific instructions NOT to comment. Instead, they are directed to bring the information back for review so that others can decide what recommendations the representative is to make at subsequent meetings. Limiting the ability of a team member to comment during a meeting can severely slow down the overall effort. Further, since these representatives are inhibited in their ability to express concerns or interact to create solutions, the team's creativity and effectiveness can also be severely limited.

- **Be perceived as leaders by peers**. It is important to select people for a task force who are respected by their peers. These people tend to be opinion leaders. When opinion leaders show support for a direction, others tend to follow. As well, opinion leaders typically ensure that any solution created addresses their concerns, which are often the concerns of others who share their opinion.

- **Be open to solutions other than their own**. While the members of a team need to be opinion leaders, they also need to be flexible and open to other solutions. A completely closed-minded opinion leader (e.g., "There is only one solution...mine.") can prevent a team from discovering solutions that satisfy multiple needs.

- **Be cross-functional and representative of all groups with a major stake in the outcome.** For teams tackling critical issues and decisions, it can be essential for groups with a significant stake in the outcome to be able to see their views reflected in one or more people selected to be on the team. This can increase confidence in the solution by a wider group. In addition, these representatives can help gain the buy-in of their constituencies.

- **Be drawn from various levels within the organization structure**. For some teams, it is important to have involvement from more than one level. For example, to address improvements in the hiring process, it might be important to create a team that includes hiring managers and human resource specialists, as well as people recently hired into entry-level and mid-management positions.

- **Be knowledgeable of all major activities in the business area.** Going back to the task force assembled to address the hiring process, no one person on that team may understand the details of all the activities in the process. However, the team should be constructed in such a way to ensure that every step is fully understood by at least one team member.

- **Represent diverse communication styles**. As shown earlier in this chapter, when one of the communication styles is missing from a team, its absence can hinder the team's performance. Therefore, it is important that the team has at least one person with strength in each of the DISC styles.

Team Norms

Another important element in equipping the team for success is to ensure that it establishes team norms. Norms set an agreed-upon level of behavior that guides how the participants will interact. Although some teams that have worked together for some time will establish their own functional, unspoken team norms, most groups benefit from a deliberate process of identifying in-bounds and out-of-bounds behavior. Over time, norms can help a team become self-correcting: team members will begin correcting themselves based on the norms that they have established and reinforced.

What follows is a sample list of team norms. Keep in mind, however, that facilitative leaders understand that norms must be developed and agreed upon by the team, not imposed by the leader.

Sample Team Norms

1. Take full responsibility for assigned tasks and deadlines.
2. Notify the team early if deadlines will be missed.
3. Arrive early for team meetings
4. In meetings, respect the speaker, have one conversation, and only work on meeting business during the meeting.
5. When we disagree, play back and question first to ensure we understand.
6. Actively use ELMO (Enough—Let's Move On!) to keep the discussions focused.
7. Keep team business within the team.
8. Address all challenges with a positive attitude and assuming positive intent.
9. If you have a problem with a project team member, take it to that person *first* before discussing it with others.

10. If a problem cannot be resolved between team members, the team members involved should bring the issue to the leader *together*.

When Do We Have a Decision?

Based on the 8 Team Essentials, the leadership process is defined as, "the method used to make decisions, assign tasks, establish policies, address issues, et cetera." But when is a decision a decision? When do you have adequate agreement to move on? An important decision for a team to make is to decide the method for decision-making.

What follows are several traditional methods for decision-making.

Traditional Decision-Making Methods

- **Leader decides.** The group will discuss the strengths and weaknesses of various alternatives, and the leader will make the final decision.

- **Leader holds veto rights.** The group will come to a decision based on one of the methods that follow, but the leader reserves the right to overrule.

- **Majority rules.** The decision is determined by the vote of a majority of the participants. Majority decision-making can be quick; however, it can also lead to less than optimal solutions and less than effective implementation because of limited discussion time and inadequate buy-in.

- **Super majority.** The group debates until a large majority of the participants agrees with one alternative. The super majority is often 60 percent, 67 percent, or 75 percent. However, supermajority can also lead to limited discussion and less buy-in.

- **Full consensus.** Full consensus encourages discussion until solutions are acceptable to everyone. Consensus is often defined as, "I can live with a decision and support it." Consensus does not mean everyone thinks the solution is the best. Instead, it typically means the solution has enough elements that every person is willing to go along with it and support it. While consensus increases buy-in, it can take considerably more time. Consensus can also result in watered-down solutions in order to gain full agreement. While the team achieves consensus on a solution, the cost of consensus may be a solution that is far from optimal and might be described as the "least common denominator." In addition, I have seen occasions in which consensus was held hostage by one person who decided he wasn't going to agree until he got exactly what he wanted. The result was clearly not the will of the group. But, in the name of getting everyone to agree, it was the solution that was put in place.

As an alternative to full consensus, in my work with teams I generally use two approaches: five-finger consensus for major decisions and informed majority for minor decisions.

Five-Finger Consensus

Five-finger consensus is designed to encourage significant agreement without jeopardizing the quality of the solution. Here's how it works.

- Once an alternative is proposed and discussed, and the group is ready to check for agreement, the team leader explains that on the count of three, each person should hold up between one and five fingers indicating the level of support for the recommendation as shown in Figure 7.13.

- **On the first vote, if everyone shows a 5, 4 or 3, consensus has been reached.** Everyone has said either they strongly agree, agree, or are willing to go with the group.

- However, if there are any 1s or 2s, those who indicate this have the opportunity to explain to the rest of the group why they gave the rating they did and can recommend changes to the alternative in order to make it acceptable to them. The originator of the alternative has the option to make the change or leave the option as it is and explains the decision to the group. If a change is made to the recommendation, then there is a new first vote. If no change is made, then it goes on to a second vote.

Figure 7.13 Five-Finger Consensus

The Decision Is
Made When

5-Finger Consensus

5 – Strongly agree

4 – Agree

1ST Vote → 3 – Will go with group's decision

2ND Vote → 2 – Disagree

1 – Strongly disagree

3RD Vote
Majority Rules

- **On the second vote, if everyone shows a 5, 4, 3 or 2, the decision is made, and we can move ahead.** The 2s are in essence saying, "I don't think it is a good idea, but if that is what the group wants to do, I won't block it."

- However, if there are any 1s, those who indicate such have another opportunity to explain to the rest of the group why they gave the rating they did and can recommend changes to the alternative in order to make it acceptable to them. Once more, the originator of the alternative has the option to make the change or leave the option as it is and explains the decision to the rest of the group. If a change is made to the recommendation, then there is a new first vote. If no change is made, then it goes on to a third vote.

- **On the third vote, majority rules.** The decision is made based on the majority of the participants.

I have seen instances where on the third vote the group went with the recommendation, as well as times when on the third vote the group felt a change to the recommendation was needed and the recommendation was voted down.

What I like about five-finger consensus is that it encourages the group to listen carefully when there is disagreement; in fact, it encourages listening carefully twice if necessary. But the approach doesn't allow a solution to be watered down because a few disagree. Though admittedly there may be one or two who don't like the alternative, five-finger consensus ensures that everyone who wants to be heard is heard, and heard well, and that the will of the group prevails.

Informed Majority

While I recommend five-finger consensus for major team decisions, for minor decisions, I recommend a simpler process called "informed majority." With informed majority the idea is to get all options on the table, have someone speak for each one to inform the group about the options, open the discussion for other comments, then take a majority vote.

To show how informed majority works, assume that a team is deciding something as simple as where to hold the team's kickoff meeting.

1. Informed majority starts with brainstorming potential options. The objective is to identify *all* the options before discussing any one of them.

2. Once options have been identified, let team members know you are going to go back over each one, and if someone believes the option is the one he/she will vote for, the person should speak up and share why. If no one speaks up for something as his/her first option, then the option is eliminated. You are looking for just one person to speak for each option at this point. Others who support the option will have an opportunity to speak later. Remember, if no one speaks for an option as his/her first choice, there is no need to vote on it and so the option goes away.

3. Note that by insisting that people speak for their first option only, this avoids having the same person speak for more than one option or wasting time on options that don't have the strong support of at least one person.

4. Once all the options have been reviewed and those that were not supported have been eliminated, if you have only one option left, that option is selected by default. If there is more than one option left, open it up for anyone else who wants to speak for or against any of the remaining options.

5. Once all comments have been made, call for a vote and go with the majority.

6. If there are multiple alternatives and no alternative receives a majority of those voting, then all but the top two alternatives are dropped. You then ask for comments for the two alternatives and then do a revote.

The point of informed majority is to make efficient and effective decisions while ensuring that all desiring to speak are heard and time is given to create and discuss alternatives. Typically, once I have used the process a couple of times with a group, they tend to catch on right away and welcome the structure to help guide their decision-making.

Happy Talk

"Michael, I need your help with something. We are the preeminent nonprofit in our city focused on bringing the community together to collectively address major community problems. We decided this year that it would be helpful if leaders in our community had stronger relationships with one another. So we are hosting a series of meetings in which the top leaders could simply network together for 90 minutes each month. The first meeting was great. We had over 40 of the top people from all sectors including corporate, government, nonprofit, faith-based, and the neighborhoods. But at the second meeting, we had only 22, and with this upcoming meeting, we only have 12 who have sent an RSVP, and most of those are neighborhood and nonprofit leaders. We don't know what to do to remedy this."

I asked the leader a few questions to ensure I understood the issue, and then explained, "It says a lot about your organization and the respect it has in the city that you could get 40 leaders together at a meeting. It is equally amazing that you were able to get 22 to come back. But it is also not at all surprising that your numbers are continuing to dwindle. See, our experience is that leaders vote with their feet. They will spend their time where they see value. They don't appreciate what I call 'happy talk,' that is, coming together and talking, then coming together again and talking, and coming together again and talking, without a clear direction of where the meetings are going and without a defined process for getting there. When leaders perceive that the only thing going on is happy talk, they find other ways to spend their time.

I counseled the leader to refocus the meetings by doing two things. First, establish a purpose other than getting to know one another. He chose: "Decide the five most important issues facing our community; select the one or two where we can collectively have an impact; and commission a team to come back with a plan for our approval that we will monitor quarterly." Second, define a step-by-step work process that the leaders would follow to achieve their purpose. This way, they can know at any time where they are in their process and what happens next. The head of the nonprofit understood the mistake with 'happy talk' and was thrilled that he had a way to transition the group out of it. The follow-up meeting and the sessions that followed it were well attended by members of all sectors.

Work Processes

Recall from earlier in this chapter that there are three team essentials that team members must create for themselves: a leadership process (i.e., decision-making), a work process, and teamwork. The prior section covered decision-making; next I am going to focus on the work process. A work process defines the steps that the team will take to address the problem or issue before it to produce the deliverables (team essential #2) that achieves the purpose (team essential #1).

Organizations have many, many unique problems. However, they often can be classified into a smaller group of problem types. As an example, one organization may have issues with its hiring process, another organization may be having problems with their event registration process, and still another with their customer order process. These are indeed three different problems; however, they are the same problem type: an inefficient or ineffective process.

Figure 7.14 demonstrates that each problem type also has a work process for solving that problem type. So whether the inefficient process is hiring, event registration, or customer ordering, the work process to solve it would be process improvement. The work process provides the team with a "generic" starting point for customizing a more specific work process for solving their problem.

Figure 7.14 Problem Types and Work Processes

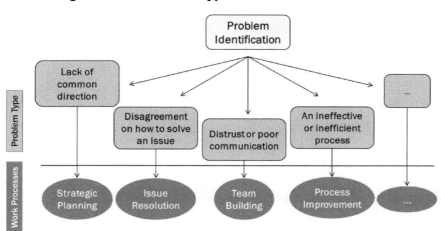

What follows are descriptions of several work processes that you can use to equip your teams with a starting point for creating a customized work process to achieve their purpose. Figure 7.15 provides a brief description of when each work process might be appropriate.

Work Process	Problem Type
Issue Resolution	There is disagreement on how to resolve a specific issue.
Process Improvement	An inefficient or ineffective process requires streamlining.
Process Reengineering	An inefficient or ineffective process requires a complete redesign.
Project Planning	A detailed plan is needed for a project or program.
Strategic Planning	An organization (e.g., enterprise, business unit, department, or team) lacks a defined shared direction and agreed upon approaches for getting there.
Team Building	A team is suffering from poor communication, low trust, or lack of alignment.

Issue Resolution

Purpose

Define an issue, identify alternative solutions, and gain consensus on an alternative.

Tasks

A. Hold scoping meeting to initiate the project.

B. Develop an issue definition statement.

C. Identify alternatives.

D. Develop specifications for each alternative.

E. Document strengths and weaknesses.

F. Identify evaluation criteria.

G. Assess alternatives against the criteria.

H. Select the most favorable alternative.

I. Document selection justification and related cost/benefit.

J. Review and assess performance.

Process Improvement

Purpose

Define the changes necessary to increase the efficiency and effectiveness of a business process.

Tasks

A. Hold scoping meeting to initiate the project.

B. Hold facilitated sessions to document how the process works currently.

C. Gather transaction counts and cost data.

D. Hold facilitated sessions to document problems, root causes, and potential solutions.

E. Perform cost/benefit analyses on top alternatives.

F. Develop and document how the process will work in the future.

G. Develop implementation plan with resource estimates and costs.

H. Present report of recommendations.

I. Review and assess performance.

Process Reengineering

Purpose

Define the changes necessary to increase the efficiency and effectiveness of a business process.

Tasks

A. Hold scoping meeting to initiate the project.

B. Hold facilitated sessions to document how the process works currently, including triggers, transactions, steps, and exceptions.

C. Document the products, customers for the products, customer expectations, and current performance against expectations.

D. Gather transaction counts and cost data.

E. Hold facilitated sessions to document problems and root causes.

F. Perform value-added/non-value-added analyses on the current process steps

G. Identify potential improvements and processing alternatives.

H. Perform cost/benefit analyses on top alternatives.

I. Develop and document how the process will work in the future.

    J.   Develop implementation plan with resource estimates and costs.

    K.   Present report of recommendations.

    L.   Review and assess performance.

Project Planning

Purpose

Identify the objectives of a project and the resources and timelines needed to complete it.

Tasks

    A.   Hold scoping meeting to initiate the project.

    B.   Define the project purpose and objectives.

    C.   Determine project scope and deliverables.

    D.   Identify critical success factors.

    E.   Develop overall approach.

    F.   Define resources, durations, and dependencies.

    G.   Define the schedule.

    H.   Identify risks and contingencies.

    I.   Document management issues.

    J.   Review and assess performance.

Strategic Planning

(The strategic planning process is described in greater detail in chapter 9.)

Purpose

Develop the mission, broad goals, measurable objectives, and specific strategies for an organization.

Tasks

    A.   Hold scoping meeting to initiate the project.

    B.   Prepare the current situation assessment.

    C.   Convene the management planning team to develop the vision, mission, goals, and objectives (strategic direction).

D. Perform research and identify current benchmarks to verify the objectives (measures).

E. Convene the management planning team to develop critical success factors, barriers, and strategies.

F. Document the plan.

G. Convene action planning teams to develop action plans.

H. Develop and execute communications plan.

I. Develop and execute monitoring plan.

J. Review and assess performance.

Team Building

Purpose

Improve a team's ability to work more effectively together.

Tasks

A. Hold scoping meeting to initiate the project.

B. Identify team's current strengths, weaknesses, and critical issues.

C. Assess the team against the 8 Essentials of a Team and the 5 Cs of Trust.

D. Define the team's visions and norms.

E. Define potential strategies to move toward our vision and norms.

F. Review communication styles.

G. Define potential strategies to improve communication.

H. Define potential strategies for critical issues not addressed already.

I. Select strategies to implement first.

J. Define our execution, monitoring, and accountability plan.

K. Document session results.

L. Review and assess performance.

Developing and Delivering Recommendations

You may note that several of the work processes include creating and presenting recommendations. However, after doing great work, a team can become highly frustrated if they aren't able to document their recommendations in a compelling way or communicate them effectively to their audience.

Figure 7.16 outlines a five-part recommendation format that I believe helps create the compelling case for implementation.

Figure 7.16 Recommendations Format

Component	Description
Finding	*Fact-based observation* regarding the environment, supported by numbers
Conclusion	*Impact* of the observation on the organization
Recommended Action	*Specific activity* to address the impact, with anticipated internal and external costs
Benefit	*Quantified advantage* to the organization of implementing the recommendation
Risk	*Potential downside* or obstacle that could impair the achievement of the recommendation

What does such a recommendation look like formatted? Figure 7.17 provides a sample.

Figure 7.17 Sample Recommendation

Finding
Our quarterly advertising expenditures averaged $30,000. Yet over 50 percent of the positions advertised in the paper were filled by in-house people.
Conclusion
The policy requiring that positions be posted in-house and advertised in the newspaper and through social media ads simultaneously is resulting in wasted dollars.
Recommended Action
Change the policy to *require* outside advertising *only if* the position is not filled within 45 days by a qualified in-house person. This recommendation requires four internal hours of research and policy development and zero out-of-pocket costs.
Benefit
Based on data from the past six months, changing this policy should result in a 30-35 percent reduction in advertising, a savings of approximately $9,000 per quarter.
Risk
For positions in which there are no qualified in-house applicants, the recommendation *could* increase time to hire if in-house posting is first chosen.

Adjusting Your Presentation Order

Now it's time to present the recommendation. How should you present it? As you can imagine, your presentation should change based on the DISC-type of the receiver.

- High-Cs are much more interested in the findings and risks. Start with the findings, end with the risks.

- For high-Is, the detailed findings are of little interest. Start with the high-level conclusion, then your recommendation. But focus on the benefits to be achieved.

- High-Ds want to know your end-point right from the beginning. So, start with the recommended action, then discuss why it needs to be done (conclusion), and finally review the benefits. Don't dive into the detailed findings unless they ask.

- High-Ss are highly flexible. They would likely want you to present the information in the order and format you find most comfortable!

Unfortunately, seldom are we presenting to a room of all one style. So, what do you do?

> The key is to tailor your presentation to the style of the most influential person in the room and have something for each of the other styles as well.

So, given the most influential person in the room, you might want to start your presentation with that piece of the recommendation in which he/she might be most interested. For example, if the most influential person in the room is a high-I, you might format the presentation so that you start with the benefits to be achieved and stop for interactive discussion following each recommendation component. At the beginning of the presentation, however, you might let the entire group know that there is an executive summary (for the high-Ds) and a detailed appendix (for the high-Cs). Similarly, if the most influential person is a high-D, you might have a brief "executive summary" type presentation that starts with the recommended action, have Q&A at the end (for the high-Is) and an appendix with all the details (for the high-Cs). For the high-Ss, they are typically satisfied as long as the atmosphere in the presentation stays friendly and cordial.

Accountability and Monitoring

The last of the 8 Team Essentials involves teamwork, which I define as trust, communication, and accountability. We have covered trust and communication in prior chapters. As such, this chapter will close with a focus on accountability.

How often have you participated in meetings or on projects or in strategy development efforts where initiatives are identified, or action plans are created, that are seldom fully executed?

Why does this happen? More times than not, the answer is *accountability and monitoring*, or more specifically the lack thereof.

Effective accountability has five critical components.

Five Key Components of Accountability

- **Clearly defined work.** This first step is often where the breakdown of accountability starts. It is often the case that work is not clearly defined, or expectations and timelines are not clearly articulated, or a plan is not delineated for achieving the work. Within the Eight Essentials of a Team, the purpose, deliverables, and work process will help with this.

- **Accepted responsibility.** Once the work is defined, someone has to accept responsibility for getting it done. Please note, *assigned* responsibility is not the same as *accepted* responsibility. Has the person been simply assigned it, or has the person accepted that it is his/her responsibility for accomplishing it?

- **Monitoring and reporting.** Accountability comes from the Latin word that literally means "to give an account." We may have accepted the responsibility for the clearly defined work. However, without a monitoring and reporting process (i.e., without a process for people to give an account), there is essentially no accountability.

- **Reward for accomplishment.** A key to effective accountability is to have a reward for accomplishing the item for which we are being held accountable. In the workplace, rewards can take a variety of forms, including recognition, time off, gift certificates, a convenient parking space, et cetera.

- **Consequences for lack of performance.** Consequences are necessary to ensure that there is both a "carrot" for performance and a "stick" for lack of performance.

While many organizations avoid consequences, I find it is an essential component for letting people know that they have let down the team. While sometimes the lack of performance is so significant and so severe that it requires "freeing up the person's future," in most cases a less severe consequence is more appropriate. One of the strategies that has proven helpful is having the team define consequences in advance. Simple consequences such as cleaning up the break room or taking another team out to lunch may be suitable. In one organization I worked with, if a team that had accepted responsibility for a strategic initiative missed accomplishing an activity one month, the entire team had to meet with the organization's CEO to explain why the miss happened and why it would not happen again!

What happens if one or more of the accountability components is missing? Not much!

Strategies for Increasing Team Accountability

Below are strategies to help team members increase their accountability to one another.

1. Maintain a separate digital file containing all actions for the team. Figure 7.18 provides a sample format.

Action	Who	Due
1. Collect annual expenses for company job postings	Joe	2/12 1/29 1/15
2. Hold interviews with each department to collect their issues with the current hiring process.	Jack	3/15
3. Schedule and hold meetings with three other companies with innovative hiring processes to document practices for us to consider.	Joanna	3/31

2. Make sure each action fully describes what is to be done to minimize at subsequent meetings confusion and guesswork about what was meant. Start each action with a verb to encourage defining the action to be performed.

3. Send a reminder to team members to update actions prior to the team meeting.

4. When a team member misses the date for an action, the team member places a new date in front of the old one (rather than delete the old one). This way, each revised date is shown and communicates the number of times a date has been revised.

5. At the beginning of the team meeting, review the actions list. This is a step that is frequently missed.

6. At the end of the meeting, review new actions added.

A critical accountability strategy: at the end of each meeting, there should be no item on the action list whose due date is prior to the date of the meeting.

---

7. In a project plan, consider using the minimum, expected, and stretch format for defining purpose and deliverables. Track and report ongoing performance and overall results.

As you equip your teams with these strategies and help them practice and implement the five keys of accountability, you will find that not only do the teams achieve at a higher level, but their sense of team and accomplishment also improves.

Summary

1. Facilitative leaders understand that their role is to equip their teams for success and then monitor their efforts as the team produces results.

2. The difference between a team and a group is based both on how they are organized and how they operate. They can be organized as a team but operate as a group. They can be organized as a group but operate as a team. An organization can also have a group of teams or a team of groups.

3. The keys for success are to be organized as a team, operate as a team, have an effective strategy, and execute it.

4. The 8 Team Essentials model identifies the eight things every team needs to be successful. With a team missing three or more of the essentials, the likelihood of success is so low that failure is highly probable.

5. In most cases, the top five of the 8 Team Essentials should be given to the team. The bottom three must be created by the team.

6. Using the DISC styles, you can anticipate the problems a team will likely have based on the style of the team leader. For example, a high-D leader would be least concerned about the team essential related to teamwork. Accordingly, as a facilitative leader you should take preventive steps to help ensure team morale stays high.

7. In documenting the purpose and deliverables for a team, consider using the minimum, expected, and stretch format for tracking and reporting ongoing performance and overall results.

8. When you select team members, consider several factors including their knowledge of the subject area, their openness to solutions from others, and their DISC style.

9. If you have a team that is missing one or more of the DISC styles, you can anticipate likely issues. As an example, a team without a high-C member might not do sufficient analysis or provide adequate detail to support recommendations.

10. Have teams establish norms to set an agreed-on level of behavior that guides how the participants will interact with one another.

11. There are a number of decision-making models for a team to use, including the leader decides, team majority, full consensus, five-finger consensus, and informed majority. Team members must define when they have a decision.

12. To keep teams efficient and to avoid wasting time in "happy talk," teams should define a work process that addresses the problem type they are facing.

13. To help ensure that recommendations developed by a team are implemented, use a five-part recommendation format: finding, conclusion, recommended action, benefit, risk.

14. When presenting recommendations, the key is to tailor the presentation to the DISC style of the most influential person in the room and to have something for each of the other styles as well.

15. There are five keys to help ensure accountability for action: clearly defined work, accepted responsibility, monitoring and reporting, rewards for accomplishment, and consequences for lack of performance.

16. To increase accountability, consider strategies such as maintaining an ongoing action list, reviewing the action list at the beginning of each team meeting, and ensuring at the end of the meeting that there is no action with a due date earlier than the meeting date.

Spring Forward

Consider each team/department under your direction and each team that you are a member on. For each team, answer the following questions:

Team: _____

1. Which of the 8 Team Essentials is the team fully or partially missing? What actions should *you* take to address this?

2. Given the leader of the team, what issues can you anticipate occurring or are likely occurring already? What actions should *you* take to address this?

3. Given the likely DISC styles of the team members, what issues can you anticipate occurring or are likely already occurring? What actions should *you* take to address this?

4. What other tools from this chapter might be helpful to the team? What actions should *you* take to influence the team to use them?

- The Three Reasons People Disagree
- Level 1: Lack of Shared Information
- Level 2: Different Values or Experiences
- Level 3: Outside Factors
- Solving Level 3: Take It to a Higher Source
- Solving Level 1: Delineation
- Solving Level 2: Strengths, Weaknesses, Merge
- Encourage Disagreement
- Summary
- Spring Forward

Chapter 8.
Engage Conflict, Encourage Disagreement

In many organizations, disagreement and conflict are things to be discouraged at best and avoided or ignored at worst. Why? It will be helpful to break down disagreement dysfunction by DISC style.

- Typical high-Ds just want to get things done. They often believe they have the answer, and disagreement slows things down. Since they know they are right, why entertain other options? Their philosophy: *I could agree with you, but then we both would be wrong.*

- For many high-I and high-S individuals, disagreements aren't fun. Disagreements don't feel good. Their experience is that when disagreements occur, people tend to act as if they are upset or angry with one another. These styles often feel that it's best to go along so as to get along. Their philosophy: *Don't rock the boat.*

- High-Cs often don't like disagreement because they recognize that people are seldom willing to take the time to gather and analyze the information needed to make thoughtful decisions. They become frustrated with conflict because they have seen multiple instances when the people in their organization haven't had the patience to do the homework needed to make a quality decision. Their philosophy: *If you don't have the time to do it right, how you are going to find the time to do it over?*

What is the result when disagreements are avoided or ignored? Here are a few.

Potential Impact of Ignoring Disagreements

- Poorer decisions
- Unspoken skepticism
- Limited buy-in to the decision
- Feelings of disempowerment
- Misalignment
- Passive-aggressive resistance

Of course, any one of these potential impacts could result in lower performance by team members and less than optimal results from the decision. Together, however, these potential impacts could doom the decision to failure even before implementation starts.

As mentioned in Chapter 5 on communication styles, without disagreement, mediocre ideas would be accepted and implemented. It is through disagreement that the process of creative abrasion unfolds. I have seen it time and time again in meetings; the first idea suggested is challenged, resulting in someone suggesting a new idea, which is challenged, and then a third idea, then a fourth, and finally the team comes to agreement on a fifth idea that is better than any of the other ideas previously suggested. And, not surprisingly perhaps, the fifth idea was not one that ANY of the team members had before they entered the room. The idea literally emerged from the disagreement.

To build on a comment from one of the leaders in our company, I describe this process of getting to agreement as follows.

> Effective collaboration is simply a series of successful disagreements.

Facilitative leaders understand that disagreements are good. They know that disagreement can achieve better decisions with higher levels of buy-in and commitment. Their experience has taught them that disagreement often means there is a better solution that the team hasn't discovered yet. However, they also know that to be able to engage disagreements effectively requires an understanding of disagreement, and effective strategies for getting to agreement, that most leaders don't have. This chapter[19] is designed to give you both an understanding of disagreement and strategies and tools you can use right away to create and benefit from successful disagreements.

> Disagreement often means that there is a better solution that the team has yet to discover.

The Three Reasons People Disagree

What follows is a statement that most people reading this book will likely find hard to believe. But it is true. Our work with literally hundreds of teams and groups over nearly three decades has revealed that there are only three reasons people disagree. Only three, literally. Every disagreement in the world can be classified as either a level-1, level-2, or level-3 disagreement. Perhaps it seems unbelievable, but we have trained over 25,000 people in the concepts I am going to cover, and to date not one of them has identified a fourth reason.

So that's the good news. There are only three reasons people disagree. Now for the bad news. Trying to solve a level-3 disagreement using a level-1 approach is highly likely to result in failure. Level-3 disagreements can't be solved with level-1 techniques. Likewise, if you have a level-1 disagreement and you try resolving it using level-2 techniques, your chances of success are very low. Therefore, it is important that facilitative leaders understand the three reasons people disagree, be able to diagnose whether a disagreement is level-1, level-2, or level-3, and have strategies they can use to successfully resolve the disagreement.

For simplicity the text will use examples of disagreements that involve two people. The same principles and techniques are adaptable for disagreements that involve groups as well. Where there is a significant distinction in the techniques for resolving two-way and group disagreements, I will highlight the distinction.

So, what are the three reasons people disagree?

Levels of Disagreement

- Level 1: Lack of shared information
- Level 2: Different values or experiences
- Level 3: Outside factors unrelated to the disagreement

It is wise to look at each of the three levels of disagreement separately and then focus on practical methods for resolving each one.

Level 1: Lack of Shared Information

In a level-1 disagreement, the people disagreeing have not clearly heard or understood each other's alternatives and the reasons for supporting them. Level-1 disagreements are often the result of an assumed understanding of what the other person is saying or meaning. Take a look at the sample below.

Pepper:	I've been thinking about the problems we have been having with our performance review process, and I think I've come up with a solution: we should have our employees write their own reviews.
Michelle:	Are you out of your mind? That can't work.
Pepper:	Sure it can. You said yourself that most supervisors can't remember all the things their employees did in the prior year, and you said that last time most of the reviews were superficial and based mostly on favoritism or on the last project people did. If employees write their own performance reviews, the focus will be on how people actually performed the entire year.
Michelle:	No, I don't think so. Pepper, we have been partners for some time. But this has to be the craziest idea you have come up with in a while.
Pepper:	I don't understand why you don't like it.
Michelle:	Well, can you say, "Fox guarding the hen house?" If we let people write their own performance reviews, every review will be rated "far exceeds expectations." People won't admit their failures. Plus, this approach completely disempowers the managers. The performance review is an opportunity managers specifically have to influence the performance of their people. Letting employees rate themselves eliminates this. And what about—

Pepper: Hold on a second. I'm not sure you are hearing me. I said have the employees write their performance reviews, not determine their ratings. That's their manager's job. But if we have the employees write about their own accomplishments, strengths, and—

Michelle: And their areas for improvement. I get it. Then you have the manager review what the employee wrote and make additions and changes as needed with the employee in the room. Then the manager sets the rating. That makes sense. But why didn't you say that in the first place?

Pepper: I did say it. You just weren't listening. I said I wanted employees to write their performance reviews. What did you think I meant?

It's fairly obvious what Michelle thought Pepper meant. When Pepper said, "We should have our employees write their own reviews," Michelle thought Pepper meant to have employees set their own ratings. Once Michelle understood what Pepper meant, they quickly realized they were in agreement.

Unfortunately, many level-1 disagreements are not resolved so quickly. People often argue without realizing that they actually agree. This situation occurs so frequently that there is a name for it: *violent agreement*. When a level-1 disagreement is resolved, you will often hear, "Oh, is that what you meant? Why didn't you say that?"

Advocacy versus Inquiry

One of the reasons that level-1 disagreements can take time to resolve is because both sides stay in what Patrick Lencioni in *Advantage*[20] refers to as "advocacy mode" instead of "inquiry mode." Both sides are advocating for their positions instead of asking questions to understand the other person's position.

If you go back and review this disagreement between Pepper and Michelle, you will see that there was a major shift in the discussion. It might appear that it happened when Michelle said, "I get it" or earlier when Pepper says, "I'm not sure you are hearing me." But the actual shift happens before either of these statements; it occurs when Pepper says, "I don't understand why you don't like it." While this is indeed a statement, it really is an implied question, "Why don't you like it?" Pepper has moved from advocacy mode to inquiry mode. She asks an implied question which Michelle then answers, and the source of the disagreement becomes obvious.

Moving from advocacy to inquiry mode can accelerate the resolution of disagreements. The next time you are in the presence of two other people arguing, listen carefully. Are they in advocacy mode where they are supporting their positions, or are they in inquiry mode where they are asking questions in an effort to understand the other's position? Facilitative leaders know that for people to reach agreement, it is important to help them move from advocacy to inquiry as quickly as possible.

Level 2: Different Values or Experiences

In a level-2 disagreement, the parties have fully heard and understood one another's alternatives. However, they have had different experiences or hold different values that result in each of them preferring one alternative over another. The sample that follows describes what on the surface appears to be a level-2 disagreement.

Terry: This course we just took on *Masterful Meetings* is fantastic. If we are going to have any chance of transforming the meetings around here, we need to get everyone trained on what a great meeting is and how to create it. I think we need to get everyone in training as soon as possible.

Jordan: *Everyone* in training? Surely, you're kidding. We can't train everyone in our organization; that's extreme. Everyone doesn't run meetings every day. Maybe just the executives and managers. They are the ones who lead most meetings anyway.

Terry: No, we can't limit this to just the executives and managers. Other individuals in our organization lead meetings. And just about everyone participates in one or more meetings every week. Everyone needs these skills. Everyone should take the course.

Jordan: When we do training, it has to be focused on the people who will get the most out of it. It never ceases to amaze me how you folks in HR want to get everybody involved in everything. You all need to keep in mind that this is a business. Training is an expense, not revenue, and it hurts revenue when you take people away from their real jobs.

Terry: Don't lecture me. I know about finances. The problem is that your managers in the field don't have a clue about what it means to empower people. If you took the time to make people feel like a part of the organization, you might be able to do something about your horrendous turnover problem.

This disagreement is going downhill rapidly. On the surface, it looks like a classic clash of perspectives, with the leader from the field valuing revenue and productivity and the human resources representative valuing people and empowerment.

Positions versus Issues

It is vital to make several points here about positions versus issues.[21]

- When in advocacy mode, the discussion stays at the position level. In the example above, Terry's position is, "Everyone should take the course" while Jordan's position is, "Only key managers should take the course." The discussion is a debate about these positions and which one is better.

- When discussions stay at the position level, the best achievable outcome is win-lose: someone is going to win and someone is going to lose. Sometimes you end up with lose-lose, where both people lose. In the example above, the organization ends up doing nothing because the two leaders can't agree.

- Positions represent the tip of the iceberg; the real issues, the source of the disagreement, are under the surface.

- One of the keys to resolving disagreement is to have tools and strategies for getting under the surface and at the real issues. Facilitative leaders know one of the best ways to get to the real issues is to move into inquiry mode and ask questions.

Level 3: Outside Factors

A level-3 disagreement is based on personality, past history, or other outside factors that have nothing to do with the alternatives.

Sean:	If our team is going to be successful with making major improvements to our performance review process, we should look at three to seven organizations known to do it well and identify their best practices.
Chris:	That's a stupid idea. There is no way that will work.
Sean:	Sure it will. We did something similar where I last worked. We just need to make sure we identify the right organizations.
Chris:	No, it won't work.
Sean:	I don't understand why you are being so difficult.
Chris:	Because it won't work.
Leader:	You may be right, Chris. It might not work. So, what do we have to do to make it work?
Chris:	There's nothing we can do. It just won't work.
Leader:	Okay. Well, how about explaining what's wrong with it?
Chris:	Everything is wrong with it. It just won't work.
Leader:	Help us understand, Chris. Why are you so convinced it won't work?
Chris:	It just won't work. *He* thought of it. It won't work!

It is obvious that the problem Chris has with the best practices idea doesn't seem to have much to do with the idea at all. Chris appears to believe that the problem is Sean, the person offering the idea. As it turns out, Chris learned some time ago that when he was interviewing to join the organization, Sean was one of the few people not in favor of hiring him. Since learning this information, Chris has felt any suggestion made by Sean can't possibly work.

Solving Level 3: Take it to a Higher Source

Level-3 disagreements are based on outside factors. Therefore, trying to analyze the issue behind, or identify alternatives to, a level-3 disagreement is a waste of time, because the disagreement does not concern either. To avoid wasting time on level-3 issues, recognize the signs.

Recognizing the Level-3 Signs

- Irrational arguments.
- No interest in considering or discussing alternatives.

How do you resolve a level-3 disagreement? Take it to a higher source. The following example uses the scenario from the earlier section featuring Chris and Sean:

Level-3 Resolution Steps

1. Agree to disagree. If a level-3 disagreement happens during a meeting, consider taking a break. Meet with the parties privately to indicate to them you do not believe the issue can be solved in the session.

   Chris and Sean, can we agree that we are not going to agree on this point?

2. Seek agreement to go to a higher source together for resolution outside the session. In essence, let a higher level in the organization make the decision by having both parties together go to the source and explain the issue.

   I would like to suggest the following. Let's the three of us go to the Vice President of Human Resources. Sean, explain what you want to do. Chris, you will have the opportunity to explain your concerns. And we'll let the VP decide what happens next.

3. Consider meeting privately to identify the core issue. Don't attempt to resolve the issue in the session. Typically, issues based on personality or past history take more time than you can afford to give.

   I appreciate all the skills you bring to the team, especially when you are giving recommendations on how to fix things. I've noticed on a few occasions that you have disagreed strongly with suggestions from Sean. Tell me more about this… Is there something I should do differently as the meeting leader? Is there something up with you and Sean that may be getting in the way?

Solving Level 1: Delineation

If a disagreement does not demonstrate level-3 signs (i.e., irrationality or no commitment to finding a solution), it is typically best to begin addressing it as if it were level-1: assume that all the key information is not necessarily known by all parties. Use techniques that slow down the conversation in order to encourage careful listening and comprehension. Facilitative leaders often find it helpful to record key information on a flip chart or some other media that allows all participants to focus on the information rather than on each other. Consider the following steps.

Level-1 Resolution Steps

1. Start with agreement. Starting with agreement helps all parties see that they already have something in common. This initial agreement can serve as a bridge for constructing the final solution.

   We all seem to agree that...

2. Confirm the source of the disagreement. Identifying the source of the disagreement shows the parties that they are not far apart, despite the fact that the discussion may have become somewhat strained.

   Where we seem to disagree is.... Is that right?

3. Identify the alternatives and record on a flip chart or other media.

   So, Terry, you are saying.... And, Sean, you are saying...

4. Ask each party specific delineating questions. For each alternative, direct specific questions at the supporter of the alternative; record the responses.

   How would this work? How much? How long? Who is involved in... ? What is involved in...?

5. Summarize the information.

   Based on what Terry has said, this alternative will cost... And it will take... And, as a result, we will have.... Based on what Sean has said...

6. Take a consensus check. Once you have delineated and summarized each alternative, check to determine if consensus has been reached. If consensus has been reached, you will be able to move on.

   Based on what we have discussed thus far, how many would be in favor of... and how many in favor of...

Delineation encourages each party to listen carefully to the other. If the disagreement is solely because of a lack of shared information, the parties quickly learn that they did not disagree at all. Either they did not hear each other, they heard but did not understand each other, or they did not share relevant information.

The sample dialogue that follows continues the disagreement between Terry and Jordan concerning who should take the meetings training. The dialogue picks up with Terry's last comment.

Terry:	Don't lecture me. I know about finances. The problem is that you guys in the field don't have a clue about what it means to empower people. If you took the time to make people feel like they are a part of the organization, you might be able to do something about your horrendous turnover problem.
Leader:	Let's slow down for a minute. It seems like you both agree that meeting training could help us, is that right?
Terry:	Definitely.
Leader:	Where you seem to disagree is on who should take the course?
Jordan:	That's right.
Leader:	So, Terry, you are saying that everyone should take the course.
Terry:	That's right. (*Using a flip chart, the leader creates a two-column chart and labels the first column "Everyone."*)
Leader:	And, Jordan, you are saying something different?
Jordan:	Yes, I think only key managers should take the class. (*Leader labels the second column "Key Managers."*)
Leader:	Terry, you said everyone would take the meetings course. How would it work? How many people is that?
Terry:	All six hundred of our employees would take the course.
Leader:	Would each one take the full two-day course that you and Jordan took?
Terry:	No. I would want the vendor to create a special half-day class at a reduced rate for our people so that they wouldn't have to spend so much time away from work.
Jordan:	A half-day course? Why didn't you say that? I have no problem with that. We can make that work.

Disagreement resolved. In this case, Terry and Jordan were in "violent agreement." They were arguing because they had made assumptions about what the other meant. Jordan thought Terry wanted everyone to take a two-day course. That's not what Terry wanted. He just wanted everyone to get trained. Terry thought Jordan was primarily concerned about everyone getting the training. That's not what Jordan was primarily concerned about. He was primarily concerned about people being away from work too long.

Recall that a level-1 disagreement is based on the lack of shared information. Delineation solves this by getting the information out for everyone to see and understand. If the disagreement is information-based, delineation addresses this.

But what if Terry really meant a two-day course? Figure 8.1 provides a sample of what a meeting leader might record on a flip chart as a result of the delineation steps.

Figure 8.1 Flipchart from Delineation

Who Should Take the Training?	
<u>Everyone</u>	<u>Key Managers Only</u>
600 people	100 people
Sign up by team	Execs select managers
2-day class	2-day class
24 people/class	24 people/class
27 classes	5 classes (one-makeup)
3 classes/month	2 classes/month
$15,000/class	$15,000/class
600 people	*100 people*
9 months	*3 months*
$405,000	*$75,000*

One of the keys to successful delineation is the questions that the facilitative leader asks. While the specific questions will differ based on the situation, in a business setting there are four general questions that need to be answered through delineation.

The Four Delineation Questions

- How much?
- How long?
- Who is involved?
- What is involved?

An easy way to start delineation is to ask the more general question, "How would that work?" and then ask follow-up questions to get answers to the four delineation questions.

At this point, Sean and Terry understand one another's alternatives but are still in disagreement. In this case, you would conclude that this is not a level-1 disagreement and would begin using level-2 resolution strategies.

Solving Level 2: Strengths, Weaknesses, Merge

If consensus has not been reached through delineation, and you have already determined that the disagreement isn't level-3, this would mean that the disagreement is level-2: different values or experiences. To resolve a level-2 disagreement, start by identifying the strengths and weaknesses of each alternative.

Level-2 Resolution Steps (Strengths and Weaknesses)

1. Identify the strengths of each alternative.

    Let's take a look at each alternative, starting with the first one. What are the strengths of this alternative?

2. Identify the weaknesses of each alternative.

    Now that we have identified the strengths of each alternative, let's look at the weaknesses. What are the weaknesses of this first alternative?

3. Take a consensus check.

    Based on these strengths and weaknesses, how many now would be in favor of.... And how many in favor of...

There are a few items to note in particular about the strengths and weaknesses process.

*   A level-2 disagreement is based on values or experiences. If you examine Figure 8.2, you will see that what is recorded are indeed values. When you ask people the strengths of an alternative, their responses typically represent the values they hold that result in them preferring one alternative over the other. For example, those who prefer the "everyone" alternative value common language and everyone benefiting. Those who prefer the "key managers only" alternative value productivity and saving dollars.

*   Always be sure to get strengths of each alternatives first before going to weaknesses. As the example reveals, when there are only two alternatives, the strengths of one are generally the weaknesses of the other. For example, if a strength of option A is "costs less," an implied weakness of option B is "costs more." Accordingly, I often skip the weaknesses step when there are only two alternatives.

*   If there are only two people involved in the disagreement, start by having each person identify the strengths of the opposing alternative. This helps bring the two people closer together as they themselves acknowledge that there are benefits to each alternative. Once the opposing person identifies strengths, then the person favoring the alternative can fill in any strengths that were missed.

Figure 8.2 Flipchart from Strengths and Weaknesses

<table>
<tr><th colspan="2" align="center">Strengths</th></tr>
<tr><th>Everyone</th><th>Key Managers</th></tr>
<tr><td>Common language</td><td>Less expensive</td></tr>
<tr><td>Everyone benefits</td><td>Completed quicker</td></tr>
<tr><td>Employees feel valued</td><td>Less time away from work</td></tr>
<tr><td>Skills throughout the
  organization</td><td>Training focused on those
  who need it</td></tr>
<tr><th colspan="2" align="center">Weaknesses</th></tr>
<tr><td>More expensive</td><td>Doesn't leverage skills or</td></tr>
<tr><td>Longer to complete</td><td> language throughout</td></tr>
<tr><td>More time away from</td><td> organization</td></tr>
<tr><td> work</td><td>People feel less valued</td></tr>
</table>

Frequently the strengths and weaknesses step resolves the disagreement as the participants have a better understanding of what is valuable about each alternative. However, if agreement is not reached, you can use the next technique, merge, to identify the key strengths and create an alternative that combines the key strengths, as outlined below.

Level-2 Resolution Steps (Merge)

1. Isolate the key strengths.

   Let's look at each alternative and identify the one or two most important strengths.

2. Create one or more new alternatives.

   Is there an alternative that might combine these key strengths?

3. Delineate the top alternative.

   Let's delineate this top alternative to ensure that we all understand how that would work. How much...

4. Take a consensus check.

   Based on what we have discussed thus far, how many would be in favor of... ?

The merge process encourages the group to create an alternative that combines the key values of all the participants. The chart that follows provides a sample of what a leader might record on a flip chart using the merge process.

Figure 8.3 Flipchart from Merge

```
                        Strengths
          Everyone                    Key Managers
    *Common language            *Less expensive
    Everyone benefits           Completed quicker
    Employees feel valued       *Less time away from work
    *Skills throughout the      Training focused on those
      organization                 who need it

    *Key strengths

    New Alternative
    Provide a 2-day course for key managers and train a
    select group of managers to deliver a half-day overview to
    all employees.
```

While some may consider the merge process to be one of compromise, merge actually tends to be a creative process: people are asked to imagine a solution that combines the key strengths of the alternatives. This question encourages people to move away from the confines of their preferred alternative and into the creative space of possibilities.

By understanding the three reasons people disagree and having strategies for addressing each one, facilitative leaders are better equipped to recognize and address conflict as it occurs on their teams. Practice these tools in low-risk personal and professional situations to move from knowledge to competency. It is also prudent to make more members of your team aware of these tools to expand the benefit to others in your organization.

Encourage Disagreement

Beyond just engaging conflict, I recommend that leaders go further by *encouraging* disagreement. This means being proactive with their teams in communicating that disagreement is acceptable.

Unfortunately, many leaders subtly avoid conflict and discourage disagreement without being aware of it. Have you ever heard leaders utter phrases such as the following?

- "If there are no better alternatives, let's move forward."
- "Since no one has objected, I am going to assume everyone is on board."
- "There aren't any questions or concerns, are there?"

While leaders may think they are inviting input, each of these phrases can subtly communicate, "I don't want disagreement, so please don't say anything."

So, how does a leader encourage disagreement? Below are several recommended strategies.

Strategies for Encouraging Disagreement

1. *Raise the conflict resolution skills of your team.*
   Ensure that every member of your team understands the three reasons people disagree, learns the strategies for addressing each level, and takes the opportunity to employ and see you employ the various methods.

2. *Always ask for other alternatives.*
   When someone makes a suggestion, whether it is you or someone else, be sure to ask for other alternatives. This communicates to the team that it is important to seek even better ways to achieve an outcome.

3. *Ask for likes and ways to improve.*
   When you or anyone else makes a suggestion, ask people to identify what they like about the suggestion first. After hearing likes, ask people to identify potential ways to improve the suggestion. Then use one of the decision-making models (e.g., five-finger consensus, informed majority) to decide which, if any, of the improvements to implement.

4. *Use small teams.*
   If your experience is that people are less likely to make critical comments in a large group, break the group into smaller teams of perhaps three to seven people each. Have the smaller teams identify ways to improve.

5. *As the leader, speak last.*
   As indicated in the first chapter, people often look to the leader to comment and then they fall in line with the leader. Facilitative leaders consciously have group members speak first and provide their input last so as to avoid swaying the group. In group meetings, facilitative leaders consciously follow the "Three before me" rule, meaning, three people have to comment before the leader comments. This prevents the leader from dominating the discussion.

Summary

1. Ignoring disagreements can result in, among other things, poor decisions, feelings of disempowerment, passive aggressive resistance, lower performance in groups, and less than optimal results.

2. It is through disagreement that the process of creative abrasion unfolds, in which second and third generation ideas emerge that are better than what was originally proposed.

3. Facilitative leaders understand that effective collaboration is simply a series of successful disagreements.

4. There are only three reasons people disagree.

   - Level 1: Lack of shared information

   - Level 2: Different values or experiences.

   - Level 3: Outside factors unrelated to the disagreement.

5. One of the reasons disagreements can take time to resolve is because both sides stay in advocacy mode instead of moving to inquiry mode.

6. As long as disagreements stay at the position level, the best solution that can be reached is win-lose: someone is going to win and someone is going to lose. Sometimes you end up with lose-lose, where both people end up losing. Positions represent the tip of the iceberg; the real issues, the sources of disagreement, are under the surface. By moving a conversation into inquiry mode, a facilitative leader helps the team get at the real issues.

7. The strategies and tools for addressing each issue type include:

   - Level 1: Delineate the alternatives.

   - Level 2: Identify strengths and weaknesses; create a merged solution.

   - Level 3: Take it to a higher source.

8. Beyond just engaging conflict, I recommend that leaders go further by being proactive with their teams in communicating that disagreement is acceptable. Strategies include:

   - Raise the conflict resolution skills of your team.

   - Always ask for other alternatives.

   - Ask for likes and ways to improve.

   - Use small teams.

   - As the leader, speak last.

Spring Forward

- With the next several disagreements that you encounter, pay close attention and make efforts to use the strategies described in this chapter. These can be disagreements in your professional or personal life, and can be disagreements between others or disagreements that involve you.

- As you listen to the disagreement, try to determine if the disagreement is likely level-1, level-2 or level-3.

- As with the strategies defined in the chapter, first determine if the disagreement is level-3. Are the arguments irrational? Does there seem to be no commitment on the part of one or more of the parties to finding a solution? If so, this may indeed be a level-3 disagreement and best resolved through a higher source.

- If you are able to rule out level 3, assume that it is a level-1 disagreement. Are the parties certain that they understand the other's alternative, or are they just assuming they do? Are they listening to one another or just making statements (advocacy mode)?

- If you can influence the discussion, consider asking permission to delineate. *We may very well understand exactly what each person is saying, but just to be sure, can we take a few minutes to have each person explain exactly how this would work? Let's start with Joe. Joe, how would we…who would be involved…how much would it cost…how long would it take?*

- If delineation does not resolve the disagreement, you can be certain that the disagreement is level-2 and can ask questions about strengths to identify the values and use the merge strategy to identify potential solutions.

- If it is not appropriate for you to play an active role in resolving the disagreement, consider taking time on your own to guess what the answers would be to the delineation, strengths and weaknesses, and merge questions.

- Strategic Thinking: Seven Key Principles
- Strategic Planning: A Special Form of Strategic Thinking
- Mission
- Vision
- Guiding Principles
- Positioning Statements
- Goals
- Objectives
- Strategic Direction versus Implementation Planning
- Critical Success Factors and Barriers
- Strategies
- Action Plans
- Drivers Model Component Definitions
- Monitoring
- How Is the Drivers Model Different?
- Your Role in Driving Strategic Thinking
- Summary
- Spring Forward

Chapter 9.
Drive Strategic Thinking
Throughout the Organization

The Atlanta Airport

As America developed during the industrial revolution, the cities on the east coast that became large metropolitan areas nearly all had major water ways: Boston, New York, Philadelphia, Washington DC, Charleston, Savannah, and so on. Atlanta is not on the list. It is landlocked with no major waterway. In essence, Atlanta was never supposed to be a big city. It originated in 1836 as a settlement called "Terminus" because it was designated as the terminating place where railroads from Savannah would meet railroads going to the Midwest. While Atlanta did grow as a railroad town, the major growth came from another transportation source.

As local folklore has it, in the early 1940s when it was time to rebuild the airport, a city alderman went to the city council to explain that there was this new type of plane being developed that would be called "jets." If Atlanta made their runways about 50 percent longer, it would be the only place in the Southeast where these new planes could land. With the approval of the city council, this was done, and in 1957 the first jet landed in Atlanta. While in 1948 1 million air passengers passed through Atlanta, by the end of 1957 the number was 2 million, making Atlanta the busiest airport in the country. By 1961, it was 9.5 million. Since 1998 it has been the busiest airport in the world. In 2018, the airport had 104 million passengers.

There is a joke told by Southerners that if you want to fly anywhere south, you will likely have to pass through Atlanta. And they are quick to add, "If you die and are 'sent south' you will surely have a two-hour layover in Atlanta."

The city council could have made a tactical decision when it upgraded the airport and gone the cheapest and most economical route. But having the vision to see where transportation was headed, a city alderman, William Hartsfield, influenced the growth of the airport that now bears his name, and helped set Atlanta on the course to becoming the transportation capital of the South.

Chapter 2 describes the level-3 leader as one who is visionary; one who is always thinking forward and considering how decisions today can impact the future. As with the Atlanta alderman, when leaders have a strategic vision they can influence the organization to make decisions along the way that bring that vision into reality.

However, strategic thinking skills should not be limited to the top people in an organization. Facilitative leaders understand the importance of spreading strategic thinking to all levels. They recognize that the more people who are thinking strategically, the more that will be making decisions that have positive, long-term, sustainable impact on the organization.

What is strategic thinking? In our courses, we define it this way:

> Strategic thinking is the process in which one or more people assess the current, envision a future, and define a path for creating that future.

Strategic thinking can be applied across a variety of situations.

- Considering launching a new product? Let's think about this strategically.

- Needing to combine two divisions? Let's think about this strategically.

- Thinking about going to lunch? This too can be considered a strategic rather than tactical decision.

How can something as simple as going to lunch be a strategic decision? Contrast strategic thinking with tactical thinking. What would a tactical lunch decision look like? Perhaps, the person might think:

I had a barbecue sandwich yesterday, a salad the day before. I think I am in the mood for Mexican today, but I only have 30 minutes so I will run downstairs and get a cheeseburger.

However, a strategic decision takes into account a longer term vision and how the present decision can further that. Perhaps the person might think:

I said this year I need to get to know people in other departments. Let me reach out this morning to a couple of people in marketing and see if they have lunch plans.

Or, with an even longer-term vision about career direction and next steps, the person might think:

If I am looking to make partner in the next three years, I need to be building relationships with more of my clients. At least weekly I want to take the opportunity to have lunch with one of my client contacts or with someone who could become a potential client. Let me check to see if....

The Drivers Model[22] is the tool we have been using with clients for over two decades to provide a robust yet simple method for strategic thinking. The Drivers Model is fully scalable and can apply to Fortune 500 companies, nonprofit organizations, government agencies, entire enterprises, single business units, field offices, individual departments, and a work team.

Figure 9.1 – The Drivers Model

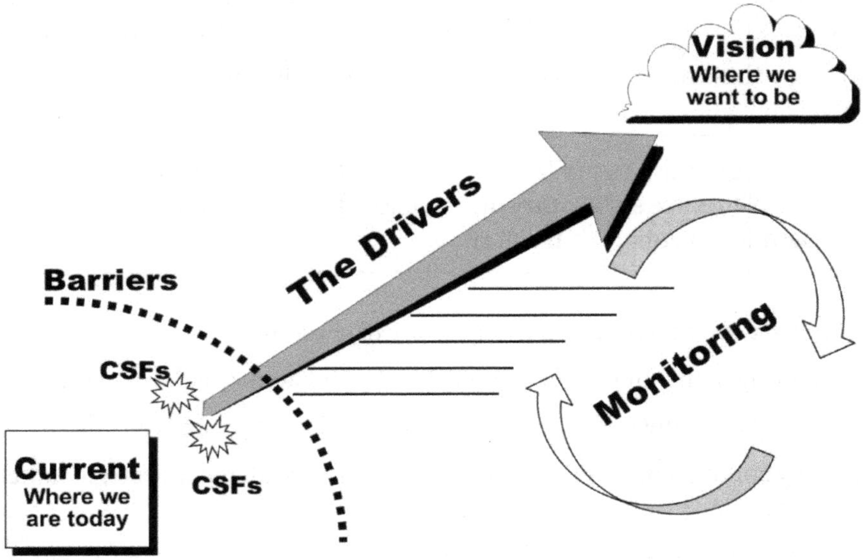

When I first introduce the Drivers Model to a team, I find that I can gain maximum buy-in to the thinking process by starting with simple, everyday examples to highlight the fundamental concepts. Accordingly, this section will start by viewing the Drivers Model through the lens of a couple buying a house. Later in the chapter I will turn to how the Drivers Model strategic thinking process can be applied to strategic planning.

Question 1: Where are we today?

The Drivers Model focuses on four core strategic questions starting with, "Where are we today?" So, with the house-buying example, the couple would start by looking at the strengths and weaknesses of the home in which they are living, as summarized in the following description.

Strengths

- It's in a nice neighborhood.
- It's rented, so we can more easily make a change.
- It's got a big attic.

Weaknesses

- The floorboards are warped.
- The paint is peeling from the plaster.
- Not enough room.

Question 2: Where do we want to be?

After understanding where you are, the next step is to understand where you want to be. In this step, you create your vision of the future. So, where does this family want to be (Figure 9.2)?

Their Vision

- The wife grew up in a family of seven with one bathroom. A key element of her vision: at least three bathrooms.
- The husband wanted the house to have a private office—the operative word being "private." He wanted his own work space that didn't have to double as a guest bedroom when people visited.
- What did the kids want? A huge playroom over the garage.

Figure 9.2 – Vision for the House

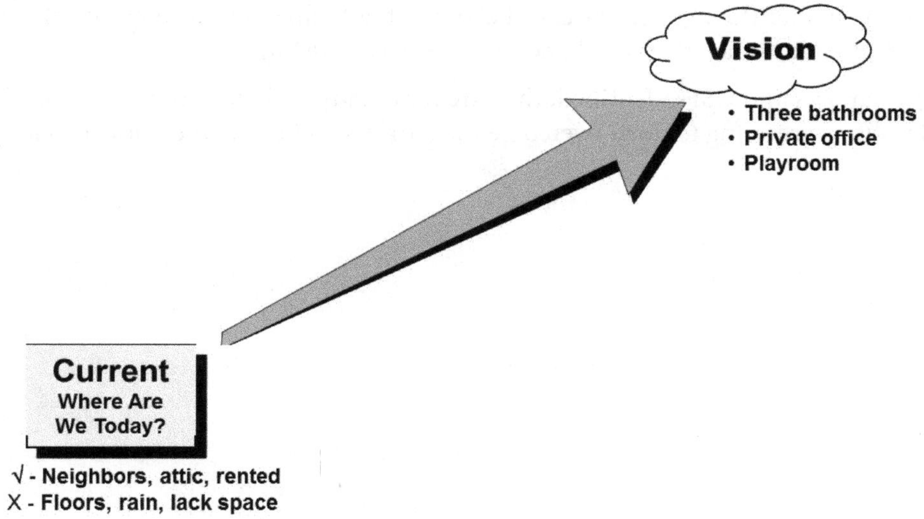

Question 3: How do we get there?

Once you have created your vision, you're ready to turn to defining your *drivers*—the actions you'll undertake to drive your success. Your drivers have to do two important things. First, the reason you are where you are is because there are certain barriers standing between you and your vision. Your drivers must break through those barriers.

For this couple the barriers were quite steep. They felt the home they were seeking was going to cost about $300,000. As first-time homebuyers, they qualified for a special loan at 5 percent down, or $15,000. Yet, they had never saved more than $5000 in their lives. So that $15,000 was a major barrier standing in the way of them achieving their vision. They could dream about the house they wanted, they could search through the newspaper for it, they could even find it and go knock on the door. However, until they overcame the $15,000 barrier, the house would never be theirs.

A second barrier for them was related to their debt-to-equity ratio. For someone to loan them the rest of the money, they had to have pretty good credit. Unfortunately, their credit card debt was high and getting higher—a clear barrier.

Along with overcoming the barriers, the drivers must also address the *critical success factors* (CSFs). The Drivers Model defines CSFs as key conditions that must be created to achieve the vision. Think of CSFs as the fuel that propels the "driver's rocket" to the vision; if you create the key conditions for success and overcome the barriers standing in your way, you achieve your vision. For this couple, a key condition was finding a house that someone wanted to sell, that had the features they desired, in a neighborhood where they wanted to live, at a price they could afford—all at the same time. In essence, if they had overcome the two barriers (the down payment and the high credit card balances) but hadn't created the critical condition (finding a suitable home), they would not have been successful.

With the barriers and CSFs identified, they are now ready to focus on the drivers. What are the things they are going to do to overcome the barriers and create the critical conditions?

Figure 9.3 – Barriers, CSFs, and Drivers

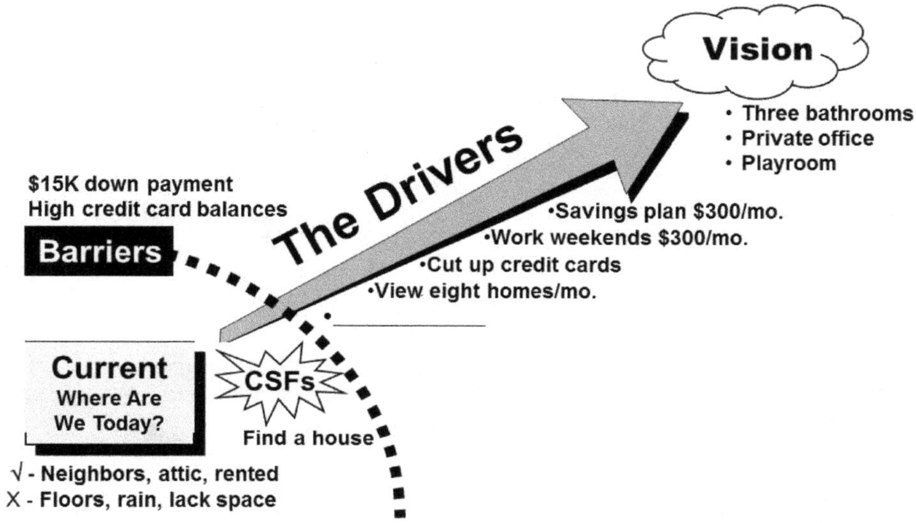

Their Barriers, CSFs, and Drivers

Barrier: $15K down payment

- Implement a savings plan to target $300 in savings per month (e.g., minimize eating out, limit unnecessary expenditures).

- Take on weekend jobs to save an additional $300 per month.

Barrier: High credit card balances

- Cut up credit cards. Pay down debt monthly.

CSF: Finding a suitable house

- Hire a realtor and target viewing eight homes per month.

Question 4: How will we monitor our progress?

There was one more driver the couple needed to put in place that was more important than any of the others. That driver was the *monitoring driver*. The purpose of the monitoring driver is to track the progress of all the other drivers. So, they did their monitoring on the first Sunday of every month at 6 p.m. At that time, all activities in their household would stop and they would ask themselves a series of questions.

- First, "How much money did we save this month?" Let's say that they saved $350, exceeding the monthly target.

- "How much did we get from the extra jobs?" Another $310. Again, over target.
- "How's the credit card debt doing?" Down 10 percent. That looks good as well.

Figure 9.4 – Monitoring

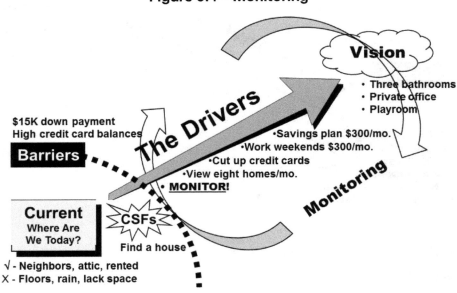

- "How many homes did we look at last month?" Five. Why only five? What was the problem? The real estate agent wasn't available and sometimes wouldn't return their calls, since the agent knew the couple wasn't going to be buying for another year. As such, they needed to find a new agent because they had a plan, and the agent was getting in the way!

Monitoring is critical to ensure that you stay on track. Monitoring also allows you to make adjustments along the way as you learn new information, encounter new barriers, or identify other CSFs. But perhaps most importantly, monitoring keeps you motivated. Typically, it takes considerable effort to move from where you are today to where you want to be. The monitoring process helps keep your vision in front of you and can give you the continual motivation needed to follow through on your drivers.

Strategic Thinking: 7 Key Principles

The Drivers Model process covers seven key principles for strategic thinking.

1. Be clear on purpose.

2. Start with an accurate assessment of today.

3. Create a shared vision of success.

4. Identify your critical successful factors and barriers.

5. Define the drivers (i.e., your strategies and priorities).

6. Monitor and report results.

7. Have rewards and consequences to build accountability.

1 | Be clear on purpose.

With any activity, start with purpose: why are we doing this? With the house example, the couple's purpose was to find a house that was more suitable to their needs. As described earlier, purpose always answers the question "Why?"

2 | Start with an accurate assessment of where you are today.

You should always start with an accurate assessment of where you are currently. Why is that important? Because you may think that you have overcome certain barriers when in reality you haven't.

An example will more clearly illustrate the importance of starting with an accurate picture of today. Imagine that you wanted to drive across the US from Atlanta, in the Southeast, to Los Angeles, on the West Coast. You would have to drive west to get there. But what if you believed you were in Atlanta, but in reality you were already on the West Coast, except way up in Seattle? What happens when you drive west? You might end up a little wet, which probably was not part of your vision! So, while you may create a compelling vision of where you want to be, if you don't clearly define where you are, you may think you're outside of certain barriers. As a result, you can end up doing the wrong things and not getting the result you want.

3 | Create a shared vision.

Once you have an accurate picture of today, you then create a shared vision—not just a vision, but a *shared* vision. Imagine the conflict that would have existed if the wife and husband had different visions of the type of home they wanted but never discussed it. The entire journey of finding a suitable home would be beset by considerable conflict and struggle. There would likely have been pushes and pulls in different directions and major fights over the smallest of things, because the couple lacked a common vision of what they were trying to achieve. By creating a shared vision up front, they have the "fight" only once. Once the vision was created, they would be able to make decisions together in line with achieving that vision.

In many organizations, there are entire departments that have different visions of where the organization needs to be. Imagine the chaos when each department goes off in a different direction. And sometimes those different directions are mutually exclusive—if one is successful, the other has to fail. This results in a profound waste of resources—all resulting from the lack of a shared vision.

4 | Identify your critical success factors and barriers.

With that shared vision defined, the fourth principle is that you then focus on identifying the major barriers to achieving that vision. Ask yourself, "Why haven't we achieved our vision already? What's standing in our way? What's keeping us where we are today?"

Then, you must isolate your CSFs. What are the key conditions that, if you create them, will drive achievement of the vision?

5 | Define your drivers.

After identifying your barriers and CSFs, the fifth principle is to define your drivers. What are the key strategies that are going to get you to your vision? Remember that the strategies must address each of the barriers and CSFs.

6 | Monitor.

With principle six, you monitor your progress to stay on track and motivated to achieve your vision.

7 | Have rewards and consequences to build accountability.

Finally, be sure to have rewards and consequences to build accountability. Even with a monitoring process, if there is no formal accountability, people quickly learn that their attention to the drivers is not required.

Strategic Planning: A Special Form of Strategic Thinking

As described earlier, strategic thinking applies to a wide range of situations; essentially, anytime there is a gap between where you are and where you want to be, strategic thinking and the Drivers Model applies.

The difference between strategic planning and strategic thinking is that strategic planning is simply a special form of strategic thinking that is applied in a more structured way with a structured set of deliverables.

The Secrets to Facilitating Strategy provides a complete description of applying the Drivers Model to strategic planning. The diagram on the next page (Figure 9.5) shows a sample document resulting from using the Drivers Model to create a strategic plan, again using a simple example. The graphic provides an extract of a strategic plan for a meeting planning organization—an association of people who plan and coordinate business meetings. The members of the association are meeting planners as well as people who supply to the meetings industry (e.g., hotel owners, audio-visual companies, and transportation companies). It will be helpful to walk through each component of this strategy document to focus on how the pieces fit together.

Mission

Definition	Example
A statement of the overall purpose of an organization that describes what you do, for whom you do it, and the benefit.	*To provide a forum for furthering the growth and professionalism of the meetings industry.*

Figure 9.5 Sample Strategy Layout

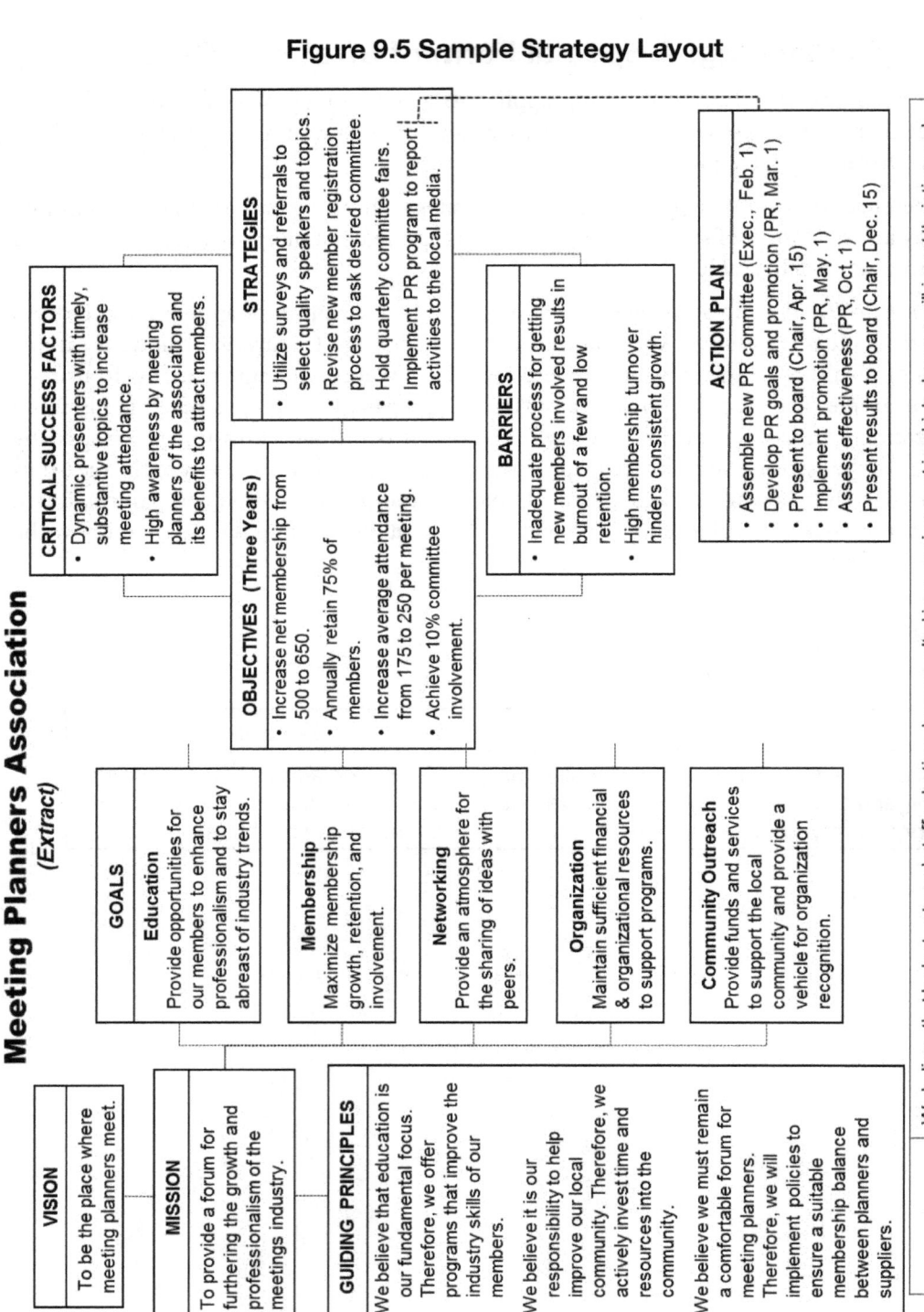

Meeting Planners Association *(Extract)*

VISION
To be the place where meeting planners meet.

MISSION
To provide a forum for furthering the growth and professionalism of the meetings industry.

GUIDING PRINCIPLES
We believe that education is our fundamental focus. Therefore, we offer programs that improve the industry skills of our members.

We believe it is our responsibility to help improve our local community. Therefore, we actively invest time and resources into the community.

We believe we must remain a comfortable forum for meeting planners. Therefore, we will implement policies to ensure a suitable membership balance between planners and suppliers.

GOALS

Education
Provide opportunities for our members to enhance professionalism and to stay abreast of industry trends.

Membership
Maximize membership growth, retention, and involvement.

Networking
Provide an atmosphere for the sharing of ideas with peers.

Organization
Maintain sufficient financial & organizational resources to support programs.

Community Outreach
Provide funds and services to support the local community and provide a vehicle for organization recognition.

CRITICAL SUCCESS FACTORS
- Dynamic presenters with timely, substantive topics to increase meeting attendance.
- High awareness by meeting planners of the association and its benefits to attract members.

STRATEGIES
- Utilize surveys and referrals to select quality speakers and topics.
- Revise new member registration process to ask desired committee.
- Hold quarterly committee fairs.
- Implement PR program to report activities to the local media.

OBJECTIVES (Three Years)
- Increase net membership from 500 to 650.
- Annually retain 75% of members.
- Increase average attendance from 175 to 250 per meeting.
- Achieve 10% committee involvement.

BARRIERS
- Inadequate process for getting new members involved results in burnout of a few and low retention.
- High membership turnover hinders consistent growth.

ACTION PLAN
- Assemble new PR committee (Exec., Feb. 1)
- Develop PR goals and promotion (PR, Mar. 1)
- Present to board (Chair, Apr. 15)
- Implement promotion (PR, May. 1)
- Assess effectiveness (PR, Oct. 1)
- Present results to board (Chair, Dec. 15)

POSITIONING STATEMENT
We believe that budget cuts and staff reductions have resulted in an environment in which planners will invest their time and money only if they can see an immediate, tangible return. Therefore, we must focus our programs on maximizing return-on-investment to planners and implement marketing campaigns that promote the association's benefit to our target audience.

With the Drivers Model, a *mission statement* answers three simple questions: (1) What do you do? (2) For whom do you do it? (3) What is the benefit? The mission statement from the Meeting Planners Association illustrates an excellent example of how a mission statement can answer these three questions succinctly.

- What do you do? Provide a forum

- For whom? The meetings industry

- What's the benefit? Furthering growth and professionalism

So, their mission statement is: *To provide a forum for furthering the growth and professionalism of the meetings industry.* It's simple, succinct, meaningful, and memorable.

Vision

Definition	Example
A picture of the "preferred future"—it's a statement that describes how the future will look if the organization fulfills its mission.	*To be the place where meeting planners meet.*

As there is a first-blush similarity between the two, it is important to clarify the difference between a mission statement and a vision statement. While a mission statement explains the overall purpose of an organization—what you do, for whom you do it, and the benefit—a vision statement gives the picture of the preferred future. A vision statement answers the question, "If the organization fulfills its mission, what will the future look like?"

Going back to our Meeting Planners Association, meeting planners find places for other people to meet. For this association, if they fulfill their mission by providing a forum for furthering the growth and professionalism of the meetings industry, the association indeed will be the place where meeting planners meet.

Guiding Principles

Definition	Example
General guidelines that set the foundation for how an organization will operate.	*We believe we must remain a comfortable forum for meeting planners. Therefore, we will implement policies to ensure a suitable membership balance between planners and suppliers.*

With the Drivers Model, guiding principles are different from *values*. *Webster's Dictionary* defines a value as "a principle, standard, or quality considered worthwhile or desirable." In organizations, values can play an important role in defining an organization's character and its culture. Values also can provide the basic foundation on which an organization is built.

When organizations define their values, it isn't unusual to hear statements similar to the following:

- We focus on the customer.

- We respect the individual.

- Integrity is non-negotiable.

- Our people are our most critical resource.

While values such as these are important, organizations using the Drivers Model gain greater benefit by transforming their values into guiding principles. Guiding principles define the value *and* describe the behaviors that the organization believes support that value. To ensure a focus on both the value and the behaviors, the Drivers Model uses the following format for guiding principles: "We believe… (value). Therefore, we will … (behaviors)."

The example from the meeting planners association illustrates the value/behavior relationship well.

> *We believe we must remain a comfortable forum for meeting planners. Therefore, we will implement policies to ensure a suitable membership balance between planners and suppliers.*

Recall that the members of this association are not only the people who plan meetings, but also all the suppliers to that industry, such as resorts, limousine companies, and audio-visual companies. The suppliers have meeting planners as their customers—wouldn't you want to attend events where all your customers gathered? However, the association was concerned that they could easily become overrun by suppliers. So, from this guiding principle, they implemented policies to prevent that from happening. For example, one of their policies was that in order for a supplier to join, a planner had to join as well.

Positioning Statements

Definition	Example
Broad determinations about the organization's direction and focus.	*We believe that budget cuts and staff reductions have resulted in an environment in which planners will invest their time and money only if they can see an immediate, tangible return. Therefore, we must focus our membership programs on maximizing ROI and invest in marketing that promotes the benefit of our association to our target audience.*

Positioning statements set the broad direction for an organization. Positioning statements are a response to the organization's current situation and identify how the organization will succeed; that is, how the organization must position itself in order to successfully respond to the current conditions. Positioning statements have a specific format: "We believe… (the current condition). Therefore, we must… (the response strategy)." The response strategy of a position statement typically is reflected later in the strategy portion of the strategic plan.

Goals

Definition	Example
Broad, long-term aims that define fulfillment of the mission.	*Maximize membership growth, retention, and involvement.*

If you were to turn back to the sample strategy layout, Figure 9.5, you would see that the meeting planning organization realized that, to fulfill its mission, it had to be successful in five areas: education, organization, membership, community outreach, and networking.

Look back at the wording of the membership goal: *Maximize membership growth, retention, and involvement.* Of course, many membership-based organizations would have this as a goal. So, goals are very broad statements. However, the key is that these statements define the five areas where this organization must succeed in order to fulfill its mission.

With the Drivers Model, goals are long-term and change infrequently. As an example, when is the Meeting Planners Association going to want to stop maximizing membership growth, or providing educational opportunities, or promoting meeting management as a viable career? Probably never. So, goals are intended to be written in broad terms. For this reason, goals don't start with finite verbs like *build, establish,* or *develop.* Once you have *built, established,* or *developed* something, the goal has been accomplished. With the Drivers Model, goals are long-term aims and therefore start with "infinite verbs," that imply "never-ending" such as *provide, promote, maximize,* and *maintain.*

What follow each goal are the measures of success, which the Drivers Model refers to as *objectives.*

Objectives

Definition	Example
Specific, quantifiable, realistic targets that measure the accomplishment of a goal over a specified period.	*Increase average attendance from 125 to 250 per meeting by the third year.*

While goals are broad aims, objectives are specific, measurable targets that define accomplishment of the goal. Going back to the sample, one of the goals for the Meeting Planners Association is to *maximize membership growth, retention, and involvement.* The organization identified four key targets that measured accomplishment of the goal over a three-year period.

By breaking down the wording of a goal, a team is able to determine what the key measures should be by asking, "At the end of the year, what would tell us that we have achieved this goal?"

- *Maximize membership **growth**.* At the end of the year, what would tell us that we maximized membership growth? (Key measure: number of members.)

- *Maximize **retention**.* At the end of the year, what would tell us that we maximized retention? (Key measure: number of members retained from the prior year.)

- *Maximize **involvement**.* At the end of the year, what would tell us that we maximized involvement? (Key measures: number of members attending meetings, number of members involved in committees.)

Based on these key measures, the following would be objectives for the membership goal.

Three-year Objectives for the Membership Goal

- Increase net membership from 500 to 650.
- Annually retain 75 percent of members from the prior year.
- Increase average attendance from 175 to 250 per meeting.
- Achieve 10 percent committee involvement.

Note that in the sample layout, I only show the membership objectives due to space limitations. Of course, each of the other four goals have objectives tied to them as well.

The point is that each objective is specifically selected because it measures accomplishment of the goal based on the way the goal is worded. This means, of course, that you have to be very careful about how you word your goals. Otherwise you could be measuring something different from your intention.

The Difference between Goals and Objectives

While goals are broad, objectives are specific and measurable targets to be reached. You need both. If you just had goals (broad aims) and no objectives (specific, measurable targets that defined accomplishment of the goal), how would you know at the end of the year, whether or not you've been successful? Suppose the meeting planners organization just had the goal of maximizing membership growth, but no specific targets? At the end of the first year, they would ask themselves, "Did we maximize membership growth?" They could respond yes, but how would they know? Without defined measurable targets, the best they could respond is, "Well, it sure feels like we maximized membership growth. We did a lot of work and we did get some new members. So yes, we maximized membership growth." Yet, without defined targets, you really don't know.

So, clearly objectives are important. However, if objectives are so important, then why not just have objectives? You don't really need goals, do you? Well, of course you do. Think of it this way. What if one year the meeting planners set objectives to increase net membership to 650, achieve average attendance of 250, and so on? Then, the following year, they set objectives to have a satellite chapter in a neighboring city, and then the following year to have at least three events with other related associations. And so on. The problem with just having objectives is that you're setting targets, but to what end? What are the targets for? What are you trying to achieve? What are your ultimate aims?

This is the purpose of goals. The goals communicate your ultimate aims. Your goals tell you the areas in which you need to have objectives. It is important to recognize that the objectives only tell you where you want to be with each of the goals by a given point in time.

By the way, it doesn't matter what you call these components. The Drivers Model calls them goals and objectives; you might reverse the names and call them objectives and goals, or key performance areas and key performance indicators, or strategic intent and strategic outcomes. The key is that you need both: something broad that defines your aims, and something specific and measurable that sets targets for a specific time period.

Results versus Activity

There is one other key point to understand about objectives: Objectives measure results, not activity. Look back again at the objectives for the membership goal. Notice that there isn't an objective that says, "Hold two membership drives this year." What would be wrong with this objective? To assess the objective, we should run it through the SMART acronym, which is often used to ensure that an objective is suitable.

Hold two membership drives this year. Is it a SMART objective?

- Is it <u>S</u>pecific? Yes, it refers to membership drives.

- Is it <u>M</u>easurable? Yes, we want to hold two of them.

- Is it <u>A</u>chievable? Presumably we can hold two membership drives in a year.

- Is it <u>R</u>ealistic? If it is achievable then it is probably realistic.

- Is it <u>T</u>ime-bound? Yes, it is a three-year objective.

The objective appears to pass the SMART test, so what is wrong with the objective? There is a big problem with the objective and a problem the Drivers Model prevents by using a different definition for the "R" in SMART. As stated above, "R" stands for "realistic," which in many ways overlaps with the "A," which stands for "achievable." In the Drivers Model, the "R" stands for "relevant." The question then becomes, "Is the objective a relevant measure of the goal?"

To answer this question, we have to go back to the wording of the goal: *Maximize membership growth, retention, and involvement.*

- Does the objective ("Hold two membership drives this year") measure membership growth? No.

- Does the objective measure retention? No.

- Does the objective measure involvement? No.

In essence, the objective doesn't measure the goal at all. In fact, the objective is measuring activity instead of results. *Holding two membership drives* is an activity to increase membership growth, not a relevant measure of whether you have achieved membership growth.

This problem of measuring activity instead of results is all too common in strategic plans for nonprofits, governments, and corporations alike. And what's worse, suppose that we had our two membership drives, but didn't get any new members. At the end of the year we would congratulate ourselves for achieving the objective—we held our two drives—but we wouldn't have achieved the goal of maximizing membership growth. That's the danger of having objectives that measure activity instead of focusing on results. If we don't measure results, we can get so caught up in the activity that we lose sight of the real goal. So, we must be careful when we create objectives to avoid measuring activity (such as holding membership drives). Instead we must focus on the true desired outcome (increasing members).

Keep in mind that activity measures aren't necessarily bad. They just don't make good objectives. Many activity measures become strategies or might serve well as leading indicators. As an example, a key strategy for increasing new members might be to have every member invite potential members to a free event hosted by the association. An activity measure might be the number of potential members attending the free event. This isn't an objective for membership growth because it doesn't serve as a measure of that goal. But, instead of serving as an objective, it could very well serve as a leading indicator of membership growth, because the number of new members each year could be highly correlated with the number of potential members attending free events.

Strategic Direction versus Implementation Planning

The objectives represent the completion of strategic direction setting, which you can consider the first half of the strategy development process as shown in Figure 9.6. Once an organization has identified its objectives, it has also defined where it is going and the measures that signal success.

The second half of strategy development is called implementation planning. During implementation planning, the entire focus is on how the organization will achieve the objectives. However, you may be tempted to jump straight to strategies to answer the question, "What do we do to accomplish the objectives?" The Drivers Model encourages you to be more thoughtful by focusing on two important areas that will help ensure you identify the most important strategies.

Critical Success Factors and Barriers

CSF Definition	CSF Example
Key conditions that must be created to achieve one or more objectives.	*High awareness by meeting planners of the association and its benefits to attract members.*

Barrier Definition	Barrier Example
Existing or potential challenges that hinder the achievement of one or more objectives.	*Inadequate process for getting new members involved results in burnout of a few and low retention.*

Critical success factor analysis is among the most important concepts in planning. CSFs encourage you to identify and focus on what factors you absolutely need in order to be successful. Once you have created your objectives, you can then identify your CSFs by asking, "What key conditions, if we create them, will drive achievement of our objectives?"

Figure 9.6 Strategic Direction versus Implementation Planning

Meeting Planners Association
(Extract)

Strategic Direction Setting

VISION

To be the place where meeting planners meet.

MISSION

To provide a forum for furthering the growth and professionalism of the meetings industry.

GUIDING PRINCIPLES

We believe that education is our fundamental focus. Therefore, we offer programs that improve the industry skills of our members.

We believe it is our responsibility to help improve our local community. Therefore, we actively invest time and resources into the community.

We believe we must remain a comfortable forum for meeting planners. Therefore, we will implement policies to ensure a suitable membership balance between planners and suppliers.

GOALS

Education

Provide opportunities for our members to enhance professionalism and to stay abreast of industry trends.

Membership

Maximize membership growth, retention, and involvement.

Networking

Provide an atmosphere for the sharing of ideas with peers.

Organization

Maintain sufficient financial & organizational resources to support programs.

Community Outreach

Provide funds and services to support the local community and provide a vehicle for organization recognition.

OBJECTIVES (Three Years)

- Increase net membership from 500 to 650.
- Annually retain 75% of members.
- Increase average attendance from 175 to 250 per meeting.
- Achieve 10% committee involvement.

Implementation Planning

CRITICAL SUCCESS FACTORS

- High awareness by meeting planners of the association and its benefits to attract members.

STRATEGIES

- Utilize surveys and referrals to select quality speakers and topics.
- Revise new member registration process to ask desired committee.
- Hold quarterly committee fairs.
- Implement PR program to report activities to the local media.

BARRIERS

- Inadequate process for getting new members involved results in burnout of a few and low retention.
- High membership turnover hinders consistent growth.

ACTION PLAN

- Assemble new PR committee (Exec., Feb. 1)
- Develop PR goals and promotion (PR, Mar. 1)
- Present to board (Chair, Apr. 15)
- Implement promotion (PR, May. 1)
- Assess effectiveness (PR, Oct. 1)
- Present results to board (Chair, Dec. 15)

POSITIONING STATEMENT

We believe that budget cuts and staff reductions have resulted in an environment in which planners will invest their time and money only if they can see an immediate, tangible return. Therefore, we must focus our programs on maximizing return-on-investment to planners and implement marketing campaigns that promote the association's benefit to our target audience.

With the meeting planners, one of their objectives was to *increase net membership from 500 to 650*. What is the CSF for increasing membership? What is the key condition that, if they create it, will drive achievement of the objective?

- High awareness by meeting planners of the association and its benefits to attract members.

Another objective is to increase meeting attendance from 175 to 250. What's the key condition?

- Dynamic presenters with timely, substantive topics to increase meeting attendance.

Along with critical success factors, you must also consider barriers before deciding which strategies to undertake. Barriers are existing or potential challenges that hinder the achievement of one or more objectives. They're the roadblocks that keep you where you are today and prevent you from getting to where you want to be. To identify your barriers, you ask the question, "What is standing in the way of our achieving these objectives? Why aren't we there already?"

When the meeting planners looked at their membership data for the prior two years, they realized that 70 percent of their turnover was made up of people who had been members for a year or less. In essence, people were joining the organization, looking around, and then leaving. The people who got involved with the organization tended to stay. Therefore, they determined that one of their major barriers was the following:

- An inadequate process for getting new members involved, resulting in burnout of a few and low retention.

Strategies

Definition	Example
Broad activities required to achieve an objective, create a critical condition, or overcome a barrier.	*Use assessment surveys and industry referrals to select quality speakers and topics.*

Once you have identified your CSFs and barriers, you're now ready to determine your *strategies*. Strategies are your drivers, the things you actually do to achieve your objectives, create a critical condition, or overcome a barrier. Note, however, that in the meeting planners example, that each strategy is designed to address a CSF, a barrier, an objective, or some combination of the three, as shown in Figure 9.7.

Figure 9.7: Tying Strategies to Objectives, CSFs, and Barriers

Strategy	Affects which Objective, CSF, or Barrier
1. Use assessment surveys and industry referrals to select quality speakers and topics.	Obj: Increase average attendance from 175 to 250 per meeting. CSF: Dynamic presenters with timely, substantive topics to increase meeting attendance.
2. Revise new member registration process to ask for member's committee preference.	Obj: Achieve 10 percent committee involvement. Obj: Annually retain 75 percent of members from prior year. Bar: Inadequate process for getting new members involved results in burnout of a few and low retention. Bar: High membership turnover hinders consistent growth.
3. Hold quarterly committee fairs after meetings.	Obj: Achieve 10 percent committee involvement. Obj: Annually retain 75 percent of members from prior year. Bar: Inadequate process for getting new members involved results in burnout of a few and low retention. Bar: High membership turnover hinders consistent growth.
4. Implement PR program to report activities to the local media.	Obj: Increase net membership from 500 to 650. CSF: High awareness by meeting planners of the association and its benefits to attract members.

Given that nearly all organizations have scarce resources, you might wonder why any organization would invest in a strategy that wasn't creating a critical condition for success or overcoming a major barrier standing in their way. Unfortunately, organizations do this very frequently.

Why? Of course, one reason is because they have no choice. For example, government organizations have legislative mandates that they must accomplish, even if a mandate is not related to their objectives, barriers, or CSFs. In the same way, a CEO of a corporation or executive director of a nonprofit may insist on implementing a strategy that others in the organization recognize isn't key to achieving any of the strategic objectives.

However, a primary reason organizations invest in strategies that don't address their CSFs and barriers is that they've never determined what their CSFs and barriers are. In essence, they were doing things (strategies), but were they doing the most important things? Maybe or maybe not. We don't know because they hadn't determined their CSFs and barriers.

Therefore, one of the keys to effective strategic planning is to identify what is critical to achieving your objectives and to isolate the barriers that are standing in your way. Only then can you make sure you invest in only the most important strategies.

Action Plans

Definition
Specific steps to be taken to implement a strategy; includes what will be done, by whom and by when, and the resources required.

In the meeting planners example, there are five goals and four strategies for the goal area called "membership." If each goal had four strategies, then this plan would generate twenty strategies. Of course, you can't do twenty strategies all at once, thus the need to prioritize to decide which strategies to focus on first. Once priority strategies are selected, your team would create action plans for each priority strategy.

An action plan provides the details for how a priority strategy will be implemented. The action plan describes what will be done, by whom and by when. The action plan also estimates both the people resources and the out-of-pocket dollars required. Figure 9.8 provides a sample action plan.

Figure 9.8 Sample Action Plan

Strategy: Implement PR plan to report activities to the local media		
Objective(s) Supported	Increase net membership from 500 to 650.	
Owner	PR chair	
Deliverables	• PR plan with measurable targets and results • Implemented promotion plan • Presentation to board on plan and results	
Due Date: December 31	**Total Costs:** $1000	**Person Days:** 27

Action Step	Who	Due	Cost	Person-days
Assemble new PR committee (Target: 5 people).	Exec. director	Feb. 1		1
Develop PR objectives.	PR comm.	Mar. 1		3
Develop promotion program.	PR comm.	Mar. 15		3
Hold board presentation.	Chair, board	Apr. 15		0.5
Begin promotion implementation.	PR comm.	May 1	$1000	15
Provide interim report of progress.	Chair, board	Aug. 15		1
Assess promotion effectiveness.	PR comm.	Nov. 1		3
Present results to board.	Chair, board	Dec. 15		0.5

Action plans also allow you to monitor the activity to ensure that the priorities are being accomplished. You should have no more than three months between action steps to ensure ongoing progress.

Drivers Model Component Definitions

Figure 9.9 summarizes the definition of each component of the Drivers Model.

Figure 9.9 Drivers Model Components

Vision	A picture of the "preferred future"; a statement that describes how the future will look if the organization fulfills its mission. *To be the place where meeting planners meet.*
Mission	A statement of the overall purpose of an organization that describes what you do, for whom you do it, and the benefit. *To provide a forum for furthering the growth and professionalism of the meetings industry.*
Guiding Principles	General guidelines that set the foundation for how an organization will operate. *We believe we must remain a comfortable forum for meeting planners. Therefore, we will implement policies to ensure a suitable membership balance between planners and suppliers.*
Goals	Broad, long-term aims that define fulfillment of the mission. *Maximize membership growth, retention, and involvement.*
Objectives	Specific, quantifiable, realistic targets that measure the accomplishment of a goal over a specified period of time. *Increase average attendance from 125 to 250 per meeting.*
Positioning Statements	Broad determinations about the organization's direction and focus. *We believe that budget cuts and staff reductions have resulted in an environment in which planners will invest their time and money only if they can see an immediate, tangible return. Therefore, we must focus our membership programs on maximizing ROI and invest in marketing that promotes the benefit of our association to our target audience.*
Critical Success Factors	Key conditions that must be created to achieve one or more objectives. *High awareness by meeting planners of the association and its benefits to attract members.*
Barriers	Existing or potential challenges that hinder the achievement of one or more objectives. *Inadequate process for getting new members involved results in burnout of a few and low retention.*
Strategies	Broad activities required to achieve an objective, create a critical condition, or overcome a barrier. *Use assessment surveys and industry referrals to select quality speakers and topics.*
Action Plans	Specific steps to be taken to implement a strategy: includes what will be done, by whom and by when, and the resources required. *Assemble new PR committee. (Exec., Feb. 1)* *Develop PR objectives. (PR, Mar. 1)* *Develop promotion. (PR, Mar. 15)*

Monitoring

Now that we have reviewed all the components of the plan, the next critical topic is the monitoring process. As described in Chapter 7, monitoring is a crucial element in ensuring accountability for execution.

Periodically, it is essential to take a full stop and grade your progress in the implementation of your strategic plan. In doing so, of course you should review all of the plan's nine components: vision, mission, guiding principles, goals, objectives, CSFs, barriers, strategies, and action plans. However, I recommend that you grade your performance by focusing on one element in particular. Which one?

- Is it vision, mission, guiding principles, or goals? No. These are too broad.

- Perhaps, CSFs or barriers? No, you can't really grade these.

- So now we're down to deciding whether to grade objectives or the strategies/action plans. Which do you grade?

The answer may be obvious. Imagine that you're at the one-year point, or the two-year point, or even the three-year point of a three-year plan, and you've achieved every one of your strategies and action plans, but you haven't achieved your objectives. Are you going to be happy? Probably not.

On the other hand, what if after a year, two years, or three years, you've achieved every one of your objectives—every single one—but you haven't done all your strategies and actions. Are you going to be happy? Absolutely. You're going to be ecstatic because you achieved your objectives and you didn't have to do all that work!

The key to grading progress is to focus on the objectives because these are your measurable targets. These are the results you're trying to achieve. If you're grading your performance based on strategies or action plans, you might give yourself an "A" for performing actions, even though you may not have achieved the results intended. Unfortunately, as indicated before, this happens frequently in corporations, government agencies, and nonprofits, especially when the organization hasn't defined measurable objectives or when its objectives focus on activities and not results.

To effectively monitor progress, the Drivers Model includes a three-step monitoring process.

The Three-Step Monitoring Process

- **Monthly**: With the Drivers Model, your team will track strategies and action plans monthly by answering the question, "Are we doing what we said we were going to do?" You'll make adjustments along the way to action plans as needed. Figure 9.10 provides an extract of a sample monthly monitoring dashboard. The color-coded dashboard would show in green those strategies that were 100 percent complete with the deliverable due that month. Those strategies in yellow are those that were at least 75 percent complete but not entirely finished. Those in red represent strategies with deliverables for that month that were less than 75 percent complete. The entire organization receives a score and a grade for the month, representing how well the organization executed on its strategic priorities.

- **Quarterly**: Every three months, however, your team will review progress on objectives and answer, "Are we getting the results we expected to get?" During these quarterly sessions, your team will adjust objectives as warranted based on issues and priorities, and will decide which current strategies to stop or continue, and which new strategies to start.

- **Annually**: The planning team will meet to answer the question, "Are we going in the right direction?" The team will review progress for the year, reassess the current conditions, identify new barriers and CSFs, update objectives, and reestablish priorities and action plans.

Figure 9.10 Sample Monitoring Dashboard (extract)

			77% C+	89% B+	91% A-	84% B	98% A
			Jan	Feb	Mar	Apr	May
		100 percent done	3	7	8	6	10
		75–95 percent done	6	3	2	3	1
		0–75 percent done	2	1	1	2	0
A1	Provide quarterly seminars on advanced meeting planning.						
B3	Partner with food bank to provide unserved food to homeless shelters.						
C1	Implement PR program to publicize events in local media.						

How Is the Drivers Model Different?

From time to time, I'm asked to explain how the Drivers Model differs from other strategic thinking and strategic planning models. Here are a few key differences.

1. **Elegantly simple**. Many executives see planning, and specifically strategic planning, as a highly challenging and complex activity. The Drivers Model provides an approach that is elegantly simple, yet robust and comprehensive enough to serve both multibillion-dollar corporations and half million-dollar nonprofits.

2. **Strategy document.** In a single, 11x17 page folded in half, you have all the core elements of your strategic plan. For management teams and employees, the strategy document serves as an easily accessible and understandable roadmap of the strategic direction. Some organizations even find it helpful to create an edited, "external" version of the strategy document to give to suppliers and customers.

3. **Clear definitions.** No more arguing about what is a goal and what is an objective! No more debates about what should be included in a vision versus a mission statement. The Drivers Model provides clear, concise, and easy-to-adapt definitions for each plan element.

4. **Mission–vision distinction.** The clear distinction between mission (*what you do, for whom, and the benefit*) and vision (*the preferred picture of the future*) helps you to be both definitive and aspirational at the same time.

5. **Goals–objectives relationship.** The relationship between goals (*broad aims that define fulfillment of the mission*) and objectives (*specific, measurable targets that define accomplishment of the goal*) ensures that your objectives focus on measuring results rather than activities.

6. **CSFs and barriers.** How do you make sure your strategies are the most important activities for your organization's focus? The Drivers Model answers the call by having you identify the critical conditions for success and the major barriers standing in your way. So, each of your strategies should create a critical condition, overcome a barrier, or both.

7. **Developing strategies.** While brainstorming potential strategies is an important part of any planning process, the Drivers Model follows the brainstorming with a rigorous review of CSFs and barriers to ensure that the plan addresses major impediments and creates the critical conditions for success.

8. **Power of verbs.** The Drivers Model defines specific differences among the verbs used for each planning component.

    - Goals start with *infinite* verbs (e.g., maximize, provide, maintain).

    - Objectives begin with *quantity* verbs (e.g., increase, decrease, and reduce).

    - Strategies use *finite* verbs (e.g., establish, develop, implement).

    - These distinctions provide a level of consistency that helps produce a quality plan.

9. **Monitoring processes.** Many plans fail in execution due to a lack of focus and commitment. The three-step monitoring model encourages both the focus and commitment needed to deliver on a plan's promise.

These differences help make the Drivers Model a practical approach to strategic thinking and strategic planning for organizations of various types and sizes.

Your Role in Driving Strategic Thinking

Promote strategic thinking

When leaders ask questions, people pay attention. By consistently asking the strategic questions, you will be advocating strategic thinking as an expectation for your people.

- What is our overall purpose with this? What are we trying to achieve?

- What are the results that will tell us that we've achieved it? What are the minimum, expected, and stretch results?

- Why aren't we there already? What are our barriers? What is standing in our way?

- What are the key conditions that, if we create them, will drive us to our results?

- What are the key things we should do to overcome our barriers and create our conditions for success so that we achieve our target results?

- How will we monitor our progress and adjust along the way?

Along with asking these strategic questions yourself, you should be very quick to acknowledge others who ask these same strategic questions.

Provide methods for improving strategic thinking skills

Whether it is through internal workshops, external training, online modules, or other means, you must build the strategic thinking muscle within your organization. Consider ways to provide these thinking skills so that there is a common language and a common approach to addressing opportunities and issues through strategic thinking.

Model strategic thinking

Whether you lead the entire enterprise, a business unit, a department, or a team, you should yourself have a strategic plan that is developed by your team and monitored and executed using the three-step monitoring process. By demonstrating strategic thinking in action, your behavior serves as a model for others to emulate.

Summary

1. Strategic thinking is the process in which one or more people assess the current, envision a future, and define a path for creating that future.

2. Facilitative leaders recognize that the more people who are thinking strategically, the more who will be making decisions that have positive, long-term, sustainable impact on the organization.

3. The Drivers Model is a strategic thinking tool that covers seven key principles.

- Be clear on purpose.

- Start with an accurate assessment of today.

- Create a shared vision of success.

- Identify your critical successful factors and barriers.

- Define the drivers (i.e., your strategies and priorities).

- Monitor and report results.

- Have rewards and consequences to build accountability.

4. Strategic planning is a special form of strategic thinking that is applied in a more structured way and with structured deliverables.

5. The Drivers Model applied to strategic thinking includes the following components

   - Mission

   - Vision

   - Guiding principles

   - Positioning statements

   - Goals

   - Objectives

   - Critical success factors

   - Barriers

   - Strategies

   - Action plans

6. There are several important distinctions to keep in mind with these components.

   - **Mission versus Vision**. Mission defines what you do, for whom you do it, and the benefit; while vision defines your preferred picture of the future.

   - **Goals versus Objectives**. Goals are broad aims that define accomplishment of the mission, while objectives are specific, quantifiable, realistic targets that measure the accomplishment of a goal.

   - **Results versus Activity**. Objectives should measure results, not the activities performed to achieve the results.

   - **Strategies.** Strategies must achieve an objective, overcome a barrier, or create a critical condition for success.

   - **Action plans.** Action plans are needed to monitor the implementation of priority strategies

7. To ensure execution of a strategic plan, use a three-step monitoring process

- **Monthly**: "Are we doing what we said we were going to do?" Track the progress of action plans to ensure progress is being made on the priority strategies.

- **Quarterly**: "Are we getting the results we expected to get?" Track the progress of the objectives to ensure the results are being achieved.

- **Annually**: "Are we going in the right direction?" Meet annually to review progress for the year, reassess the current condition, identify new barriers and CSFs, update objectives, and reestablish priorities and action plans.

8. A facilitative leader has three critical roles in driving strategic thinking throughout the organization.

- Promote strategic thinking by consistently asking the strategic questions.

- Provide training, resources, and tools for your people to build and exercise strategic thinking skills.

- Model strategic thinking by having and executing a strategic plan for your area.

Spring Forward

As described in this chapter, facilitative leaders play three critical roles in driving strategic thinking in their organization to help more and more leaders move to level-3 leadership. What are you doing today in each of these roles, and what might you do differently to help improve your organization's strategic thinking capability?

Role	What are you doing today?	What steps can you take to enhance even more?
PROMOTE strategic thinking by consistently asking the strategic questions.		
PROVIDE training, resources and tools for your people to build and exercise strategic thinking skills.		
MODEL strategic thinking by having and executing a strategic plan for your area.		

- The Masterful Meeting Quiz
- What Is a Masterful Meeting?
- Meeting Rights
- Masterful Preparation
- Meeting Participants
- Masterful Start
- The Type-B Question
- Maintaining Focus
- PeDeQs to Provide Clear Directions
- Recording Information
- Preventing, Detecting, and Resolving Dysfunction
- Closing the Meeting
- Sample Meeting Notes
- Leading Virtual Meetings
- Checklists
- Summary
- Spring Forward

Chapter 10.
Start, Execute, and Close
Every Meeting Masterfully

In the business world, meetings are the arena in which leaders make decisions that impact organizational success. Whether the meeting is with two people or 200, the decisions that come out of meetings are critical. However, as described in Chapter 1, facilitative leaders understand that it is not the decision alone that matters. The effectiveness of that decision will be highly impacted by the buy-in and commitment of those impacted. Therefore, facilitative leaders pay close attention to ensure they run meetings in such a way as to maximize efficiency, effectiveness, and buy-in.

Unfortunately, based on comments from our workshop participants, meetings in most organizations don't come anywhere close to achieving these aspects. If you are the leader of a team, a department, or an entire organization, ask your people about the meetings they attend. You will find that many of the meetings your people attend are unproductive, ineffective, demotivating, or completely unnecessary.

Bad meetings waste time, consume resources, and wear down people's energy and passion. Still worse, bad meetings often result in decisions which are poorly thought through, void of innovation, and missing the necessary buy-in for success. And yet even worse, we have lowered the bar so far that bad meetings have become the norm. We have accepted them as a necessary evil.

Perhaps not surprising is the conclusion that, judging from our workshops, bad meetings have become so common that most people don't know what a masterful meeting is. How do we know? We start our meetings workshops with a simple ten-question, true-or-false assessment about what makes a meeting masterful. If you were to randomly guess the answers, on average you would get 50 percent correct. So, if we assume that 65 percent is a passing grade, the results are quite surprising. **Less than half the people who take the masterful meeting quiz at the beginning of our classes pass!**

Why do so few people pass? I think it is because people have gotten so used to poor meeting behaviors that a bad meeting has become what is expected.

> In essence, people have become so accustomed to poor meetings, that a bad meeting is considered good.

The Masterful Meeting Quiz

The Masterful Meeting Quiz, Figure 10.1, provides ten true or false questions. Take the quiz before going through this chapter to determine if you know what a truly masterful meeting is.

Figure 10.1 – The Masterful Meetings Quiz

		True	False
1.	A key strategy in transforming meetings in an organization is to **establish meeting rights**.		
2.	Outside of logistics, the three **most important** things to know in preparing for a meeting are the 3 Ps: the participants, the desired products, and the process or agenda.		
3.	For **all or nearly all meetings**, the people you invite should understand the topics to be discussed, have a stake in the outcome, and be empowered to make a decision or a recommendation.		
4.	After introductions if necessary, meetings should **generally start** with a review of the agenda.		
5.	When formulating questions to get lots of ideas, the **most important attribute** of the question is that it is open-ended.		
6.	If the conversation goes off focus, the meeting leader should **allow the discussion to go on for a few minutes** to see if it gets back on topic.		
7.	When recording information on a flip chart, it is **okay to paraphrase** as long as you ask people for permission.		
8.	It is best if **no dysfunctions** occur in a meeting.		
9.	Before a meeting ends, the meeting leader should **always or almost always** review what was done, identify open issues, and define next steps.		
10.	A key strategy to keep people engaged in teleconferences and other virtual meetings is to **randomly call on people** during discussions.		

What is a Masterful Meeting?

I define a "Masterful Meeting" as follows:[23]

> A Masterful Meeting is a well-prepared, well-executed, and results-oriented meeting with a timely start, a decisive close, and a clear follow-up plan.

A masterful meeting has 18 key characteristics. As you read through the list, think about the percentage of the meetings you attend that have at least 12 of these 18 characteristics; that is, what percentage of the meetings you attend would receive a passing grade of 65% or more.

Figure 10.2 Characteristics of Masterful Meetings

<u>Preparation</u>

1. **Clear purpose, products, and agenda**
   The meeting leader defines the purpose, products, and agenda that validate the need for a meeting.

2. **Advance notification**
   Participants know the purpose, products, proposed agenda, and other key information about the meeting in advance.

3. **Right people—prepared and present**
   The right people are at the meeting. They arrive prepared, they arrive on time, and they stay for the duration.

4. **Right information**
   All necessary information is available at the meeting.

<u>Start</u>

5. **Timely start**
   The meeting starts on time.

6. **Purpose and products reviewed**
   At the start of the meeting, the meeting leader reviews the meeting's purpose and desired products.

7. **Key issues identified**
   Either during the meeting or in advance, all participants have a chance to identify key issues or topics that need to be discussed to achieve the purpose and products.

8. **Agenda confirmed**
   The meeting leader confirms the agenda and establishes time limits for each item. The leader may choose to adjust the agenda to ensure all key issues are discussed.

9. **Ground rules reviewed**
   The meeting leader reminds the participants of ground rules. Participants honor the ground rules throughout the meeting.

Execution

10. **Steady meeting flow**
    As the meeting flows from one agenda item to the next, the meeting leader reminds the participants of the purpose for each agenda item, how the agenda item fits into the overall meeting objective, and what the group is being asked to accomplish with the agenda item.

11. **Focused discussion**
    The discussion remains focused on the topic at hand. A topic is allowed to exceed its allotted time only with the expressed agreement of a majority and with full knowledge of the effect on the remaining agenda items.

12. **Positive, energetic participation**
    All participants are actively engaged throughout the meeting. They feel safe to speak openly and honestly. People talk and listen with respect. There is energized discussion and debate. No one dominates the discussion.

13. **Constructive conflict**
    Disagreement is encouraged and conflict is handled by participants asking questions, identifying strengths, defining concerns, and seeking new alternatives that maximize strengths and reduce concerns.

14. **Thoughtful decision making**
    Prior to making decisions, appropriate time is given to inviting input, identifying alternatives, and evaluating potential solutions.

Close and Follow-up

15. **Decisions and actions reviewed**
    During the meeting, issues that arise that are inappropriate for discussion are deferred to an issues list; decisions made and actions to be taken are documented. Prior to ending the meeting, all issues, decisions, and actions are reviewed, and appropriate action designated.

16. **Timely finish**
    The meeting ends on time.

17. **Summary provided**
    Following the meeting, a meeting summary is distributed to all participants. The meeting summary includes issues, decisions, actions, and relevant analysis.

18. **Follow up on actions**
    A follow-up process is put in place to ensure all assigned actions are performed.

This chapter will walk through the 10 survey questions and provide strategies that facilitative leaders use to make all of their meetings masterful.

Meeting Rights

	Meeting Quiz Question
True	1. A key strategy in transforming meetings in an organization is to **establish meeting rights**.

People often sit through bad meetings because they feel powerless to do anything about it. Often, when meetings start late, it is considered typical and acceptable. When the meeting leader is unprepared, no one says anything. Discussions go off topic over and over again, participants constantly interrupt one another, individuals check out, and meetings end without a clear understanding of what is going to happen next. Meetings feature all or some of the dysfunctions listed, or a host of others, and more times than not people sit through them and let it happen.

Imagine the impact if everyone in your organization was granted and exercised a set of meeting rights designed to empower participants to make bad meetings unacceptable. Consider what meetings would feel like if bad meeting behavior wasn't tolerated. Think about how much more effective and productive meetings could be if people were actually empowered to "just say no" to bad meetings by exercising their meeting rights.

Figure 10.3 provides an abbreviated version of a set of sample meeting rights. The abbreviated version gives the right but doesn't indicate an action the person can take to exercise the right. What follows is an example of an expanded version of the second meeting right. Leaders who adopt meeting rights should decide how each right should be exercised given the specific circumstances of their organization

Meeting Right II – Sample Expanded Version

You have the right to attend meetings that start on time. If, despite your repeated request for the meeting to begin, a meeting does not start within eight minutes of the scheduled start time, you have the right to leave the meeting unless a majority of participants agrees to delay the start.

However, granting a provocative list of rights could result in anarchy if you don't provide meeting leaders with a vision of what a masterful meeting looks like and strategies for executing masterful meetings on a regular basis.

Figure 10.3 Sample Meeting Rights

I. **Meeting Notice.**
You have the right to be informed about the purpose, expected products, and proposed agenda for a meeting, verbally or in writ¬ing, at least twenty-four hours in advance of the meeting.

II. **Timely Start.**
You have the right to attend meetings that start on time.

III. **Right People.**
You have the right to have all major viewpoints critical to decision-making represented at the meeting.

IV. **Right Information.**
You have the right to have the information necessary to facilitate decision-making available at the meeting.

V. **Ground Rules.**
You have the right to have agreed-upon ground rules respected in the meeting.

VI. **Focused Discussion.**
You have the right for meetings to stay focused on the topic of the meeting.

VII. **Input Opportunity.**
You have the right to have the opportunity to provide input and alternative views before decision-making occurs in the meeting.

VIII. **Meeting Recap.**
You have the right to hear a recap of (a) decisions made during the meeting, (b) actions to be taken, when and by whom, following the meeting, and (c) any outstanding issues to be discussed at a future meeting.

IX. **Timely Completion.**
You have the right to have your time respected by having meetings finish at or before the scheduled end time.

X. **No Retribution.**
You have the right to exercise Your Meeting Rights without fear of retribution or other consequences.

Masterful Preparation

	Meeting Quiz Question
False	2. Outside of logistics, the three **most important** things to know in preparing for a meeting are the 3 Ps: the participants, the desired products, and the process or agenda.

Many meetings fail due to a lack of planning and preparation. I have been told by several leaders that they frequently prepare for a meeting during the two minutes it takes to walk from their office to the room where the meeting is being held!

The 6 Ps of Preparation

Facilitative leaders understand that to do masterful preparation, at a minimum they should know the answers to the 6 Ps.

The 6 Ps of Preparation

- **Purpose**. Why am I holding this meeting?
- **Product**. What do I want to have when we are done that says the purpose has been achieved?
- **Participants**. Who are the participants who need to attend the meeting to create the products to achieve the purpose?
- **Probable Issues**. What are the issues that will likely need to be addressed by the participants to achieve the purpose and create the products?
- **Process**. What process or steps should we go through (i.e., the agenda) to develop the products that achieve the purpose, given the participants and probable issues?
- **Place**. Where will the meeting be held? What time? What materials? What room setup?

As you probably have surmised, purpose is the most important item in the list, as nearly all of the other Ps stem from it. Accordingly, the answer to the meetings quiz is "false" because the most important item, purpose, is missing from the list of the three most important Ps.

The 3 Hs of Product

In identifying the product for the session, I recommend that facilitative leaders break the product into the "3 Hs" by asking the following questions.

- **Hands**. What do I want people to have in their hands when the meeting is over?
- **Heads**. What do I want people to have in their heads when the meeting is over? That is, what do I want them to know that they didn't know before the meeting started?
- **Hearts**. What do I want people to have in their hearts when the meeting is over? That is, what do I want them to believe that they didn't believe before the meeting started?

Meeting Types

To effectively plan masterful meetings, facilitative leaders recognize two basic meeting types: status meetings and working meetings. The meeting type is determined by whether the primary focus of the participants will be reviewing or creating, as outlined in Figure 10.4.

Figure 10.4 Status versus Working Meetings

	Status Meeting	Working Meeting
Meeting Focus	Review	Creation
Meeting Flow	Primarily one-way	Primarily two-way
Typical Products	Information update, idea generation, feedback	Decision, issue resolution, action plan
Recommended Group Size	Unlimited	3–16
Typical Length	30–90 minutes	1–8 hours
Typical Frequency	Weekly, monthly	As needed

The Differences

- While status meetings are designed to review progress or gain feedback, working meetings are designed to create a decision, action plan, or some other product.

- Status meetings are primarily one-way communication and therefore can have three, thirty, or even three hundred people in attendance.

- Working meetings require two-way communication and should have a much smaller number of participants.

- Finally, while status meetings tend to be relatively short since they are review meetings, working meetings tend to be longer because creation typically takes more time.

Unfortunately, one of the most common problems with status meetings is that they become working meetings! That is, in the middle of the status meeting, the meeting leader discovers a problem and then takes the meeting off course by transforming it from a status meeting to a working meeting focused on solving problems. This transformation from status to working meeting happens so frequently that many reading this book may wonder why I might consider it a negative activity. Think about the following example.

- Consider a status meeting with eight people, each one of whom is allocated about seven minutes to provide a status update as part of a one-hour meeting.

- Suppose that, during the second person's status update, the meeting leader identifies a problem and takes five minutes with this person to identify ways to solve it and six minutes on the status update.

- Then, during the fourth person's turn, the leader identifies another problem and takes an additional eight minutes with the fourth person to address it along with five minutes for the status update.

- You probably get the point: By the time the seventh and eighth people get their turns, they will be rushing through their status updates because there will be limited time remaining. And what if the most critical issues needing to be addressed are in their areas, but they are given short shrift because the meeting focused on less important issues?

- But perhaps worse, consider what the other team members in the status meeting may have been doing while the leader was holding ad hoc working meetings with a couple of individuals in the middle of the status meeting. Essentially, the leader may have been wasting the time of the other team members who may have been unaffected, uninterested, or unable to provide any worthwhile input during these ad hoc working meetings.

> Facilitative leaders understand: Status meetings are for status; working meetings are for working; and never the twain shall meet!

When an issue that requires solving is identified in a status meeting, facilitative leaders add the issue to the "Issue List" of items to be addressed when the status meeting is over. Prior to the close of the status meeting, the facilitative leader with the team prioritizes the items on the issues list and sets duration times for each one; then the working meeting begins. What do people do who can't contribute to the issues? They can exit the meeting and use their time in a much more productive way.

And just as status meetings can degenerate into working meetings, working meetings can degenerate into multiple working meetings. That is, while a working meeting is typically designed to address a specific issue, meeting leaders often permit the discussion to wander off into other topics. The result: time is wasted debating issues that would be better addressed in a different working meeting.

Meeting Participants

False	Meeting Quiz Question 3. For **all or nearly all meetings**, the people you invite should understand the topics to be discussed, have a stake in the outcome, and be empowered to make a decision or recommendation.

Who are the right participants for a meeting? That depends on the meeting type as follows.

Participants for a Status Meeting

- Those who need to know or their representatives

Participants for a Working Meeting

Each participant should:

- Understand the issue

- Have a stake in the outcome

- Be empowered to make a decision or recommendation

The answer to the quiz question is "false" because the question asks, *"For all or nearly all meetings..."* The criteria given are just appropriate for working meetings and do not cover the criteria for status meetings. Why should each participant in a working meeting have the characteristics listed above? See the discussion of the selection of team members in Chapter 7 for a more detailed explanation.

Masterful Start

False	Meeting Quiz Question 4. After introductions if necessary, meetings should **generally start** with a review of the agenda.

Meeting leaders often start meetings by reviewing the agenda—if they have one—and then diving straight into the first agenda item. As a result, participants often aren't sure of the purpose of the meeting, the products to be produced, why the meeting is beneficial, or why the meeting should be important to them. In essence, meetings often have an ineffective start that can negatively affect the rest of the meeting.

Inform, Excite, Empower, Involve

As described in Chapter 3, facilitative leaders understand the importance of starting every meeting with *the why*, that is, starting with the purpose. A masterful start to a meeting accomplishes four goals in particular.

Inform   Provide the purpose and product; that is, explain why the meeting is being held and what products will be produced as a result of the meeting.

Excite   Describe the benefits to the participants for achieving the purpose and the products.

Empower   Let participants know what they are being asked to do. Are they making a decision, making a recommendation, just brainstorming ideas, et cetera?

Involve   Get participants involved and interacting by posing a question to them that will further the work of the meeting.

As a model for starting a meeting masterfully, consider the following:

- The purpose of this meeting is… (Inform: purpose)
- When we are done, we will walk away with… (Inform: product)
- This is exciting because… (Excite: benefits)
- You have been empowered by… to… (Empower: their role)
- Before we get started, I would like to ask a question about… (Involve: key topics)

Review the Agenda and Ground Rules

After you inform, excite, empower, and involve, the next step is to review the agenda and remind participants of the ground rules and the parking boards. Ground rules provide a vehicle for gaining agreement on a set of behaviors that will guide how participants interact with one another. A sample set of ground rules follows.

Sample Ground Rules

- Start and end on time.
- Everyone speaks.
- Have one conversation.
- No beeps, buzzes, or ringy-dingies.
- Only work on the meeting during the meeting.
- Take a stand.
- Be soft on people, hard on ideas.
- Use the parking boards.

Explain the Parking Boards

During a meeting, people will often bring up topics that are not directly related to the meeting's purpose but will be covered in a later agenda item. Additionally, there will be times during the meeting that decisions will be made or follow-up actions identified. In each of these cases, consider "parking" the information on a flip chart or some other vehicle so that everyone is aware of it.

For most meetings, I find three parking boards are particularly useful as follows.

Three Common Parking Boards

- **Issues list**: Topics that need to be discussed later in the meeting or entirely outside the meeting.

- **Decisions list**: Decisions made by the group that should be documented for future reference.

- **Actions list**: Actions to be performed sometime after the completion of the meeting.

At the beginning of the meeting, quickly review the purpose of the parking boards. Note that the parking boards appear as the last ground rule, making for an easy transition to discussing them.

The Type-B Question

	Meeting Quiz Question
False	5. When formulating questions to get many ideas, the **most important attribute** of the question is that it is open-ended.

Recall that in the "involve" step of a masterful start, you get participants involved and interacting by posing a question to them that will further the work of the meeting. This step engages everyone early in interaction and prepares them for the rest of the meeting.

What question do you ask and, more importantly, how do you ask it? Here are three sample "involve" questions which I classify as type-A questions.

Sample Involve Questions (Type-A)

- What are the key topics we need to talk about?

- What are the outcomes you personally would like to see come out of today's meeting?

- What is a significant event that has happened to you since we were last together?

Contrast these three questions with the type-B questions that follow, which attempt to get at the same answers but in a different way. Which question type is more likely to generate many responses, type-A or type-B, and why?

Sample Involve Questions (Type-B)

- Key Topics
    - I have just gone over the purpose of today's meeting.
    - Given this purpose, think about the topics that you know we need to cover to accomplish the purpose.
    - Think about the specific issues that we have to address or maybe specific ideas that we should discuss.
    - Let's build the list. If we are going to be successful today, what are the key topics we need to talk about?

- Personal Outcomes
    - Let's assume this meeting was highly successful.
    - Think about the results, the outcomes that occurred, and the things that would make you say, "This was a great meeting."
    - Let's build the list. Given our purpose and products, what are the outcomes you personally would like to see from today's meeting?

- One-Minute Check-In Approach
    - It has been several days since we were all together. Let's start with each person giving a quick one-minute check-in.
    - We were last together on [date]. Think about the significant events that have happened since that time, either personally or professionally.
    - Think about things that have made your smile, or things that may have been challenging since we were last together.
    - Let's go around the room. What is a significant event that has happened to you since we were last together?

Why is Type-B Better?

In our workshops our participants tell us repeatedly that, although they are wordy, the type-B questions are far superior to the type-A questions. But did you notice? All six questions are open ended. Therefore, the reason the type-B questions are better can't be because they are open-ended. It must be something else. Therefore, the answer to the quiz question is indeed false.

What makes the type-B questions better?

> Type-B questions are better because they create an image
> that helps participants visualize their answers. When that
> happens, participants respond right away.

The Format of a Type-B Question

How do you create a type-B question? Type-B questions use a specific format based on what I call the secret of the starting question.[24] To construct a type-B question, use the three steps shown in figure 10.5.

Figure 10.5 Formatting Type-B Questions

> - **Start with an image-building phrase** (e.g., "Think about... Imagine... Consider... If...").
> - **Extend the image** so the participants can see their answers. This usually takes two or three additional phrases.
> - **Ask the direct question** (type-A) to which you desire to know the answer.

By contrast, type-A questions ask what you, the meeting leader, want to know. If you want to know the key topics your meeting participants want to discuss, you ask, "What key topics do you want to discuss?" If you want to know what significant events have happened to them since the team was last together, you ask, "What significant events have happened to you since we were last together?" Type-A questions are asked frequently because they are easy. However, if you simply ask the type-A question, participants tend to become silent as they try to visualize their answers. With the type-B starting question, however, you make it easier for your participants to respond, because you create the image for them and they can begin answering right away because they can see their answers.

When to Use a Type-B Question

When do you use type-B questions? You should use type-B questions at the beginning of a meeting to engage participants and also at any time you want them to provide a lot of responses, such as when identifying steps in a process, brainstorming potential strategies, and listing alternatives.

Figure 10.6 includes samples of type-A questions and the much better type-B questions.

Figure 10.6 Sample Type-A and Type-B Questions

Type-A Question	Type-B Question
How does the performance review process work today; what are the steps?	I would like to build a list of the steps in the current performance review process. Imagine that you have a great employee who performs extremely well year after year, and you want to make sure you cover all the bases in the performance review process to ensure that she receives a very positive review. Think about all the steps that you or she would have to take as part of the performance review process, all the things that would have to be done early in the year, late in the year, et cetera. Let's build the list. What are the steps in our current performance review process?
What are the problems with the current process?	Think about our last performance review cycle. Consider the things that were real problems, the things that frustrated you, the things that worked very poorly, or the things that were just real problems. What things made you say, "There's got to be a better way to do this?" What are some of those frustrating problems with the current performance review process?
What are things we could do to improve the current process?	We are ready to build a list of things to do to improve the performance review process. Look over the problems we need to fix. Consider things we could do to solve them. Think about things you have seen implemented in other places. Consider how technology might be used to improve the performance review process or ways that we can better organize to get the work done. Let your mind see all the possibilities that we might consider. Let's list some of the ideas that could be put in place to improve our process. Who wants to start?

Maintaining Focus

	Meeting Quiz Question
False	6. If the conversation goes off focus, the meeting leader should **allow the discussion to go on for a few minutes** to see if it gets back on topic.

Facilitative leaders know the importance of carefully monitoring the discussion in a meeting to ensure that comments and questions are related to the topic at hand. If the group begins to detour to an unrelated topic, they bring the group back on course by using a redirection question and placing the topic on the issues list if needed.

The Redirection Question

For example, the leader might say:

"That's an interesting point. Can we put it on the issues list so we don't lose it, and then focus back on...?"

As indicated by the response to the meeting quiz question, I do not recommend allowing the conversation to continue in hopes that it gets back on track. Off-topic comments are, significantly more times than not, followed by another off-topic comment which can take the discussion even further away from the subject of the meeting. Accordingly, redirect conversations immediately to avoid wasting time on unrelated topics.

In addition, to prevent potential dysfunction, remember to always ask permission before redirecting a comment to the issues list. By asking, you secure the participant's buy-in. What do you do if you ask for permission to table an issue and the participant disagrees? You may find it helpful to put the question to the group.

The Checkpoint

While there are numerous strategies for maintaining focus in a meeting, there are two that are critical and worth mentioning here: the checkpoint and "PeDeQs" for giving directions.

At the beginning of every agenda item, facilitative leaders should take a checkpoint to get everyone on the same page.

Taking a Checkpoint

- **Review**: Quickly cover what has been done to date.

- **Preview**: Describe briefly what the group is about to do.

- **Big View**: Explain how the previewed agenda item fits into the meeting's overall purpose.

The checkpoint serves to ensure that all participants are aware that a transition is occurring. It also helps participants understand why the item is on the agenda and how it fits into the meeting's purpose. Finally, when you give a checkpoint at the beginning of every agenda item, the participants experience a smooth transition as you guide them through the meeting.

Sample Checkpoint

- ❑ We have just talked about how the performance review process works today. (*Review*)

- ❑ Our next step is to identify the problems and root causes to those problems. (*Preview*)

- ❑ This is important because by identifying the problems and their root causes, we will be able to create solutions to the causes of these problems which will result in a much better performance review process. (*Big View*)

PeDeQs to Provide Clear Directions

After the checkpoint, you might ask your meeting participants to engage in some type of activity, such as brainstorming or working in small teams. Depending on the activity, the quality of the directions that you provide can affect the success of that next step. A key to running masterful meetings is delivering quality directions.

When giving directions, good meeting leaders describe what the participants are to do. However, facilitative leaders describe what to do, how to do it, and why doing it is important.

To ensure you cover the what, how, and why, consider giving directions by stepping through the PeDeQs.

Providing Directions Using PeDeQs

- Give the overall **P**urpose of the activity.

- When appropriate, use a simple **E**xample that is outside the topic area.

- Give general **D**irections, using verbal pictures and gestures.

- Give specific **E**xceptions and special cases.

- Ask for **Q**uestions.

- Ask a **S**tarting Question that gets participants visualizing the answers.

As an example, suppose you want the participants in the meeting to identify the problems that occur in the organization's performance review process. Along with identifying the problems, you also want to identify the symptom and root causes for each of the problems. Figure 10.7 provides a sample of the table that might be used for such an activity.

Figure 10.7 Sample Table for Problems, Symptoms, and Root Causes

Problem	Symptom	Root Cause

What follows is the dialogue you might use to give PeDeQs directions for completing the table.

Sample PeDeQs Dialogue

- We will use this table to help identify the problems, symptoms, and root causes related to the performance review process. *(Purpose)*

- For example, if we wanted to drive our car to take a trip, a problem might be a flat tire. The symptom might be that there is no air in the tire. The root cause might be that I haven't put air in the tire for a while. What else might be a root cause? *(Example)*

- Of course, we're not taking a trip in a car. We are analyzing the problems with the performance review process. Here's how we will do it. First we will list all the problems. Then, once we have identified the problems, we will then determine the symptom and root cause for each problem. *(Directions)*

- Now, there are a few other things you need to know. While we are discussing problems, you may come up with a root cause. I will place it in the root cause list until we identify the problem related to it. Likewise, after we list all the problems and are talking about symptoms and root causes you may mention a new problem, and I will add it to the bottom of the problem list. *(Exceptions)*

- Any questions? *(Questions)*

- Okay, think about our last performance review cycle. Consider the things that were real problems, the things that frustrated you, and the things that worked very poorly, took too long, or were problematic in other ways. What things made you say, "There's got to be a better way to do this?" What are some of those frustrating problems with the current performance review process? *(Type-B Starting Question)*

Recording Information

	Meeting Quiz Question
False	7. When recording information on a flip chart, it is **okay to paraphrase** as long as you ask people for permission.

After doing a checkpoint, providing directions, and getting the agenda item initiated, the meeting leader should record—or have someone else record—the information provided by the participants. Unfortunately, few meeting leaders truly understand the power of the pen. For when meeting leaders don't record what participants say or when meeting leaders paraphrase by recording their own words and not the words of the participants, they are abusing the power of the pen. And, unfortunately, the meeting leader's abuse of the pen can very easily lead to dysfunctional behavior by the participants—such as dropping out, arguing with the facilitator, and not buying in to the overall result.

How Leaders Abuse the Power of the Pen

How do leaders "abuse" the power of the pen? One very common occurrence is when meeting leaders listen to a participant's statement, then transform what is said into words more "acceptable" to the meeting leader. Why do they change the words?

- Some meeting leaders indicate they change the words to summarize the idea.
- Others say they transform the words to promote clarity.
- And still others say they are just trying to shorten the comment to make it easier to write.

Whatever the reason for changing a participant's words, the potential negative impact on empowerment may far outweigh the benefit.

- If you try to clean up the speaker's words by writing words he or she did not say, you as the meeting leader are implicitly saying, "You don't know how to speak; let me speak for you."
- Over time, less assertive participants will tend to get lazy and look to you to "make all their words better;" more assertive participants will tend to compete with you to come up with suitable words for the other participants.
- In addition, rewriting comments in your own words decreases the likelihood that participants will still be able to understand what was meant after time has passed. This effect is a result of you using words and expressions in ways that are familiar to you, but which might not be the way the participants express these same ideas.
- Finally, writing your words can decrease the participants' ownership of the result, since the words are yours, not theirs.

Write First, Discuss Second

How do facilitative leaders avoid abusing the power of the pen? One of the ways is to write first and discuss second. Consider the following:

- If what is said is incomplete, you should write it.
- If what is said can be improved upon, write it.
- If what is said is not the answer you were looking for, write it.
- If what is said is obviously wrong, still write it.

By recording what is said, you, as the meeting leader, are implicitly saying, "Thank you for making a contribution." It is vital to positive group dynamics that this happen regardless of whether the contribution is good, bad, or indifferent. Each time you record a contribution, you are saying "thank you." If you stop saying thank you, participants may very well stop contributing.

There are other benefits to writing first as well.

- Writing first helps prevent your opinion about a comment influencing whether the comment gets recorded.

- Writing first prevents you from slowing down the activity because you have to ask, "What did you say again?"

- Writing first helps make sure you record their words and not yours.

- Writing first helps you—the meeting leader—stay on track. Should a long discussion ensue, you will always be able to refocus by looking at the last thing you wrote.

What Should be Recorded?

Facilitative leaders know that there are only four items that need to be documented in a meeting.

Items to Document in a Meeting

- **Decisions** made during the meeting.
- **Actions** assigned during the meeting.
- **Issues** that come up in the meeting to be discussed later.
- **Relevant analysis and comments** covered during the meeting.

Consider using a flip chart, LCD projection, or some other vehicle so that people can see the recorded comments. Why is it important for people to see what is recorded?

Benefits of Having Participants See what is Recorded

- Keeps everyone focused on the same topic.
- Discourages participants from repeating comments previously made.
- Helps ensure that comments are recorded accurately.
- Allows participants to easily and accurately refer to earlier comments.

Preventing, Detecting, and Resolving Dysfunction

True	Meeting Quiz Question
	8. It is best if **no dysfunctions** occur in a meeting.

In our workshops, we define dysfunctional behavior as follows.[25]

> Dysfunctional behavior is any participant activity that is consciously or unconsciously a substitution for expressing displeasure with the meeting content, the meeting process, or outside factors.

This definition has three important implications.

- **Behavior, not the person, is dysfunctional.** In one meeting a person may be actively and cooperatively participating, but in the next meeting that same person's behavior may turn dysfunctional. In fact, the transition from functional to dysfunctional can occur in the same meeting multiple times!

- **Dysfunctional behavior may be conscious or unconscious.** Oftentimes people exhibiting signs of dysfunction are not aware of the behavior. Other times the behavior is intentional in an effort to bring about change, disruption, or some other action.

- **Dysfunction is a substitution**. Dysfunctional meeting behavior often serves as a substitute for expressing displeasure related to the meeting content or process or to an outside factor. For example, the content issue might be that a comment was made with which the participant strongly disagrees. If the displeasure is with the process, it might be that the participant feels that the pace is too fast or that the process is interfering with the real work. If the displeasure relates to an outside factor, it might be that there is an issue in the participant's personal life that has left the participant distracted and unable to focus on the session.

Since dysfunctional behavior is a substitute for expressing displeasure, facilitative leaders know that the best dysfunctions are those that don't occur. Why? Because their goal is to do the preparation work to prevent displeasure from occurring; but if displeasure does occur, they want participants to express it openly and not substitute a dysfunctional behavior. Accordingly, "true" is the answer to the meeting quiz question.

How should you respond to a dysfunction? Of course, this depends on the dysfunction and other factors, including when it occurs, the number of people affected, and the probable root cause. However, consider the following general formula.

General Formula for Addressing Dysfunction

- Approach privately or generally.
  - Either speak with the person one-on-one during a break, or address the behaviors generally to the group without singling out any individuals. At times, however, singling out an individual during the meeting may be unavoidable.

- Empathize with the symptom.
  - Praise an appropriate aspect of their behavior or express concern about the situation in which they find themselves.
- Address the root cause.
  - Make an effort to get at the real issue by asking a question that will yield a response that confirms the issue.
- Get agreement on the solution.
  - Get agreement on how the situation will be handled going forward. Be sure that the solution addresses the root cause and not just the symptom.

With each of the common dysfunctions that follow, I have provided a description of the dysfunction, strategies to take to prevent the dysfunction, and what to do "in the moment" when the dysfunction occurs. While most descriptions are for individual dysfunctions, the last two are dysfunctions related to the entire group.

Cell Phone Junkie

The person's cell phone constantly rings, or the person is on and off the cell phone frequently.

Prevention

- Establish a ground rule: no cell phone calls during the meeting.

In the Moment

If a private conversation is possible:

- "It looks like people don't know you're in an important meeting, so they keep interrupting you. Have you been able to get the problem addressed? Is it okay then to turn the cell phone off for the rest of the meeting?"

If a private conversation is *not* possible:

- "When I heard Tony's phone, it was a reminder to me that we need to keep cell phones off if we can. I want to check in with the group to make sure this won't be a problem."

Door Slammer

The person leaves the room in apparent disgust.

Prevention

- Establish a ground rule: everyone speaks about issues in the room; we will discuss the undiscussable.

In the Moment

- "Wow, Bill just got up and left the room. Given what felt like abruptness, I don't think it was because he had to go to the rest room."

- "We could try to continue working, but I bet many people are thinking about Bill's departure. So I would like to take a few minutes to get clarity on what just happened. Who can take a shot at explaining what happened and why you think it happened?"

- "So we have talked about what happened, and we have a guess as to why it may have happened. Now I have two other questions. What should we do about Bill? And what needs to happen differently to keep the rest of us from doing what Bill just did?"

- By taking a few minutes for debriefing, the group creates a common view of the incident.

Drop-out

The person does not participate in the discussion.

Prevention

- Establish a ground rule: everyone speaks.

In the Moment

- "Let's hear from everyone on this next point. With this question, I would like to start with [give the name of a person two seats to the right of the drop-out] and go around the room to her left. The question is..."

- A round-robin brainstorming activity such as this gets everyone involved. By starting two people before the dropout, you avoid putting the person on the spot and provide the person time to prepare an answer.

Interrupter

The person interrupts others or finishes their sentences.

Prevention

- Establish a ground rule: have one conversation; respect the speaker.

In the Moment

- Interrupt the person.

- "It can be hard sometimes to avoid interrupting when you really want to say something, but we should stick to our ground rules. Can you hold that thought for a moment so that the person who was speaking has the opportunity to finish?"

Late Arriver/Early Leaver

The person habitually arrives late to the meeting or leaves early.

Prevention

- Distribute the meeting notice ahead of time. Indicate a gathering time of five to ten minutes prior to the start time. Indicate the importance of the purpose and products for the meeting.

- Contact the person in advance to gain commitment to be present for the entire meeting. Get agreement that the meeting should start on time with whomever is present.

In the Moment

- "I want to thank everyone for being here when you could get here and for continuing to do all you can to arrange your schedules so that we can start on time. Our next topic..."

Loudmouth

The person dominates the discussion.

Prevention

- Establish a ground rule: have one conversation; share the air.

- Meet in advance to let the person know that you will be trying to get others to speak.

- "I appreciate you being willing to speak, especially given that most have been pretty quiet. I need to get other people speaking more so that we can get their views on the table. So, during this next meeting, there will be times when you might hear me say, 'Nice point. Let's hear from some others on this.' This way, we'll get everyone's input."

In the Moment

- "Let's hear from everyone on this next point. With this question, I would like to start with [give the name of a person to the left of the loudmouth] and go around the room to his left. The question is..."

- A round-robin brainstorming activity such as this gets everyone involved. By directing the conversation away from the loudmouth, everyone else will be able to provide input first.

Naysayer

The person makes audible sighs of displeasure or negative statements such as "That won't work" without offering solutions.

Prevention

- Establish ground rules: benefits first (i.e., give the strengths of an idea before identifying problems); take a stand (i.e., rather than describe what won't work, describe what will).

In the Moment

- Say with optimism, "You may be right. How do we make it better?"
- Naysayers often express their views negatively without offering alternatives. Avoid a debate about whether something is wrong by focusing their attention on creating something better.

Physical Attacker

The person physically attacks someone.

Prevention

- Identify probable issues prior to the meeting.
- Establish ground rules: discuss the undiscussable; be soft on people but hard on ideas.
- Actively keep the conversation focused on seeking solutions rather than assigning blame.

In the Moment

- Stop the meeting immediately.
- Let the group know they will be notified when the next meeting is scheduled.
- It is inappropriate to try to reschedule the meeting then since a physical attack can restart while the attempt to reschedule is going on.
- Contact security or the human resources department if appropriate.

Storyteller

The person likes to tell long-winded stories. Establish a ground rule: share the air.

Prevention

- Meet in advance to let the person know that you will have limited discussion time in the meeting.
- "I can readily see how stories give people a stronger picture of the point you are making. One of the concerns I have is that I've noticed sometimes people drop out when you begin a story. Is there a way that you can make your end point first and then shorten the story so that most will be able to follow? This may also mean that

we can get to more things during our meeting... . So, during this next meeting, if I perceive that you may be starting a story, you might hear me say, 'Let's give the end point first so that people will be able to follow you better.'"

In the Moment

- "Let's remember the ground rule to give the end point first and keep it brief so that people will be able to follow along better."

Topic Jumper

The person frequently takes the group off topic.

Prevention

- Establish a ground rule: have one conversation; one topic at a time.

In the Moment

- Consider seeking an agreement with the person to make an effort to use the issues list when new topics come up.

Verbal Attacker

The person makes a negative comment about or directed at someone.

Prevention

- Identify probable issues prior to the meeting.
- Establish ground rules: discuss the undiscussable; be soft on people but hard on ideas.
- Actively keep the conversation focused on seeking solutions rather than assigning blame.

In the Moment

- Move between the people to cut off the debate, then slow down the discussion and reestablish order.
- "Let's take a timeout here. We have important issues to discuss, and we have established ground rules to help us do this. One of our ground rules is to be soft on people and hard on ideas. We will unlikely be successful if our focus is on blame or finger-pointing. I would like to continue the discussion, if we can, but only if we can do so respectfully and with an understanding of the problems and a focus on developing solutions. Can we do this?"

Whisperer

The person holds side conversations during the meeting.

Prevention

- Establish a ground rule: one conversation.

In the Moment

- "Let's remember the ground rule that we want to have one conversation in the room so that we are respectful of the speaker and other listeners."
- Privately, if possible, give the "shhh" sign with one finger to your lips if the whispering continues.

Workaholic

The person does other work during the meeting.

Prevention

- Establish a ground rule: meeting work only (i.e., work on only the meeting during the meeting).

In the Moment

If a private conversation is possible:

- "It looks like you have some important work to get done and this meeting has put you in a crunch. We do need your full attention if we can get it. Is this work something you can do later?"

If a private conversation is *not* possible:

- "I know we established the ground rule of only doing meeting work during the meeting. I want to make sure that the ground rule will still work for everyone."

Group: Low Energy

Energy in the room is low.

Prevention

- Ensure topics and speakers are appropriate for the audience.
- Plan the agenda to ensure that the group is highly engaged during low-energy periods.
- Have the group establish a simple recharge activity (e.g., "the wave") for use when the energy dips.

In the Moment

- "I'm sensing that the energy in the room is dipping pretty low. Let's quickly do our recharge activity to get the energy up."

- During low energy times, consider using round-robins in order to get everyone involved, (e.g., "Let's go around the room and get everyone's answer to this next question...")

Group: Time Pressures

You are running out of time.

Prevention

- While reviewing the agenda at the start of the meeting, establish target times for each agenda item.
- Put the items that are less critical near the end of the agenda.
- Use a timer to track time spent; alert the group when nearing the scheduled time for an item.
- Be flexible, allowing additional time when warranted and acceptable to the group but ending discussions when appropriate.

In the Moment

- "We have hit our time limit with this item. Can we end the discussion here, or do we need additional time... ? Okay, let's give it an additional five minutes, but let's see if we can wrap it up even sooner."
- "It looks like that at the rate we are going we will not be able to spend the time we need to have a thoughtful discussion on the last agenda item. Does it make sense to move this one to our next meeting, or is another alternative more appropriate?"

Closing the Meeting

	Meeting Quiz Question
True	9. Before a meeting ends, the meeting leader should **always or almost always** review what was done, identify open issues, and define next steps.

Once all agenda items have been covered, it is time to close the meeting. Before closing, however, there are a number of items to be covered, and after closing follow-up is often needed. The closing typically can take as little as five minutes, but often can go 45 minutes or longer depending on the size of the group and the steps you use.

While the list that follows shows all the steps for closing, facilitative leaders adjust the list as appropriate for each meeting. However, those items asterisked (*) should be done for every meeting regardless of the length or number of participants.

Closing Steps

- *Review the items covered in the meeting.
- *Confirm the decisions made.
- *Address outstanding issues.
- *Ensure that all actions have names and dates assigned.
- Evaluate the meeting.
- *Thank participants, and end the meeting.
- Document and distribute meeting notes.
- *Follow-up to hold people accountable for assigned actions.

*Recommended for all meetings

In the sections that follow, I review strategies for each of these steps.

Review Items Covered in the Meeting

Before ending the meeting, go back to the agenda and review all the activities completed during the meeting.

- The review provides the participants with a reminder of what was done. It also can provide a sense of accomplishment.
  - "Let's step through the agenda and identify what has been accomplished during this meeting."
- If key topics or participant outcomes were identified, review each one to ensure coverage.
  - "Let's also ensure that each key topic you identified earlier has been covered, and determine if we need to add any of them to the agenda for our next meeting."

Confirm Decisions Made

Next, review the decision list, found on the parking board used to record decisions.

- The goal of the decision review is to **remind the team of the decisions** that have been made.
  - "Let's next review the decisions we made during this meeting. I will walk through each one. Stop me if any one of them is not recorded correctly."
- Following the meeting, participants may be asked why specific decisions were made. To prepare participants for the discussion, as an optional activity, consider taking time in the closing to **document the benefits of each decision**.

- "To help ensure that we all understand why each decision was made, let's take a moment to add one or two bullet points to each decision to document the benefit we expect to gain. Let's start with this first one, which says... . Think about the benefits to be gained from this. Let's list one or two of these."

Address Outstanding Issues

The issues list was the place that you parked topics that arose during the meeting that either needed to be covered at a later time or were completely irrelevant to the meeting. At the end of the meeting, it is important to clear all remaining items off of the issues list.

Questions to Ask to Clear the Issues List

As a systematic way to quickly process the issue list, ask these questions in the following order for each issue:

- "Have we covered it?" (If so, move on to the next issue.)
- "Do we need to cover it?" (If not, move on to the next issue and ask the first question.)
- "Do we need to cover it now?"
  - Yes: Set a time limit and lead the discussion.
  - No: Move the issue to the action list.

Assign Actions

The actions list contains activities to be performed sometime after the completion of the meeting. Figure 10.8 provides a format for the action list.

Figure 10.8 Action List Table

Action	Who	When
1.		
2.		
3.		

Questions to Ask about Actions

- "Does this action still need to be accomplished?" (If no, discard it and move on to the next action.)
- "Who should do it?"

- It is not appropriate to assign an action to someone not in the room.

- If the action is best performed by someone outside the room, assign it to a person of authority in the room who will then ask the other person to perform the action.

- "By what date will you have it completed?"

  - Note that the date for the action is set AFTER determining the person who will take on the action.

  - Facilitative leaders know that having the person responsible for the action set the date for completion builds accountability and a sense of responsibility for action.

Evaluate the Meeting

Feedback from meeting participants can provide valuable insights on how to continuously improve meetings. Consider the following feedback steps.

1. Start with strengths.

   - "Let's start with strengths. I would like to go around the room, starting with Andrea. I would like all of us to identify one thing we liked about the meeting and the way we worked together. If someone has already said the thing you like, feel free to say, for example, 'Ditto number one.'"

   - "So, think about the things you liked about the meeting, the things that went well, the times that people seemed to be engaged, and the things that really worked. Let's build the list. Andrea, get me started. What did you like about the meeting? What went well?"

2. Rate the meeting.

   - "Let's rate the meeting on our key criteria. Remember our rating system: three means the meeting was well done, two means it was adequate, and one means it was insufficient. How would you rate..."

Preparation and start?	The meeting notice, participants preparation, on-time start, clear purpose, and appropriate agenda
Staying focused?	Keeping on track and at the appropriate level of detail
Group dynamics?	Working together, everyone engaged, handling conflict, and minimizing dysfunction
The results?	Good decisions, clear actions, and follow-up plan
Overall?	All aspects of the meeting

3. Move on to ways to improve.

- "We've talked about strengths and rated the meeting. Let's move on to ways to improve. I would like to open it up. We do not have to go in any order. Take a look at the ratings, especially the lower ones. Think about the things that could have happened that would have improved these ratings. Consider things we might want to do differently next time. What would you suggest are things that would have made the meeting even better? Who wants to go first?"

4. Review each improvement suggestion and ask for a show of hands of those who support each.

- "Let's go back now over each improvement suggestion. I would like to get a rough indication of the level of support for each one. As I read each suggestion, please raise your hand if you agree with that suggestion. The first says... . How many people agree that this suggestion would have improved the meeting? That looks like about eighty percent. Let's move on to the next... ."

Thank Participants and End the Meeting

Finally, end the meeting by expressing to the participants your appreciation for their attendance, reminding them of the next steps, and adjourning the meeting.

- "Thank you for participating in this meeting."
- "You should be receiving documentation of this meeting within seven days."
- "Our next meeting is on [date] at [time] in this same room. I will see you all then."
- "This meeting is officially adjourned!"

Document and Distribute Meeting Notes

What should be documented and included in the meeting notes? Consider the following (as above, while not all items are required in the documentation that follows every meeting, the asterisked (*) items should always be documented):

Items to Document in Meeting Notes

- *Decisions** made during the meeting.
- *Actions** assigned during the meeting.
- **Issues** that come up in the meeting to be discussed later.
- **Relevant analysis and comments** covered during the meeting.

The final documentation will also include notes added by the documenter to add clarity or build context for the reader. Consider italicizing notes added by the documenter to differentiate these notes from information provided by the participants. An example of meeting notes appears on the next page.

Follow Up to Hold People Accountable

To ensure that actions assigned during the meeting are accomplished, consider follow-up actions such as the following:

Strategies to Encourage Follow-Through on Actions

- In the body of the letter or e-mail that accompanies the meeting notes, remind the participants that actions are included that need to be completed prior to the next meeting.

- Several days before the next meeting, distribute a letter or e-mail that highlights the actions to be completed prior to the next meeting.

- On the agenda for the next meeting, include a review of prior actions as the first or second agenda item.

- At the next meeting, ask people to report on those actions.

    - Applaud those items completed on time.

    - For those items not completed, ask the person responsible to provide a revised deadline.

If follow-through appears to be a problem, consider having the team agree on a consequence list (e.g., buying everyone lunch, providing the minutes for the next three meetings) when an assigned date for an action is missed more than once.

Sample Meeting Notes

The Meetings Transformation Team
Meeting Notes from xx/xx/xx

The Meetings Transformation Team held its first meeting on xx/xx/xx from 9:00 a.m. to 11:30 a.m. The meeting was held in Conference Room A. Attendees of the meeting were the following people:

- Cleve C.—Team Leader
- Ken M.
- Bill G.—Documenter
- Vanessa R.—Executive Sponsor
- Trina J.
- Andrea T.

The following are the meeting notes from the meeting. *Items appearing in italics indicate information added by the documenter for clarity or to provide context.*

A. Welcome, Purpose and Agenda

Following the welcome, the team leader presented and gained agreement on the following purpose and agenda for the meeting.

Meeting's Purpose

To confirm the project objective and gain agreement on the work process and our operating norms.

Meeting Agenda

A.   Welcome, purpose, and agenda

B.   Review the team's objective.

C.   Identify critical issues for accomplishing the team's objective.

D.   Confirm the team's work process (*the master plan*).

E.   Define team norms and decision-making method.

F.   Decide logistics for meetings.

G.   Begin team work process (if time permits).

H.   Define next steps.

B. Review the Team's Objective

The team leader provided team members copies of the team's objective below which was crafted by the organization's leadership team.

> The overall objective of the Meetings Transformation Team is to help make our meetings more effective, more efficient, and more productive.

C. Identify Critical Issues

Team members were asked to identify the key items that they felt needed to be addressed in order to ensure we achieved our objective. These items are listed below. The team leader indicated that, throughout the process, we will be coming back to this list and adding to it to ensure that all issues are covered.

- o Getting everyone on board
- o Addressing managers who chronically lead bad meetings
- o Avoiding starting with a bang and then fizzling out
- o Determining how to measure our success
- o Participating on this team while maintaining full work responsibilities
- o Identifying when we are done

D. Confirm the Team's Work Process

The team leader presented the master plan—a proposed work process. After a lengthy discussion, during which modifications were made to the proposed process, the team agreed to the following work tasks.

- o Identify the problems we see in our meetings to provide a starting list of what needs to be fixed.
- o Conduct a meeting survey to document a baseline of how successful we are with meetings.
- o Finalize Your Meeting Rights, Our Meeting Vision, and The Master Plan.
- o Finalize measurable outcomes that will define success for the initiative.
- o Develop a support plan—including training, tutorials, and samples—to build up skills in those who lead or participate in meetings.
- o Develop our plan for rewards and accountability.
- o Develop our plan for monitoring progress and communicating results.
- o Present a draft to senior management for approval.
- o Refine recommendations based on senior management input.
- o Execute *The Master Plan*, including monitoring results.

E. Define Team Norms and Decision-Making Method

The participants agreed to the following norms for the team:

- o Everyone will participate.
- o We will have one conversation in the room.
- o We will fully participate in each meeting.
- o We will leave cell phones, Blackberries, and computers off (except for the documenter).
- o We will speak positively of the team and of each other.
- o We will respect one another's time by arriving at least five minutes in advance for all meetings so that we can start on time.
- o We will take personal responsibility to be prepared for each meeting by reading all materials in advance.
- o We will speak up about any issues or concerns we have.
- o We will use five-finger consensus for all major decisions.
- o We will operate all meetings as masterful meetings.

F. Decide Logistics for Meetings

The participants agreed to the following parameters for our meetings:

- o We will meet every other Thursday from 9:00 a.m. to 11:30 a.m. in Conference Room A.

G. Identify Existing Problems with Meetings

The team began its work process by identifying existing problems with meetings.

- o No agenda
- o Minimal participation
- o Going off track
- o Side conversations
- o No decisions
- o No results
- o Sarcastic comments
- o Too many agenda items
- o No real purpose to meet
- o One person dominating
- o Too much detail
- o No follow-up

H. Next Steps

The team will meet again on zz/zz/zz from 9:00 a.m. to 11:30 a.m. Our focus will be on the following:

- o   Review action list.

- o   Define Step 2: Meeting Survey.

- o   Define Step 3: Meeting Vision Components.

- o   Discuss how to participate on the team and still get a full workload done. (This may entail a recommendation to the Leadership Team.)

I. Decisions List

The following is an ongoing list of decisions made by the team with the date that the decision was made.

1.   We agreed to team norms (xx/xx/xx).

2.   We agreed on our work process (xx/xx/xx).

3.   We will meet every other Thursday from 9:00 a.m. to 11:30 a.m. in Conference Room A (xx/xx/xx).

J. Actions List

The following is an ongoing list of actions to be taken outside of the meeting along with the due dates and the person responsible for each action. When an action is completed, it appears in the next meeting notes as "done" and is then removed from subsequent meeting notes.

1.   Document and distribute the meeting notes. (Bill G., xx/xx/xx)

2.   Review the draft survey and the draft meeting vision components from the book, and come to the meeting with recommended changes. (All, xx/xx/xx)

Leading Virtual Meetings

	Meeting Quiz Question
False	10. A key strategy to keep people engaged in teleconferences and other virtual meetings is to **randomly call on people** during discussions.

How do you manage a meeting in which some, if not all, of the participants are in different places around the globe? Whether through audio-conferencing, videoconferencing, or web-conferencing, more and more virtual meetings are being held where some or all participants are no longer face-to-face.

Leading a masterful meeting using technology presents an additional level of complexity for the facilitative leader. Despite the geographic dispersion, the leader must still: find a way to get the participants excited from the very beginning; keep everyone engaged and focused on the objective; gather and document the critical information; build consensus; manage dysfunction; and close with a clear understanding of what was accomplished, the value of the accomplishment, and the steps to be taken once the meeting ends.

Consider the following tips for managing virtual meetings.

Preparing for the Virtual Meeting

1. Prior to the meeting, distribute the meeting notice including purpose, products, agenda, ground rules, and any relevant handouts. If multiple time zones are included in the meeting, be sure to specify the time zone when informing participants of the start and end times.

2. In planning the meeting, limit agenda items so that the entire call can be completed in two hours or less. If necessary, break the meeting into several calls.

3. Consider having participants do preliminary brainstorming and submit ideas prior to the meeting. You can summarize these ideas into "brainstorm lists" and send them in advance to participants along with the agenda and other written materials.

4. Consider having multiple people at the same location assemble for the meeting in a conference room or some other suitable environment. Having as many as possible in the same room promotes teamwork and helps people avoid the temptation to multitask.

5. Create a roll-call list that shows the name and location of each person expected in the meeting.

Executing a Virtual Meeting

1. At the beginning of the meeting, conduct a roll call: ask all participants to state their names and locations. Try to address participants by name throughout the meeting to help people link names with voices.

2. In getting the meeting started, perform a traditional "inform-excite-empower-engage."

    -   Explain the purpose of the meeting.

    -   Get the participants excited about participating by explaining the benefits they will see from a successful outcome.

    -   Let them know the authority that has been given them.

    -   Get them involved by asking a starting question that engages them in meaningful discussion that will contribute to the work to be done.

3. Add specific ground rules to assist with "virtual meeting etiquette," such as the following:

    -   Announce yourself when joining the meeting, and inform the group if you leave prior to the end of the meeting.

    -   Always identify yourself before speaking.

    -   Avoid using the "hold" button, especially when music or other sounds result.

4. Use round-robins frequently to get input from all participants. Instead of calling on people randomly as indicated in the masterful meeting question, use the roll call list to follow the same order every time. This method encourages everyone to listen because they know they will be asked to provide input each time. To avoid having the same person go first and last every time, start at a different position in the roll call list with each round-robin.

5. Be sure to have an engagement activity at least every 10-15 minutes to ensure focus and attention.

6. Establish a verbal method for doing consensus checks, such as a round-robin, by which each person indicates agreement or disagreement.

7. Consider using meeting software that allows all participants to view on a computer the information that is recorded while the meeting is ongoing.

8. Do considerable summarizing to make sure that everyone understands the focus of the discussion and what is being said.

Closing a Virtual Meeting

1. Review all issues, decisions, and action items prior to ending the meeting to help ensure full understanding and commitment to action.

2. Publish a recap immediately after the meeting.

Checklists

Use the checklists that follow as an easy reminder for running masterful meetings. As above, while not all items are required, the asterisked (*) items should always be followed.

Checklist for Preparing

- ❏ *Decide the meeting's purpose.
- ❏ *Define the meeting's products.
- ❏ *Confirm the meeting is necessary.
- ❏ *Select the participants.
- ❏ *Identify probable issues.
- ❏ *Develop the agenda.
- ❏ Determine key processes and timings.
- ❏ *Determine meeting date, time, and location.
- ❏ *Develop and distribute the meeting notice.
- ❏ Hold preliminary discussions beforehand as needed.
- ❏ Prepare the room and other logistics.
- ❏ Prepare your opening words.

*Recommended for all meetings

Checklist for Starting

- ❑ *Start the meeting on time.
- ❑ *Deliver the opening, including purpose and products.
- ❑ *Engage the participants.
- ❑ *Confirm the agenda.
- ❑ Review the ground rules.
- ❑ Review the parking boards.
- ❑ Make introductions if needed.

*Recommended for all meetings

Checklist for Running a Meeting (FIRST CLASS)

For each agenda item:

- ❑ **F**ocus the participants by providing an explanation of how the item furthers the meeting's purpose.
- ❑ **I**nstruct by providing clear and concise directions on how the agenda item will be executed.
- ❑ **R**ecord the appropriate information during the meeting.
- ❑ **S**eek consensus before moving on.
- ❑ **T**rack time to ensure it is spent appropriately.

As needed:

- ❑ **C**ontrol and resolve any dysfunctional behavior quickly and effectively.
- ❑ **L**isten for off-topic discussions and redirect to a parking board to keep the meeting focused.
- ❑ **A**ddress disagreements or conflicts that emerge.
- ❑ **S**eek all opinions and invite people into the discussion.
- ❑ **S**ummarize and close the meeting.

Checklist for Closing and Follow-Up

- ❑ *Review the items covered in the meeting.
- ❑ *Confirm the decisions made.
- ❑ *Address outstanding issues.
- ❑ *Ensure that all actions have names and dates assigned.
- ❑ Evaluate the meeting.
- ❑ *Thank participants, and end the meeting.
- ❑ Document and distribute meeting notes.
- ❑ *Follow-up to hold people accountable for assigned actions.

*Recommended for all meetings

Summary

1. Though meetings are the arena where leaders make decisions that impact the success of their organization, unfortunately the effectiveness of the average meeting is so low that bad meetings have become the norm.

2. Facilitative leaders pay close attention to run "masterful" meetings to maximize efficiency, effectiveness, and buy-in.

3. A masterful meeting is a well-prepared, well-executed, and results-oriented meeting with a timely start, a decisive close, and a clear follow-up plan.

4. A masterful meeting has 18 specific characteristics.

Preparation

- Clear purpose, products, and agenda
- Advance notification
- Right people—prepared and present
- Right information

Start

- Timely start
- Purpose and products reviewed
- Key issues identified
- Agenda confirmed
- Ground rules reviewed

Execution

- Steady meeting flow
- Focused discussion
- Positive, energetic participation
- Constructive conflict
- Thoughtful decision-making

Close

- Timely finish
- Decisions and actions reviewed
- Summary provided
- Follow up on actions

5. People often sit through bad meetings because they feel powerless to do anything about it. Establish a set of meeting rights designed to empower meeting participants to make bad meetings unacceptable.

6. Facilitative leaders understand that to do masterful preparation, at a minimum they should know the answers to the 6 Ps.

   - **Purpose**. Why am I holding this meeting?

   - **Product**. What do I want to have when we are done that says the purpose has been achieved?

   - **Participants**. Who are the participants who need to attend the meeting to create the products to achieve the purpose?

   - **Probable Issues**. What are the issues that will likely need to be addressed by the participants to achieve the purpose and create the products?

   - **Process**. What process or steps should we go through (i.e., the agenda) to develop the products that achieve the purpose, given the participants and probable issues?

   - **Place**. Where will the meeting be held? What time? What materials? What room setup?

7. To effectively plan masterful meetings, facilitative leaders recognize two basic meeting types: status meetings and working meetings.

   - Status meetings are designed to review progress or gain feedback, are primarily one-way communication, and can have three, thirty, or even three hundred people in attendance.

   - Working meetings are designed to create a decision, action plan, or some other product, require two-way communication, and should have a much smaller number of participants.

   - One of the most common problems with status meetings is that they become working meetings when participants attempt to address issues or solve problems.

- Instead of transforming a status meeting into a working meeting on the fly, participants should identify issues in status meetings and address them in subsequent working meetings.

8. The right participants for a meeting depend on the meeting.

Status	**Working**
• People who need to know or their representatives	• People who understand the issue, have a stake in the outcome, and are empowered to make a decision or recommendation

9. A masterful start to a meeting accomplishes four goals in particular.

Inform Provide the purpose and product; that is, explain why the meeting is being held and what products will be produced as a result of the meeting.

Excite Describe the benefits to the participants for achieving the purpose and the products.

Empower Let participants know what they are being asked to do. Are they making a decision, making a recommendation, just brainstorming ideas, et cetera?

Involve Get participants involved and interacting by posing a question to them that will further the work of the meeting.

10. After you inform, excite, empower, and involve, the next thing is to review the agenda and remind participants of the ground rules and the parking boards.

11. During the meeting, when formulating questions to get lots of ideas, ask type-B questions, that is, questions that help participants visualize their answers. A type-B question is formatted as follows:

- **Start with an image building phrase** (e.g., "Think about... Imagine... Consider... If...").

- **Extend the image** so the participants can see their answers. This usually takes two or three additional phrases.

- **Ask the direct question** (type-A) that you desire to know.

12. If the group begins to detour to an unrelated topic, facilitative leaders bring the group back on course by using a redirection question: "That's an interesting point. Can we put it on the issues list so we don't lose it, and then focus back on...?"

13. At the beginning of every agenda item, facilitative leaders should take a checkpoint to get everyone on the same page.

- **Review**: Quickly cover what has been done to date.

- **Preview**: Describe briefly what the group is about to do.

- **Big View**: Explain how the previewed agenda item fits into meeting's overall purpose.

14. When giving directions, facilitative leaders use PeDeQs to describe what to do, how to do it, and why doing it is important.

   - Give the overall **P**urpose of the activity.

   - When appropriate, use a simple **E**xample that is outside the topic area.

   - Give general **D**irections, using verbal pictures and gestures.

   - Give specific **E**xceptions and special cases.

   - Ask for **Q**uestions.

   - Ask a **S**tarting Question that gets participants visualizing the answers.

15. Facilitative leaders avoid abusing the pen by writing first, discussing second, and by using the words that participants say instead of substituting their own words.

16. Facilitative leaders know that there are only four items that need to be documented in a meeting.

   - **Decisions** made during the meeting.

   - **Actions** assigned during the meeting.

   - **Issues** that come up in the meeting to be discussed later.

   - **Relevant analysis and comments** covered during the meeting.

17. Dysfunctional behavior is any activity by a participant that is consciously or unconsciously a substitution for expressing displeasure with the meeting content, the meeting process, or outside factors. Facilitative leaders takes steps to prevent dysfunction in meetings and to address dysfunction should any occur.

18. Facilitative leaders close meetings by reviewing what was done, identifying open issues, and defining next steps.

19. With meetings that are virtual, facilitative leaders use additional strategies to maintain high levels of engagement, including frequent round-robins in which all participants are asked to respond.

Spring Forward

Use the Masterful Meeting Preparation and Starting Tool that follows for the next few meetings that you lead. The tool uses the strategies from this chapter to help you prepare and start your meetings masterfully.

Masterful Meeting Preparation and Starting Tool

Note: Some items you record in the tool are for preparation purposes only. These items aren't lettered. The lettered items you use both in your preparation and in your starting. The letters indicate the order in which you will say these items when you start the meeting.

1. Use the space below to record the purpose and the product for the meeting.

Purpose (inform). The purpose of this meeting is to...	
A	

Product (inform). When we are done we will have...	
B	

2. Next, identify the people you will need to invite to achieve the purpose and product.

Participants. The people who will be invited to the meeting are…

3. Now, give some thought to why these people should attend this meeting. What's in it for them? What benefits will they get if the meeting achieves its purpose? Provide at least two sentences.

Excite. This is exciting because, when we achieve our purpose, you…	
C	

4. Why were these participants selected and what are they empowered to do? Are they being asked to represent a viewpoint? To be creative? To make a decision or recommendation?

Empower. You were selected to be a part of this meeting because...	
D	

5. Next, decide the involvement question. As an example, you might ask participants to identify key topics they want to cover. Make sure to use the type-B format for the question.

Involve. Before going over the agenda, I would like to get you involved by asking…

	Start with an image building phrase:
E	*Expand the image to the answers:*
	Ask the direct question:

6. Next, think about the issues that will need to be addressed to achieve the purpose and product. What topics need to be covered? What will people want to talk about? What concerns will likely be expressed?

Probable Issues. To achieve the purpose and create the product, the following issues will need to be addressed or will likely come up...

7. Decide the agenda items you will have to cover during the meeting to achieve the purpose, create the products, and address the relevant probable issues.

Process. To help us achieve our purpose, I propose we use the following agenda...	

8. For each agenda item, determine the process details.

- What question will you ask (Type-B)?

- What directions will you give (PeDeQs)?

- How will you record the responses?

- What supplies do you need?

- How much time do you expect the agenda item to take?

Now you are prepared and ready. To start the session, run through the six lettered elements you have prepared in order.

- Knowing Yourself
- Developing Individuals
- Leading Your Team
- A Final Word

Chapter 11.
Pulling It All Together

The prior chapters reviewed the eight practices of a facilitative leader. Though each practice was treated as a separate chapter, generally this is not how the practices are used. They are not independent of one another, nor are they always applied in the order in which they have been presented. This chapter will demonstrate how the strategies within the practices come together across the following three areas.

- Knowing Yourself
- Developing Individuals
- Leading your Team

Knowing Yourself

Consider the following activities to increase your leadership effectiveness by improving your own self-awareness related to the TAFA practices.

1. Determine on which **leadership level** you are operating today and what you have to do to move to a higher level and increase your contribution to the organization. (Chapter 2)

2. Use the **Leadership Scorecard** to evaluate your own performance as a leader. (Chapter 2)

3. Review how your **role changes with TAFA**; evaluate which changes will likely be most challenging for you and identify steps you can take to better adjust. (Chapter 2)

4. Determine **your own "why"** to increase your focus and motivation. Ask yourself why you choose to be in the position you occupy. Ask yourself what is motivating you. (Chapter 3)

5. Assess your **communication style** and practice **identifying and adapting to the styles** of others to increase your effectiveness with your boss, your peers, and your subordinates. (Chapter 5)

6. Determine how you naturally respond to conflict and select your strategies for **encouraging disagreement** to achieve better solutions and higher levels of creativity and innovation. (Chapter 8)

7. Use the **Drivers Model** to draft your strategic vision for the organization to prepare your own thoughts prior to doing strategic planning with your team. (Chapter 9)

Developing Individuals

Consider the following activities to increase your effectiveness in applying the TAFA practices to developing the people who work for you.

1. Develop your **"Managing Your Boss"** memo and distribute to your direct reports to help them understand how to be more effective with you. (Chapter 4)

2. For your direct reports, identify their likely **communication style** and the appropriate **leadership style** to principally employ to help you be more effective with them. (Chapters 4 and 5)

3. Utilize the steps for **effective directing, effective delegation**, and **effective coaching** as appropriate to support the development of your people. (Chapter 4)

4. Develop **decision trees** with each direct report to provide them clarity on their level of empowerment. (Chapter 4)

5. Have those direct reports who have subordinates complete quarterly the **Leadership Scorecard** and utilize it during your 1-2-1 sessions to help them focus on how well they are leading others. (Chapter 2)

6. Make sure each of your people understand the **5 Cs of Trust** and the **Decision Matrix**, so that they are aware of where they stand with you. (Chapter 4)

7. Hold the **Trust Conversation** and/or the **Decision Matrix Conversation** as needed to address issues. (Chapter 4)

8. Be aware of the **natural communication style clashes** and use the strategies to recognize and **recover when you miscommunicate**. (Chapter 5)

9. When you praise be sure to give a **GIFT** to maximize the positive impact. (Chapter 6)

10. When you disagree use **PAC** to connect then challenge. (Chapter 6)

11. In giving constructive feedback using the **PERCS** approach, be sure to separate the **facts from your story**. (Chapter 6)

12. If you have a person with a behavioral issue, be sure to recognize the **behavioral issue types** and apply insights from the **reasons people change** based on DISC type. (Chapter 6)

Leading Your Team

Consider the following activities to increase your effectiveness in applying the TAFA practices in equipping, guiding, and inspiring teams.

1. With your team use the **Drivers Model** to develop a strategic plan for your area to provide a clear vision, the measures of success, and the key priorities for getting there. (Chapter 9)

2. Implement the **three-step monitoring process** to ensure accountability, adjustment, and follow-through. (Chapter 9)

3. Develop your **principles of operation** for your area to ensure your entire team understands the basic guidelines you want used in making day-to-day decisions. (Chapter 4)

4. Utilize the **masterful meeting** framework to help ensure you prepare, start, execute, and close every meeting effectively, efficiently, and productively. (Chapter 10)

5. When a disagreement occurs, utilize the **3 Reasons People Disagree** model to assess the disagreement and apply the appropriate strategy to resolve it. (Chapter 8)

6. With every team you charter, document the **first five of the Eight Team Essentials** to ensure you equip the team for success. (Chapter 7)

7. **Compose each team** to maximize its effectiveness based on knowledge, skills, and communication styles. (Chapter 7)

8. Based on the team leader and the team composition, anticipate the **likely team issues** and take appropriate steps to prevent them. (Chapter 7)

9. Help increase team effectiveness by ensuring the team **creates the last three of the Eight Team Essentials** by determining a leadership process, a work process, and team norms. (Chapter 7)

10. Instruct the team in **developing and delivering recommendations** to help increase the likelihood of adoption. (Chapter 7)

A Final Word

I am very excited about the possibility of more and more leaders experiencing the amazing impact they can have by taking a facilitative approach to leading their people. My hope is that this book has given you a treasure chest of practical and beneficial strategies you can use to improve the level of engagement, buy-in, and commitment from your people. Engagement fosters buy-in; buy-in yields commitment; and commitment produces results.

Use the eight core TAFA practices, and the strategies that support them, in your decision making, problem solving, coaching, and leadership.

- **S**tart with the why, engage with the how
- **U**nderstand and empower, don't command and control
- **C**ommunicate in their language, not yours
- **C**onnect first, correct second
- **E**quip for success, monitor for results
- **E**ngage conflict, encourage disagreement
- **D**rive strategic thinking throughout the organization
- **S**tart, execute, and close every meeting masterfully

If there were a ninth TAFA practice it would focus on spreading the TAFA approach and strategies throughout the organization. Consider helping more people gain an understanding of the power of such strategies as giving a GIFT, applying DISC, using the 5 Cs of Trust, resolving disagreements, et cetera. Join me and thousands of other leaders in spreading the word and demonstrating the positive difference that comes from taking a facilitative approach to leadership!

About the Author

Michael Wilkinson is the Managing Director of Leadership Strategies—The Facilitation Company, an organization that specializes in training, facilitation, consulting, and leadership skills. Leadership Strategies also provides professional facilitators to help organizations with strategic planning, issue resolution, focus groups, and a variety of other processes.

Michael is a leader in the facilitation industry. He is the author of *The Secrets of Facilitation, The Executive Guide to Facilitating Strategy, CLICK: The Virtual Meetings Book, The Secrets to Masterful Meetings,* and *Buying Styles.* He is founder of the FindaFacilitator.com database and serves on the board of the International Institute for Facilitation. He was one of the first five Certified Professional Facilitators in North America and has been awarded the prestigious Certified *Master* Facilitator designation. In 2016, he was inducted into the International Facilitation Hall of Fame by the International Association of Facilitators.

Michael is a much sought-after facilitator, trainer, and speaker, both in the United States and internationally. He has worked with hundreds of public and private sector organizations and has completed international assignments in over 25 cities around the world, including Bangkok, Beijing, Geneva, Glasgow, Hamburg, Helsinki, Hong Kong, Istanbul, London, Melbourne, Milan, Moscow, Riyadh, Saint Petersburg, Stockholm, Sydney, Vienna, and Warsaw.

Prior to his current post, he was a Senior Manager in Ernst & Young's Management Consulting Group. As an accomplished information technology consultant, he was selected by the governor of his state to serve for two terms on the state's twelve-member Information Technology Policy Council.

Michael resides in Atlanta. He gets a thrill out of teaching and facilitating, is a passionate football fan, and recognizes God as his source.

Assistance in Facilitative Leadership

Clients frequently ask about our services to assist in training their people in Facilitative Leadership. I have provided brief descriptions below.

Training

The Facilitative Leader is our flagship leadership course designed to equip new and experienced managers alike with the TAFA framework: the eight core practices that facilitative leaders use to create the level of engagement, buy-in, and commitment that yield results. The curriculum has a customizable design that includes eight half-day modules:

1. Getting Started, Facilitating Yourself
2. Facilitating Communication
3. Facilitating and Coaching Individuals
4. Facilitating Your Team
5. Facilitating Your Strategy
6. Facilitating Agreement
7. Facilitating Meetings: Part 1
8. Facilitating Meetings: Part 2

Clients are able to customize the delivery of the eight half-day modules to suit their schedules and leadership team preferences. For example:

- Eight half-day sessions delivered on weekly basis
- Four full-day sessions (two modules per day)
- One full-day session, six half-day sessions

By the end of this dynamic training, your leaders walk away with an action plan for skillfully and confidently empowering, engaging, inspiring, and leading.

Consulting Services

We provide professional facilitators who will guide your team through critical activities including the following.

- Strategic planning
- Project and program planning

8 Core Practices of Facilitative Leaders

- Team acceleration
- Process improvement
- Issue resolution
- Partnering

Our team members bring defined processes and methods that they customize to address your specific needs. In addition, as expert facilitators, they use proven strategies for managing even the toughest group dynamics to effectively and efficiently produce results. Let us help you.

800.824.2850 Leadership Strategies, Inc. www.leadstrat.com

Reference Notes

1   Robert Zawacki, *Transforming the Mature Information Technology Organization* (Eagle Star Publishing, 1995).

2   Simon Sinek, *Start with Why: How Great Leaders Inspire Everyone to Take Action*, (New York: Portfolio, 2009).

3   Kevin Kruse, *Employee Engagement 2.0: How to Motivate Your Team for High Performance (A Real-World Guide for Busy Managers)*, 2nd Edition (Charleston: CreateSpace, 2012).

4   Adapted from Michael Wilkinson, *The Secrets of Facilitation*, 2nd Edition (San Francisco: Jossey-Bass, 2012), 8.

5   In *Good to Great*, Jim Collins describes the level-5 leader. How does the Level-3 Leadership Model compare to what Collins describes? Collins describes his five levels as: 1-highly capable individual, 2-contributing team member, 3-competent manager, 4-effective leader, 5-great leader. The first two levels are individual contributors without supervisory responsibility and therefore not addressed in our Level-3 Leadership Model. While level-1 and level-2 leaders in the Level-3 Leadership Model are roughly akin to Collin's level-3 and level-4, Collin's level-5 is characterized by a unique blend of personal will and humility that are not covered in our Level-3 Leadership Model.

6   Simon Sinek, ibid.

7   The mission statements listed in this chapter were taken from information available to the author at the time and may not reflect the current mission of the cited organizations.

8   Adapted from Michael Wilkinson, *The Secrets to Masterful Meetings* (Atlanta: Leadership Strategies Publishing, 2005).

9   Paul Hersey and Kenneth Blanchard, *Management of Organizational Behavior: Utilizing Human Resources*, 4th Edition (Englewood Cliffs, NJ: Prentice-Hall, 1982).

10   The name has been changed to provide anonymity.

11   Stephen Covey, *The Seven Habits of Highly Effective People* (New York: Free Press, 1989). Habit #2: Start with the end in mind.

12   Susan Scott, *Fierce Conversations* (London: Penguin Group, 2002).

13   The discussion of communication styles is adapted from Michael Wilkinson, *Buying Styles* (New York: AMACOM, 2009).

14   Ibid, 67-69.

15   Ibid, 71-72.

16   Kerry Patterson, Joseph Grenny, Ron McMillan, Al Switzler, *Crucial Conversations: Tools for Talking When Stakes are High* (New York: McGraw Hill, 2002).

17   Kenneth Blanchard, *Whale Done!: The Power of Positive Relationships* (New York: Free Press, 2002).

18   Creative abrasion is a term whose origin has been credited to Jerry Hirshberg, founder of Nissan Design International.

19   The information in this chapter is largely adapted from *The Secrets to Masterful Meetings* and *The Secrets of Facilitation*. For a deeper discussion of disagreement and consensus building, see Chapter 10 of *The Secrets of Facilitation*.

20   Patrick Lencioni, *The Advantage* (Hoboken, NJ: Collins Business-Wiley, 2012).

21   Positions and interests are described more thoroughly in Roger Fisher, William Ury, and Bruce Patton, *Getting to Yes*, 3rd Edition (London: Penguin Group, 2011).

22   This chapter is adapted from *The Secrets to Facilitating Strategy* (Atlanta: Leadership Strategies Publishing, 2011), Chapter 1.

23   Unless otherwise indicated, this chapter is adapted from *The Secrets to Masterful Meetings* (Atlanta: Leadership Strategies Publishing, 2005).

24   Ibid., 34.

25   Adapted from Michael Wilkinson, *The Secrets of Facilitation*, 2nd Edition (San Francisco: Jossey-Bass, 2012), 178.

CPSIA information can be obtained
at www.ICGtesting.com
Printed in the USA
FFHW011544190719
53709092-59418FF